Understanding Environmental Policy Processes

To the memory of Michael John Keeley
JK

To Andrea, Jake and Kate
IS

Understanding Environmental Policy Processes

Cases from Africa

James Keeley
and
Ian Scoones

Earthscan Publications Ltd
London • Sterling, VA

First published in the UK and USA in 2003 by
Earthscan Publications Ltd

ISBN: 1-85383-975-2 (paperback)
     1-85383-980-9 (hardback)

Typesetting by JS Typesetting Ltd, Wellingborough, Northants
Printed and bound by Creative Print and Design (Wales), Ebbw Vale
Cover design by Danny Gillespie

For a full list of publications please contact:

Earthscan Publications Ltd
120 Pentonville Road
London, N1 9JN, UK
Tel: +44 (0)20 7278 0433
Fax: +44 (0)20 7278 1142
Email: earthinfo@earthscan.co.uk
Web: **www.earthscan.co.uk**

22883 Quicksilver Drive, Sterling, VA 20166–2012, USA

A catalogue record for this book is available from the British Library

Library of Congress Cataloging-in-Publication Data applied for

Earthscan is an editorially independent subsidiary of Kogan Page Ltd and publishes
in association with WWF-UK and the International Institute for Environment and
Development

This book is printed on elemental chlorine-free paper

Contents

Preface

It is now over ten years since the major United Nations (UN) Conference on Environment and Development held in Rio. The Rio conference, or Earth Summit, heralded much hype and expectation about the potential for policy change regarding the environment, especially in Africa. Following the Johannesburg summit of 2002, it is perhaps time for some critical reflection. What has been achieved? What have been the disappointments? What needs rethinking?

In this book our focus is on policy *processes*: how policies are made, and how they change. While there has been lots of work on the technical details of environmental policies and the pros and cons of different options, there has, surprisingly, been less reflection on the nature of the process by which policies arise and how they do – or often don't – change.

This book, then, asks why do particular perspectives on environmental change become so entrenched in policy? Which actors are involved? Whose interests are served? Whose knowledge is included and whose excluded? Our focus is, therefore, on the intersections and negotiations of knowledge, power and politics.

In the environment and development arena there has been a key role for science. In the post-Rio era, in particular, there has also been an internationalization of environment and development science, with a range of different actors implicated in the policy-making process.

One reader of an earlier discussion paper, which forms the basis of one of the chapters here, described it as 'dangerous'. He implied that, by questioning the policy process, we were undermining the cause of environmental protection and sustainability in Africa. But by opening up policy processes for detailed scrutiny, this book should not be misconstrued as a simplistic attack on environmental positions, as some recent anti-environmental literature has been prone. It is definitely not about whether or not soil fertility decline is occurring, the extent of and damage caused by soil erosion and so on. It is, however, about how knowledge – from experts and others – comes to be incorporated in, or left out of, policy positions, and the politics of this process.

If the post-Rio agenda means discounting uncertainties, avoiding debate about the framing of problems and imposing rigid, centrally developed frameworks and planning processes, we, of course, do object. And so, we are sure, would our disappointed reader. Yet, many of the plans and initiatives generated by the international scientific and environmental community in the wake of Rio have failed to address some real key problems on the ground, often missing their target through inappropriate diagnosis and inadequate reflection in formulating and implementing new policies.

The real challenge, we would argue, is to recognize and encompass complexity and dynamism in policy processes, and to ensure that the range of different, always partial, perspectives is heard. An exclusionary, narrow policy process often acts to reinforce particular knowledges and interests and, in the longer term, does the cause of sustainability no favours by preventing or dissuading learning and innovation.

The chapters in this book, then, take a series of case studies, explored in detailed research over a number of years, in Ethiopia, Mali and Zimbabwe, as well as in 'international' contexts associated with the land management/soils debate in Africa. Chapter 1 introduces the main themes of the book and offers an overview of some of the key features of the case study countries. Chapter 2 provides a conceptual route map to the approach adopted in the book, briefly reviewing a range of literatures that have informed our analysis. Chapter 3 takes the international Soil Fertility Initiative (SFI) for Africa as a case study and examines how this was framed, tracing the links between the global and the local. Chapters 4 to 6 comprise the three country case studies, which each examine how debates about land and soil management have been played out in particular contexts. By examining particular policy moments and histories, the chapters offer insights into how policies are made and change. Chapter 7 is the concluding chapter, which draws the themes of the book together and asks what prospects there are for a more inclusive and participatory form of policy process.

James Keeley and Ian Scoones
Institute of Development Studies
Brighton
January 2003

Acknowledgements

The research for this book is based primarily on around 250 semi-structured interviews with informants in Ethiopia, Mali and Zimbabwe, as well as Kenya, Italy, the Netherlands, the UK and the US (approximately 50 'international' interviews, 80 in Ethiopia, 40 in Mali and 70 in Zimbabwe). These have been combined with documentary analysis based on published and grey literature, available in text and web formats, and active participation in a number of workshops, seminars, conferences and policy reviews as 'participant observers'. The research was carried out intermittently between 1996 and 2001 in collaboration with a wide range of partners. It was supported by a grant from the Economic and Social Research Council (ESRC) (Understanding Environmental Policy Processes: the Case of Soil Management in Africa, Award No R 000 222 765), and was linked to two research-action networks dealing with soils management in Africa – Nutrient Networking in Africa (NUTNET) and Indigenous Soil and Water Conservation (ISWC, Phase II), coordinated by the Research Institute for Agrobiology and Soil Fertility (AB-DLO), Wageningen, and CDCS (Centre for Development Cooperation Services), Free University, Amsterdam, both supported by the Netherlands aid agency (NEDA). These projects brought together researchers and practitioners in the fields of soil and natural resource management from nine African countries. Discussions at project workshops and interactions in the field with project partners have helped to develop our understanding of these issues from an African perspective. In addition, we have been involved in preparing a review on policy issues relating to soil fertility management for the UK Department for International Development (DFID), and have been partners in the International Institute for Environment and Development (IIED) co-ordinated and European Union International Cooperation (EU-INCO)-funded networking project Enhancing Soil Fertility in Africa: from Field to Policy-Maker. All of these activities – beyond the actual research – afforded the opportunity to debate with a range of policy actors, as well as researchers and field practitioners, and to test our ideas out as we went along.

Research for Chapter 3 was carried out in Africa, Europe and North America with the help of people in a range of different organizations, including scientists and managers in institutes that are part of, or linked to, the Consultative Group on International Agricultural Research (CGIAR) (including the International Centre for Research in Agroforestry, Nairobi – ICRAF); the International Food Policy Research Institute, Washington (IFPRI);

the International Maize and Wheat Improvement Center, Harare (CIMMYT); the International Fertilizer Development Center, US (IFDC); the Tropical Soil Biology and Fertility Programme, Nairobi (TSBF); the United Nations Environment Programme, Nairobi (UNEP); and the International Soil Reference and Information Centre, the Netherlands (ISRIC); universities and research organizations (including Wageningen Agricultural University, the Netherlands; Reading University, UK; Wye College, UK; Natural Resources Institute, UK; the IIED, UK; and various university/national agricultural research institutes in Ethiopia, Mali and Zimbabwe); bilateral aid agencies (including DFID, UK; NEDA, the Netherlands; the Deutsche Gesellschaft für Technische Zusammenarbeit GmbH, Germany – GTZ; the Swedish International Development Cooperation Agency – SIDA; the Swiss Agency for Development and Cooperation – SDC); and multilateral agencies (including the Food and Agriculture Organization – FAO; the United Nations Sudano–Sahelian Office – UNSO; the United Nations Development Programme – UNDP; and the World Bank).

For the Ethiopia work reported in Chapter 4, we are most grateful to our collaborators at Mekelle University College in Tigray (notably Dr Haile Mitiku), SOS-Sahel (including Feyera Abdi and Dr Eyasu Elias), FARM-Africa (particularly Ejigu Jonfa and colleagues in the Farmers' Research Project), and Awassa College of Agriculture (Worku Tessema). We have also benefited from comments on earlier versions of this chapter presented at the Ethiopia–Eritrea Network Conference at the University of East Anglia in June 1998, and to the Africa Studies Association Biennial Conference on Comparisons and Transitions in September 1998, subsequently published in the *Journal of Modern African Studies* (JMAS, 2000). We would like to thank Simon Maxwell (Overseas Development Institute), Deryke Belshaw (University of East Anglia) and Adrian Wood (University of Huddersfield), and the JMAS editor Christopher Clapham and two anonymous reviewers for their comments.

For the work on Mali covered in Chapter 5, we benefited from help and guidance from many colleagues, particularly in the Institute d'Economique Rurale, Mali (IER), especially Alpha Maïga, director of IER, and the Equipe Systeme de Production et Gestion des Resources Naturelles (ESPGRN) team based in Niono. The assistance with interviews of Daouda Koné and Yenizie Koné from ESPGRN was invaluable. Also in Mali, Djeidi Sylla at UNDP provided much appreciated support to the process. In Europe, we were also helped by several people with long experience of working in Mali, especially Arnoud Budelman and Toon DeFoer at KIT, Thea Hilhorst and Camilla Toulmin of the IIED Drylands Programme and Jeremy Swift of the Environment Group at the Institute of Development Studies (IDS).

For the Zimbabwe research we have benefited from long-term collaboration with the Department of Research and Specialist Services' Farming Systems Research team, with the team leader Bright Mombeshora, as well as the Chivi team led by BZ Mavedzenge, who provided many insights. Our links with the Institute of Environmental Studies at the University of Zimbabwe have also been important, especially through joint work with Edward Chuma,

Billy Mukamuri and Bev Sithole over the years. Kuda Murwirwa from the Intermediate Technology Development Group, Zimbabwe (ITDG) has also been a close collaborator. In addition, colleagues in the Department of Soil Science at the University of Zimbabwe (UZ), Agritex in Harare, Masvingo and Chivi and others in a range of government departments, research institutes and non-governmental organizations (NGOs) have provided encouragement at various points. Earlier versions of Chapter 6 were read and commented on by Gilles Kleitz and William Wolmer at IDS, as well as colleagues in Zimbabwe.

But perhaps most of our thanks should go to the many informants – ministry and parastatal officials; politicians, NGO workers; media personnel; donor staff; expatriate technical advisors; scientists and policy researchers; farmers and their representatives; and others – who offered their time to discuss with us. The responsibility for the content of the book is, however, solely ours.

List of Acronyms and Abbreviations

AB-DLO   Research Institute for Agrobiology and Soil Fertility
ADB   African Development Bank
AIDS   acquired immune deficiency syndrome
AOF   Afrique Oriental Française
AREX   Department for Agricultural Research and Extension, Zimbabwe
AVs   *associations villageoises*
BSE   bovine spongiform encephalopathy (or 'mad cow disease')
CADU   Chilalo Agricultural Development Unit, Ethiopia
CAMPFIRE   Communal Areas Management Programme for Indigenous Resources, Zimbabwe
CAP   *connaissances, attitudes, pratiques*
CDCS   Centre for Development Cooperation Services
CCD   Convention to Combat Desertification
CFA   West African Franc
CFDT   Compagnie Française pour le Développement des Fibres Textiles
CFU   Commercial Farmers' Union
CG   consultative group
CGIAR   Consultative Group on International Agricultural Research
CIDA   Canadian International Development Agency
CILSS   Comité Inter-Etat de Lutte Contre la Secheresse au Sahel
CIMMYT   International Maize and Wheat Improvement Center
CIRAD   Centre de Coopération Internationale en Recherche Agronomique pour le Développement
CLUSA   League of the Cooperatives of the United States of America in Mali
CMDT   Compagnie Malienne pour le Développement des Fibres Textiles
CPS   Cellule de Planification et Statistiques, Mali
CSDS   Centre for Development Cooperation Services, Free University, Amsterdam
DA   development agent
DEAP   District Environmental Action Plan
DFID   Department for International Development, UK
DIPs   deliberative inclusionary processes

DNR	Department of Natural Resources, Ministry of Mines, Environment and Tourism, Zimbabwe
DRSS	Department of Research and Specialist Services, Ministry of Agriculture, Zimbabwe
EHRS	Ethiopian Highland Reclamation Study
ENDA	Environment and Development Activities, Zimbabwe
EPA	Environmental Protection Agency, Ethiopia
EPRDF	Ethiopian People's Revolutionary Democratic Front
ESPGRN	Equipe Systeme de Production et Gestion des Resources Naturelles, Mali
ESRC	Economic and Social Research Council, UK
ETC	ETC Foundation, the Netherlands
EU	European Union
EU-INCO	European Union International Cooperation (developing country research programme)
FAO	Food and Agriculture Organization, United Nations
FDRE	Federal Democratic Republic of Ethiopia
GDP	gross domestic product
GERENAT	Gestion des Resources Naturelles, Mali
GLASOD	global assessment of the status of human-induced soil degradation
GM	genetically modified
GNI	gross national income
GTZ	Deutsche Gesellschaft für Technische Zusammenarbeit, GmbH
ha	hectare
HIPC	Highly Indebted Poor Countries Initiative (of the IMF)
HQs	headquarters
HYVs	high-yielding varieties
ICRAF	International Centre for Research in Agroforestry
ICRISAT	International Crops Research Institute for Semi-Arid Tropics
IDS	Institute of Development Studies
IER	Institute d'Economie Rurale, MDRE, Mali
IFA	International Fertilizer Industry Association
IFDC	International Fertilizer Development Center
IFPRI	International Food Policy Research Institute
IIED	International Institute for Environment and Development
ILEIA	Centre for Information on Low External Input Agriculture
IMF	International Monetary Fund
IPM	integrated pest management
IRCT	cotton and other textiles department, CIRAD
IRD	integrated rural development
IRDEP	Integrated Rural Development Programme, Zimbabwe
ISRIC	International Soil Reference and Information Centre
ISWC	Indigenous Soil and Water Conservation Project
ITDG	Intermediate Technology Development Group

ITK	indigenous technical knowledge
IUCN	World Conservation Union
JMAS	*Journal of Modern African Studies*
K	potassium
KARI	Kenyan Agricultural Research Institute
kg	kilogrammes
km	kilometre
MDC	Movement for Democratic Change, Zimbabwe
MDRE	Ministère pour le Développement Rural et de l'Eau, Mali
MEDAC	Ministry of Economic Development and Cooperation, Ethiopia
mm	millimetres
MMET	Ministry of Mines, Environment and Tourism, Zimbabwe
MMR	mumps, measles and rubella
MoE	Ministry of Environment, Mali
N	nitrogen
NCS	National Conservation Strategy
NEAP	National Environmental Action Plan
NEDA	National Economic and Development Authority, the Netherlands
NFIA	National Fertilizer Industry Association, Ethiopia
NGO	non-governmental organization
NPK	nitrogen, phosphorus and potassium
NUTNET	Nutrient Networking in Africa
ODR	Operations Développement Rurales, Mali
OECD	Organization for Economic Cooperation and Development
ON	Office du Niger, Mali
ORSTOM	French Institute for Scientific Research in Overseas Development and Cooperation; now the Institut de Recherche pour le Développement
P	phosphorus
PA	Peasant Association, Ethiopia
PADEP	Peasant Agricultural Development Exchange Programme
PADETES	Participatory Agricultural Demonstration and Extension Training System
PGRN	Programme Gestion des Ressources Naturelles, Mali
PNAE	Plan National d'Action Environnemental, Mali
PNT	*phosphate naturel de Tilemsi*
PNVA	Projet National de Vulgarisation Agricole, MDRE, Mali
PPS	Primary Production in the Sahel
PR	rock phosphate
PRA	participatory rural appraisal
PSS	Production Soudano-Sahélienne
RPI	Rock Phosphate Initiative
SADC	Southern African Development Community
SAFIRE	Southern Alliance for Indigenous Resources, Zimbabwe

SARDC	Southern African Research and Documentation Centre, Zimbabwe
SCRP	Soil Conservation Research Project, Ethiopia
SDC	Swiss Agency for Development and Cooperation
SFI	Soil Fertility Initiative
SG2000	Sasakawa Global 2000
SIDA	Swedish International Development Cooperation Agency
SNNPR	Southern Nations, Nationalities and Peoples' Region, Ethiopia
SSA	sub-Saharan Africa
SYCOV	Malian Union of Cotton and Food Crop Producers
TPLF	Tigrayan People's Liberation Front, Ethiopia
TSBF	Tropical Soil Biology and Fertility Programme, Nairobi
TSP	triple superphosphate fertilizer
T&V	training and visit
UDI	unilateral declaration of independence
UK	United Kingdom
UN	United Nations
UNCED	United Nations Conference on Environment and Development
UNDP	United Nations Development Programme
UNEP	United Nations Environment Programme
UNSO	United Nations Sudano-Sahelian Office
US	United States
USAID	US Agency for International Development
UZ	University of Zimbabwe
WADU	Wolaita Agricultural Development Unit, Ethiopia
WFP	World Food Programme
ZANU–PF	Zimbabwe African National Union–Patriotic Front
ZERO	Zimbabwe Environmental Research Organization
ZFU	Zimbabwe Farmers' Union

1

Knowledge, Power and Politics: Environmental Policy Processes in Africa

INTRODUCTION

Why is it that particular views about the nature and causes of environmental 'problems' seem to stick with such tenacity in policy debates? What processes create and reinforce 'received wisdoms', such as the view that population increase and poverty inevitably result in cycles of worsening land degradation? How are these wisdoms challenged? This book seeks to unravel some of the complex linkages connecting knowledge, power and politics in the policy-making process in Africa. Our aim is to understand environmental policy processes, with a focus on issues of land management – and particularly that key agricultural resource for farmers across the continent: soils.

Why is this important? Today there is much talk of the importance of policy – getting things right in terms of policy frameworks is seen to be central to much development effort. In the area of land and natural resources management this is seen as particularly key, as a whole range of policies impinge upon it – agricultural services, environmental protection, land tenure, credit, input supply and so on. This brings in a range of different actors from within and outside government, from local-level bureaucrats to global conventions and initiatives, in both the formulation and implementation of policy. Understanding how policies are made and, in turn, seen through on the ground is therefore central. In order to understand such policy processes, we must ask how policies are framed, who is included and who is excluded in the process, which actors and which interests are dominant, and how policy changes over time.

One feature of policy on the African environment is the remarkable degree of similarity and consistency of approach from the colonial era to the present (Leach and Mearns, 1996). Perceptions of crisis, in particular, have informed and shaped environmental policy-making. For example, the issues of soil fertility decline, deforestation and desertification are deeply entrenched as problems for policy concern. Accordingly, projects, strategies and legislation have consistently been formulated to address such perceived crises. However, the frame of reference for much policy debate is 'what tools are there to better attack these problems?', rather than an examination of whether the questions that are being posed are appropriate in the first place.

The aim of this book is to look beyond specific policy debates to the more general, but critically important, underlying question of how particular perspectives, and the interests they reflect, find their way into policy. An important theme throughout the book is the relationship between science and policy, and how particular forms of expertise engage in the policy-making process. Soil erosion engineers, biologists, agronomists, economists and others all make inputs into the policy debate. Our examination of this process must take account of the institutional location of such experts, and the political context within which decisions are made. Thus, the cast of characters in the case study analyses that form the core of this book includes scientists, bureaucrats, non-governmental organization (NGO) activists, farmers' leaders, media professionals and others. Through a detailed examination of land management policy-making, we draw on case material from Ethiopia, Mali and Zimbabwe, and reflect on the role of international initiatives, networks and organizations in influencing debates.

In the contemporary policy world the intersection of national and international policy processes is, we argue, particularly important. Since the 1992 Earth Summit in Rio, in particular, environmental issues have shot to the top of global policy agendas, and have been reinforced by a swathe of projects, programmes and initiatives that have followed in the wake of the Rio commitments. Of particular relevance to Africa has been the Convention to Combat Desertification (CCD), ratified in 1994 and by early 2003 signed, ratified or accepted by 185 countries, which sets out an international agenda for the management of dryland resources. The Soil Fertility Initiative (SFI) that we examine in Chapter 3 is a particular example of one of the multiplying initiatives that have emerged from the global debate, and is illustrative of an important dynamic in the contemporary policy-making process – the interactive relationship between local, national and international settings in the framing and interpretation of policy positions.

While international policy initiatives are important – and perhaps increasingly so – we should not underestimate national and regional settings. For this reason the bulk of this book concentrates on three detailed country case studies that explore different policy contexts. These case studies emerge from longterm research engagement in Ethiopia, Mali and Zimbabwe, and are based primarily on several hundred interviews carried out between 1996 and 2001, as well as informal observation and interaction over longer periods. An analysis of these cases provokes some interesting comparisons in styles of policy-making, which, in turn, relate to different histories, forms of state organization, relationships with civil society, engagement with donors and international organizations and so on. Through an examination of how policies are made and implemented in these different settings, the prospects for participation and inclusion, particularly of poorer and marginal farmers, are explored throughout and returned to as a central theme in the final chapter of the book.

A focus on understanding the relationship between knowledge and the policy process shifts our attention, therefore, from policy analysis to policy *process* analysis. One response to 'bad' policy is to explain why it is misguided and suggest how it might be improved – the technical approach. However, if there is something intrinsic to the policy process that means that policies invariably take a particular shape – that certain people and perspectives are repeatedly excluded – then what may be needed is a more wide-ranging examination of the processes of policy-making themselves. This is, then, the aim of this book. While our case studies are necessarily focused on one area of environmental and agricultural policy and on three countries, we believe that the insights emerging have more broad relevance, not only in Africa but more widely.

SCIENCE, POLICY AND DEVELOPMENT

Everyone agrees that contexts for policy-making are changing quickly. Debates involve new actors and take place in new locations. As illustrated in the chapters that follow, trends of internationalization and localization are occurring in parallel. International initiatives, conventions and flows of donor funds create links between African settings and those elsewhere (usually Europe or the US, but sometimes other 'international' settings in Africa). A key theme we explore, particularly through the case of the SFI (Chapter 3), concerns the relationships of knowledge and power that are created as international science is refracted by more local processes. International science in the area of soils and land management – through the Consultative Group on International Agricultural Research (CGIAR) system, university collaborations, and NGO projects, for example – has an important effect both on the framing of issues and on the day-to-day practice of science and policy. Policy can be said to be 'co-constructed' across space, through particular networks and connections linking global and local sites. This, we argue, is an important feature of the contemporary policy process, particularly in settings where national science capacity is weak or under-confident.

But the influence on policy processes is not only one way. Policy 'actors' operating in the international arena have local reference points – many expatriate Africans working in Rome or Washington, for instance, bring with them a particular located understanding of issues, problems and solutions. And in constructing international networks, connections to the local are vital. Alliances must be struck with national scientists and bureaucrats. Farmers in pilot projects in particular locations must be enlisted to give institutional authority and credibility, to provide opportunities to 'witness' facts, such as the efficacy of particular techniques or the reality of certain problems, and so offer empirical support to the development of policy positions. Thus, an examination of the located nature of particular policy processes is vital. As

Chapters 3 to 6 amply demonstrate, no matter what the apparent influence of the international arena (read, in most cases, North American or European), what happens in national bureaucracies, in the context of local interest group politics, and in field settings through the interactions of farmers and extension workers, national and local contexts really do matter.

Such contexts matter, in particular, given the importance of 'globalized' policy processes. Various forms of decentralization, community-based initiative and micro-project, for example, are very much in vogue in current natural-resource management policy thinking and practice, and are being pushed by donors and national governments alike (Leach et al, 1997). As our case study analysis shows, in some instances these create spaces for experimentation and debate at a more local level, offering opportunities for innovation and the recasting of the policy debate from below. In other cases, such spaces allow the further penetration of external influences and a deepening centralization of control and regulation.

Mediating such relationships across scales are 'structures' (particular configurations of politics and bureaucracy) and 'actors' who are largely associated with the state. With increasingly constrained fiscal resources, the reach of the state in Africa is highly variable, and the efficacy and impact of national policy highly differentiated (Herbst, 2000). Thus, in addition to our understanding of local and international contexts, the changing nature of the state and associated bureaucracies is a key theme of the book. Such an analysis requires an assessment of the historical process of state formation, and the way bureaucratic functions and practices have been defined (Young, 1998).

The importance of science as a route to state control through the deployment of expertise is an important comparative theme of the book, throwing up different stories in different places. An analysis of the relationships between science, expertise and the state has, in turn, implications for the styles of engagement that exist with people – and, in our case, particularly rural farmers – and the degree to which different forms of 'participation' are encouraged, or even allowed, by the state.

Across these sites of policy-making – from the local to the global – connections, networks, alliances and coalitions are created. Such linkages are forged by knowledge and power relationships of varying sorts. It is through these networks of knowledge and power that policies are created and development practice is played out. What emerges from such an analysis is a picture that both rejects the simplistic monolithic view of a hegemonic dominance of international development discourse and practice, that sweeps aside all that is local and differentiated in its wake. But it also rejects a simplistic populist vision of bottom-up emancipated development. Power, interests and politics are very much part of the picture. Instead, a more complex and nuanced perspective emerges. Networks and alliances often interact in unexpected ways; apparently all-powerful modernist visions of top-down technocratic development may be subverted, diverted or simply ignored; and seemingly empowering and participatory processes may be captured, controlled or manipulated. Thus, for us, understanding policy processes means understanding the interaction of networks and relationships, agency and practice, and knowledge and power dynamics in particular contexts.

In the area of environmental and land management policy, science plays a critical role in development. By shaping the way development problems are thought about, science influences the nature of networks and relationships between states, within and across bureaucracies and in relation to how alternative expertise is thought about. It is surprising, perhaps, that the role of science and scientists in development policy processes has not been a focus for much study until recently. A core argument in this book, however, is that science is central, and that a lack of interrogation of the nature of expertise in the policy-making process conceals important power dynamics.

By examining how cases for policy positions are built, we attempt to uncover the 'fact-building' processes of scientists and other experts, both lay and professional. The practices of science can be seen as far from neutral. In order for a particular policy perspective to gain ascendancy, very often uncertainties must be black-boxed and controversies downplayed. As Epstein (1991: 28) points out: 'Masked behind [scientific fact's] hard exterior is an entire social history of actions and decisions, experiments and arguments, claims and counterclaims.' It is this social and political history of 'fact-building' that we explore in relation to a number of policy-making processes in the following chapters. What this reveals, of course, is that technical and political processes are deeply intertwined, and that the practices of science – field and lab experiments, models and so on – help co-construct policies in particular ways.

How such science becomes credible and authoritative is another theme of the book. The institutionalization of scientific practice links science to bureaucracies and the administration of development. Science, particularly when linked to international networks, offers authority through the enlistment of accredited experts, the production of formal publications and the use of statistics. This is reinforced by the location of such expertise in state (and international) bureaucracies. The way such mainstream knowledge is counteracted, subverted or resisted by others offering different knowledge claims is also an important theme. While particular styles of science can be identified as dominant, they are not all-enveloping, and alternatives can and do arise. The degree to which these have purchase on the policy process, and offer opportunities for recasting the debate, is also explored in the chapters that follow. Thus, in order to understand 'science in practice' (following Latour, 1987), we trace the actors and networks which are creating the 'facts' that make up policy, as well as uncover alternative practices of 'fact-building' sitting outside the mainstream. This, therefore, required an analysis of how particular types of knowledge, and styles of knowledge creation, become embedded in particular institutional and organizational forms, and how, as a result, others are excluded.

Starting with a focus on relationships, processes and connections, and moving to a situated analysis of institutions, organizations and structures, allows us to see the more permeable, malleable and often contingent nature of policy-making. As people move across locales, practices are linked through initiatives (such as the SFI; see Chapter 3), funding networks (such as Rocke-feller-funded research in Southern Africa; see Chapter 6) and professional alliances of various sorts. As the international, national and local intersect, particular networks and policy positions stabilize around particular ways of speaking and acting. But what legitimacy and authority do these have, emerging as they often do from international initiatives promoted by the World Bank, the UN Food and Agricultural Organization (FAO), the CGIAR, or Northern NGOs and researchers? As new social and political relations are created around particular policy positions, new relations of knowledge, power, meaning and practice also emerge.

While recognizing the dispersed nature of policy connections, the practices of science and policy must be firmly located; scientific practice is necessarily shaped by particular histories and politics, suggesting different relationships between science, expertise and publics (Fischer, 2000). For example, debates emanating from Europe dominate the literature and point to the emergence of a post-industrial risk society (Beck, 1992, 1995; Adam et al, 2000). But different contexts in Africa suggest a different diagnosis. In the chapters that follow we trace the historical relationships between science, local knowledges and political styles, as influenced by different types of engagement with colon-ialism, post-independence development efforts and international science. Thus, across the case study countries we see different forms of interaction conditioned by such histories, and influenced by such factors as media freedom, educational qualifications, civil society organization, and so on. Following this, a variegated and located form of 'modernity' emerges, one that defies universalist descriptions and prognoses (Comaroff and Comaroff, 1999; Agarwal and Sivaramakrishnan, 2000).

Our understanding of the relationships between science, policy and development, and the way in which policies are co-constructed, persist or get challenged, emerges, therefore, through a simultaneous examination of science in context, policy in context and, in turn, science–policy in context. Our emphasis on policy processes encourages an analysis that looks at relation-ships and interactions, linkages and networks and pushes us to go beyond the conventional categories that often guide policy analysis. While categories such as 'the state' or 'civil society' or 'the bureaucracy' or even 'local', 'national' and 'international' may be useful shorthand, they must be unpacked. As the case study chapters show, policy processes cut across such divides, blurring boundaries and encouraging a more nuanced view of the power and relation-ships than is sometimes offered in the more blunt structuralist analyses of policy-making and development. This is important, as it highlights how, in different settings, policy responses may be quite divergent and that contexts really do make a difference. Thus, the notion of a standard development policy – or, by extension, a standard policy-making process – must be fundamentally questioned.

AFRICAN CONTEXTS

What are the particular contexts explored in this book? The core of the book looks at three country case studies from Ethiopia, Mali and Zimbabwe. These countries are some of the poorest in the world. The per capita gross national income (GNI) is only US$6.3 billion, 2.6 billion, and 6.5 billion for Ethiopia, Mali and Zimbabwe, respectively, according to 1999 figures (World Bank, 2001a, b). Broader human development indices put them at 158, 153 and 139 in a global ranking of 162 countries (UNDP, 2001). With substantial numbers of people defined as 'below the poverty line', all three countries have been recipients of substantial amounts of development aid, bringing with it a range of initiatives, projects and technical expertise. In all three countries, natural resource-based agriculture is essential to the livelihoods of the majority of the population, and soils management is a key component of this. In this section, we explore some of the similarities and contrasts across the three country settings.

AGRICULTURE, NATURAL RESOURCES AND LIVELIHOODS

The management of soils has long been a policy concern in Ethiopia, Mali and Zimbabwe. Narratives of soil fertility decline and soil erosion, leading to desertification, have often framed debates, resulting in major development efforts. Thus, for example, in Ethiopia, rural poverty and famine in the highlands has been attributed, at least in part, to the consequences of long-term soil erosion and declines in productive potential. Following the droughts of the 1970s, and particularly after the major famine of 1984, government and donor initiatives have engaged in major soil erosion works – including bunding, terracing and hillside closures – along with a push towards the modernization of agriculture through the supply of external inputs, and, in particular, fertilizer (Chapter 4). Similarly, in Mali, concerns about land degradation in the cash crop enclaves of the Office du Niger and the cotton zone in Mali Sud have prompted a range of programmes aimed at reducing erosion and improving land productivity (Chapter 5). In Zimbabwe, colonial interventions in the former 'reserves' (now communal lands) concentrated on creating a particular model of sustainable farming centred on the mixed farm, with associated erosion structures implemented, often through force and compulsion, to protect arable lands. While the more draconian interventions of the colonial era have largely been abandoned, a similar diagnosis and technical approach persists at the centre of much extension thinking in Zimbabwe to this day (Chapter 6).

Our concern in this book is not to debate the technical pros and cons of such initiatives.[1] Instead, we focus on how such policy diagnoses arise, and how they are implemented, adapted, abandoned, changed, subverted or rein-vented. While there is a striking commonality in the basic framing of problems

– and, indeed, the menu of solutions recommended – there are important differences in the contexts for such policy interventions across the three countries. All countries rely on agriculture, and it makes up 52 per cent, 45 per cent and 11 per cent of the national GDP in Ethiopia, Mali and Zimbabwe, respectively (World Bank, 2001a). But the structure of the agricultural economy varies significantly.

In Ethiopia, a predominantly agricultural economy contributes the bulk of output, with the major production zones being in the central highland areas. Our work in Ethiopia, however, took us to two more marginal zones where infrastructure is poor, markets remote and livelihoods precarious, subject to frequent droughts and, in the recent past, famines. In the dry northern highlands of Tigray and the southern root crop and enset zone of the south, agriculture, while vitally important for people's livelihoods, is but one component of a more complex livelihood system, where off-farm work, migration and other livelihood sources complement agricultural production on often very small plots (Chapter 4).

In Mali we contrast dryland agricultural zones with the cash crop enclaves – particularly the cotton zone in the south of the country – which were set up in the colonial era as sites for agricultural production for export to France. In the cotton zone, farmers are linked into an integrated production and marketing system that is overseen by a parastatal company, where input and credit packages are provided and an extension system is geared towards the efficient production of cotton. By contrast, the dryland zones have very little external support beyond sporadic NGO and donor projects, and livelihoods are necessarily more diverse, given the lack of reliable rainfall or irrigation (Chapter 5).

In Zimbabwe, a dual agricultural system is evident: the inheritance of colonial settlement and racial land segregation. The large-scale commercial farming areas, created largely by white European settlers, sit alongside so-called communal areas, many of which are located in the dry, marginal areas of the country. Here, livelihoods are derived from a mix of agriculture, off-farm income earning and circular migration of various sorts, with the importance of agriculture being dependent on a combination of rainfall amount and reliability, market access, infrastructure development and access to credit and inputs. In the Zimbabwe case study chapter we focus on policy initiatives in the communal areas; but the broader context for agriculture and land access – and particularly the contested large-scale farming sector – is important for any assessment of the political economy of policy-making in the country (Chapter 6).

SCIENCE AND POLICY PROCESSES

In the shaping and promotion of particular development initiatives around agriculture, natural resources and land management, science has played an important role in all three countries. As part of the modernizing project of development, science has served a variety of ends. In the colonial era in Zimbabwe, for example, a significant scientific capacity was developed to service the development of settler commercial agriculture. Alongside this, scientific advice was applied to the development of the African farming areas, resulting in a range of recommendations on how farming should be done, and a set of restrictions, enshrined in law, about the management of natural resources. A technocratic style became embedded in state institutions and the practices of government bureaucracies, with scientific expertise providing legitimating authority for a range of interventions, with far-reaching consequences (Chapter 6). In Ethiopia, a comparable technocratic style emerged in the imperial era, often drawing on expertise from the then British colonies of East Africa. US support for the establishment of land grant-style agricultural universities during the 1960s set a pattern for modernizing interventions in the agricultural sector that continued through integrated rural development and minimum package programmes, to the Sasakawa-Global extension and input supply model of the 1990s. Again, scientific advice on appropriate agricultural practices has remained key throughout (Chapter 4). In Mali, the commercial interests of France in the cotton and irrigated rice zones resulted in significant investments of research expertise, often through long-term placement of expatriate technical advisors. Such connections, reinforced by the educational links of Malians educated in Europe, became well embedded in the cultures and practices of the research and extension organizations of the country (Chapter 5).

During the last decades, with the rise of the involvement of aid donors, many of the previous patterns of technocratic dominance have been reinforced. Scientific expertise, often in the form of technical assistance, has been seen as central to the modernizing project of development. In the contemporary era, as discussed above, the scientific networks created have been transformed in important ways. In Mali, for instance, the dominance of French technical expertise has been challenged – at least to some extent, and certainly in the field of land and soils management – by investments of Dutch foreign aid and links to Wageningen Agricultural University in the Netherlands. In Ethiopia, a range of connections were forged with the Soviet bloc, for instance, in the Mengistu era from 1974, and then with the West and such institutions as the World Bank since 1991. In Zimbabwe, while a relatively strong national research presence existed, transformed, to some extent, from its earlier colonial incarnation following independence in 1980, dependence on foreign assistance for research has become increasingly important, particularly following the declines in state support as a result of adjustment policies instituted from 1991. Thus, in all countries, while national research institutions exist, their dependence on external funding and expertise is an important feature influencing the emergence of contemporary scientific styles.

Beyond the national level, in all three countries connections with regional, continental and international scientific networks are important. Thus, in Ethiopia links to other East African countries in the field of soil management have been forged through funding from the Swedish International

Development Cooperation Agency (SIDA) and the FAO, while in Mali connections across Francophone West Africa are important. In Zimbabwe, Southern African connections are significant, both as part of the Southern African Development Community (SADC) and in other regional networks, such as SoilFertNet, supported by the Rockefeller Foundation and coordinated through the International Maize and Wheat Improvement Center in Harare (CIMMYT). Other linkages are broader in scope. For instance, the Tropical Soil Biology and Fertility Programme based in Nairobi, together with CGIAR centres such as the International Centre for Research in Agroforestry (ICRAF), attempt Africa-wide research interaction through a variety of networks and research collaborations. The Soil Fertility Initiative (SFI), coordinated by the World Bank and the FAO (Chapter 3), included Mali and Ethiopia as focal countries and is another attempt at addressing soil management on a continental scale. With the emergence of international accords on environmental issues – notably following the Earth Summit in Rio – further connections are forged at even wider scales. As signatories of the Convention to Combat Desertification (CCD), all countries have, for example, been engaged in various forms of desertification assessment, sometimes linked to World Bank-funded National Environmental Action Plans (NEAPs). Thus, through these types of connections, national scientists are both exposed to, and have the potential to influence, wider agendas, framings and implementation practices. The interaction of national scientific styles and practices with international processes is key, informing and reconfiguring the relationships of science with policy at the national level.

Scientific styles, cultures and practices thus emerge from a variety of historical experiences and influences, and continue to be shaped by interactions within and outside the countries concerned. The relationship between science and the state is thus conditioned by such interactions. As an important source of authority for the state, the place of science within governmental institutions is significant in our analysis of the contexts for policy processes. As discussed already, in the colonial era in Mali and Zimbabwe, for example, science provided a set of justifications for forms of intervention – for example, support for cotton cash-crop production in Mali, the maintenance of a commercial farming sector in Zimbabwe, and the control of production practices by small-scale farmers in Zimbabwe's communal areas.

As a result, bureaucratic and administrative control was predicated upon a set of scientific analyses, framed in particular ways by certain groups of experts and in the context of a particular political economy of agriculture. This historically situated and institutionally embedded nature of science provides the foundation for particular scientific practices, which become routinized in policy and implementation processes. Thus, in Zimbabwe, statistics on soil erosion in the communal areas, collected in particular ways through often very narrow sets of methods, provided the direct justification for certain types of intervention – soil bunds, wetland protection and so on – and with this the exercise of certain types of state control (Chapter 6). Science and politics are thus closely intertwined, as are science and bureaucratic practice. In the case study chapters that follow, these relationships are examined through particular policy stories. These highlight how an attention to wider political processes, interest group alliances and institutional formations is a necessary element of any understanding of science and development in practice.

PEOPLE–STATE RELATIONS

The relationship between the state, and hence state-led science (and its various incarnations as supported by international development aid), and the wider population again provides some points of comparison between the three countries. Each country has seen the emergence of the contemporary state through quite different pathways.

The contemporary state in Ethiopia emerged from an imperial power based on centres of control in the highlands, spreading during the late 19th century as a result of conquest in the south, through a revolutionary transition that brought with it major social and political upheaval in the period from 1974. With the overthrow of Haile Selassie by Mengistu Haile Mariam, a more unified state system was created on the basis of a socialist model, involving state acquisition of industries and large-scale farmland and major land reform initiatives in most parts of the country. However, maintaining a hold over such a diverse and large country has always been a challenge for Ethiopian rulers. In 1991, Mengistu Haile Mariam was overthrown by a Tigrayan-led rebellion from the north after a long civil war. The new government, while allowing Eritrea independence, has attempted a regional form of control, giving some level of (often notional) independence to the regions. Over time, then, the degree to which state policy emanating from Addis Ababa has had an impact in the remoter regions, especially away from the central highlands, has been variable and has depended upon the extent to which state agents were able to control the countryside through various means – including taxation, land administration or incentives such as food aid. In Chapter 4 we explore two contrasting regions – Tigray and Southern Nations, Nationalities and People's Region – which, under post-1991 regionalization policies, have developed different relationships with the centre and different degrees of decentralized autonomy, resulting in different types of policy process.

Mali is a vast and sparsely populated country where administrative control over the more marginal areas is, to this day, very limited. Indeed, secessionist movements in the north led by Tuareg pastoralists have been a thorn in the side of Bamako-based governments for many years. With limited capacity and reach, state efforts have, since the colonial period, concentrated on the core economic zones of the country.

As Chapter 5 describes, the politics of cotton are at the heart of the politics of Mali and so the relationship between the state, the powerful parastatal Compagnie Malienne pour le Développement des Fibres Textiles (CMDT) and the cotton farmers of Mali Sud is critical to the political regime. Since independence in 1960, the country was ruled by a series of authoritarian regimes. In

1991, *'les evennements'* resulted in the overthrow of the military government
and the installation of a democratically elected one. Electoral politics in the
contemporary era, just as politics before, is very much dominated by the
fortunes and allegiances of the farming communities in the cash-crop zones.
While attempts have been made at decentralizing democratic authority to
communes, the degree to which such new institutions are sites for policy-
making is yet to be established. What persists today, however, is the
concentration on the cash-crop zones, where the politics of cotton (and, to a
lesser extent, irrigated rice) reigns supreme. It is here that state policies do
matter, and, as explored in Chapter 5, where the contests over meanings and
interpretations of policy issues are played out.

As the settler economy grew in Zimbabwe, the influence of the white settler
population over the politics of the country became more and more entrenched.
With the unilateral declaration of independence (UDI) in 1965, a separation
from the colonial power was established, and state interests became even more
associated with a limited group of white farmers and industrialists. With
independence in 1980, the racial division was eliminated and all citizens were
given the opportunity to vote. However, in many respects the colonial inheritance remained, both in the structure of land holdings (despite some attempts
at resettlement during the 1980s), and in forms of governance in practice
(despite some attempts at encouraging decentralized democratic authorities
in the communal areas from 1984).

Unlike in Ethiopia and Mali, the Zimbabwean state has, until recently at
least, considerably more of its own resources. Infrastructure, except to the
remotest areas, is relatively well developed, and the reach of state agents –
extension workers, land development officers, police and so on – is more
extensive and comprehensive. The consequence for communal area inhabitants, both before and after independence, has been that policies made at the
centre have had an impact on the ground. Laws, regulations and recommendations – on soil protection measures, cultivation methods and locations,
and livestock keeping, for example – were rigorously enforced, often with
strict penalties for disobeying. A technocratic state, with effective reach, has
dominated, with remarkable continuities in style and content between the pre-
and post-independence eras (Chapter 6). In recent years, however, this has
changed somewhat. Firstly, there has been a decline in state capacity through
adjustment-imposed fiscal constraints during the 1990s, resulting in fewer
people on the ground, with fewer resources. Secondly, more recently, there has
been a shift in the locus of authority, as the central state, and so the ruling party,
the Zimbabwe African National Union–Patriotic Front (ZANU–PF), was
contested for the first time in large parts of the country by opposition groups
and became heavily influenced by disillusioned war veterans, creating new
and often variable and dynamic forms of governance on the ground.

Thus, the origins of different forms of state, and, with them, state bureaucracies and the practice and culture of science and expertise, have differed
significantly across the three case study countries. This has had major consequences for the ways in which democracy and participation are conceived

and practised, and the implications this has for the relationships between science, expertise and citizens in the policy-making process. In all countries, as already mentioned, there have been moves towards democracy – multiparty representative democracy has been established (at least on paper) in Ethiopia, Mali and Zimbabwe within the last decade or so. The degree to which this has resulted in an active flourishing of democratic practice, and civic engagement in policy processes, is, however, variable, as is discussed in the case study chapters and, more synthetically, in Chapter 7.

CITIZEN ENGAGEMENT AND THE POLICY PROCESS

One notable feature across all countries has been the emergence of various forms of civil society grouping, particularly over the last decade or so. There has been much commentary in the literature on the emergence of civil society in Africa in the post-Cold War era, and much debate about whether this will usher in a new era of revived democracy and governance. Much of this discussion, however, fails to examine the social and political nature of civil societies, and how these relate to the state, and is geared at a more ideological, programmatic commitment to the benefits of community-based organizations, NGOs and other civic groups as democratic forces. In the cases of Ethiopia, Mali and Zimbabwe, there are different stories to report.

Following the major 1980s droughts in Ethiopia, a veritable flood of relief-and-rehabilitation NGOs arrived in the country and became engaged in a variety of development projects on the ground. Much of this was very focused project work, and was closely regulated by the government. The degree to which such initiatives brought with them alternative framings of policy is therefore questionable. Thus, for example, the highly influential NGO Sasakawa Global 2000 (SG2000) provided the impetus for a major new thrust in extension policy in the mid-1990s. Their activities essentially continued a long-established technocratic tradition embedded in Ethiopian agricultural research and extension institutions, albeit with expanded scope and ambition. There have been a few exceptions that have managed to develop a broader social and policy agenda, as discussed in Chapter 4; but, overall, there have been only highly constrained opportunities for wider policy debate. Rein-forcing this, with strong central state control, even in the regionalized system, there has also been limited scope for autonomous development of local organizations. Most local organizations that do exist have strong ties to the state and to various incarnations of the ruling party, the Ethiopian People's Revolutionary Democratic Front (EPRDF). The consequences of this in different parts of the country are important, with a sense of inclusion and engagement with state policy-making in the Tigray region contrasting quite dramatically with a lack of involvement and a disenchantment with the state and its functioning in the Southern region. This has sometimes resulted in violent regional, ethnically based backlashes in the southern region (Chapter 4). Thus, cultures of participation vary significantly across regions, depending on the relationship with those in power at the centre, and the history of interaction between people and the ruling party.

In Mali there has been a similar deluge of development NGOs in the last decade, focusing their efforts most particularly in the more marginal zones, where, as we have discussed, formal state presence remains limited. Again, most of these have engaged in the standard range of development activities, with relatively little impact on wider policy processes. However, as discussed in Chapter 5, there have been some impacts, particularly through alliances made across NGOs – for example, in the Segou region, where more coord- inated action and civic capacity-building has been attempted around such issues as resource tenure and management. With the advent of decentralized local government, the opportunities for the engagement of emerging civic groups with government may grow. However, it is too early to tell whether local government will have enough authority and resources to make a differ- ence. The degree to which such groupings – except as ventriloquized by international NGOs or elite Malian NGO leaders based in Bamako – have an influence on national policy processes is unclear. Most assessments suggest that this is limited. Despite the rhetoric of participation and consultation, attempts at instituting this have, as discussed in relation to the SFI and the National Environmental Action Plan (NEAP) in Chapter 5, been half-hearted at best.

Participation, then, is seen more as part of playing the development game, particularly in the more remote dryland areas, and a necessary part of often donor-funded state activity. Where things really matter politically – in the cash- crop zones – a different dynamic is evident. Here, the stakes are high, with both politicians and senior bureaucrats and parastatal officials wrapped up in a complex web of political patronage and favours. Keeping the lid on dissent in the cotton zone is of prime political importance, hence the reluctance to countenance loosening state control through privatization and deregulation of the cotton sector. Protests over cotton prices, including withdrawal of cotton from the market by farmers' organizations, have sent shock waves through the political and economic establishment in recent years. Usually various accom- modations have been made; but there are limits. With declining cotton prices worldwide and pressure from the World Bank and the International Monetary Fund (IMF) on debt relief and loan conditions, room for manoeuvre is increas- ingly constrained. It is this political dynamic – between the state (and the various actors allied to the state and associated with cotton) and Mali Sud cotton farmers – that, we argue, is perhaps of more significance in Mali when defining the nature of citizen engagement in policy, than the often perfunctory forms of participatory consultation carried out in the name of the development in the dryland zones.

Zimbabwe, too, has no shortage of NGOs and 'community-based' projects of various sorts. While many have sunk without trace with the collapse of donor funding to the country in the last few years, at its height during the late 1980s there were several hundred registered NGOs in the country. Again, the degree to which these really represented an up-welling of civil society or a cashing-in on a donor trend is difficult to discern. As Chapter 6 discusses, however, there have been some opportunities for interesting local-level experimentation and innovation that have, through alliances with other non-government groups and government, resulted in important policy shifts in particular areas. Along with Ethiopia and Mali, this process has been enriched by the expansion of networks, both within the country and outside, afforded by linking up with international or regional donors and others. Thus, the flow of ideas has expanded beyond the confines of state bureaucracies, often allowing the opportunity for cross-over exchanges when particular networks are created. The case of the transformation of the agricultural extension system discussed in Chapter 6 towards a more bottom-up and participatory mode is an example of where the increasing permeability of the state was evident. Staff mobility between government and non-government organizations, and national and international settings, therefore potentially allows for innovation and experimentation, on the one hand, or, on the other, the consolidation and the further embedding of mainstream narratives and policy perspectives.

Organized civil society, outside the urban areas, however, remains relatively weak in Zimbabwe. For example, the farmers' union, which notionally represents small-scale farmers, is seen to be dominated by a particular elite and has had since independence, some would say, an uneasily cosy relationship with government. The emergence of an opposition party from the ranks of the trade unions has been largely an urban phenomenon, and opposition and contest in the rural areas has been sporadic and fairly limited. Rural politics has almost exclusively been dominated, until recently, by the ruling party who consolidated its power through village and ward-level authorities as part of a centralized form of decentralization. Although more powers have been allocated to so-called traditional leaders in recent years, as representatives of broad rural interests their role can be questioned. Yet, this is not to say that more informal forms of organization and protest are unimportant, beyond the conventional definitional boundaries of 'civil society'. The rise of the new Christian churches has been, for example, an important trend, with implications at the local level for associational life and collective activity in rural areas. Similarly, self-styled prophets calling for a return to traditional ways and a rejection of much state-imposed development activity have had an important influence in some parts of the country, particularly following and during the early 1990s' drought (Chapter 6).

The escalation of farm invasions and the intervention of the war veterans' lobby (and associated allies, both linked to and separate from the ruling party) have been important new developments during the last few years, resulting in a fundamental shift in the balance of power in rural areas, with variable and uncertain consequences. While focused on land reform and resettlement, this will, inevitably, recast the way rural politics is played out, with formal governmental district authorities, technocrats from the line ministries, chiefs and headmen often being by-passed or coopted into new political alliances that appear to vary dramatically from area to area. Quite what the longer-term implications of this change are for rural governance is as yet unclear; but the parameters for participation, and even the engagement of NGOs and other development players, have changed significantly.

The consequences of these contexts for participation are examined in more depth in Chapter 7, which explores the possibilities of citizen participation in the policy process through a reflection on the various case studies. What can be said at this point, however, is that such contexts vary massively both across and within countries. An understanding of these broader contexts that frame the relationships between science, expertise and the state and citizens is, therefore, for us a key starting point for any analysis of policy change processes.

A COMPARATIVE AND MULTI-SITED APPROACH

By taking three countries as cases representing such diverse contexts, and exploring policy processes around land management over time through a number of detailed examples, the book aims to identify what works where and why. A comparative approach allows for an assessment of different contexts and an analysis of the implications that these have. Nevertheless, this is not an exercise in direct comparison with a similar methodology applied across all sites in relation to a fixed set of variables. The complexities and particularities of individual policy processes would not allow for such an approach. Instead, in each case we pursue a number of specific policy stories, uncovering their histories, investigating their contexts, mapping the networks and coalitions and evaluating their impact.

The methodology is, therefore, necessarily both qualitative and eclectic. The case studies are based on over 250 interviews, conducted during a number of visits to Ethiopia, Mali and Zimbabwe, as well as Nairobi, Rome, Washington, DC, and London between 1996 and 2001. Our interest in examining policy processes – and particularly the question of why particular policies persist and how some change – emerged from a longer-term engagement at a more local level. This village-based collaborative research on soil fertility dynamics (Hilhorst and Muchena, 2000; Scoones, ed, 2001) took place over several years from 1995 in a number of sample villages in Wolayta in southern Ethiopia, Dilaba, Siguné, M'Peresso and Tissana villages in Mali, and Chivi and Mangwende communal areas in Zimbabwe. This research revealed the immense diversity of soil management practices implemented by farmers, and the startling disjuncture between local knowledge and practice and policy positions at both the national and international level.

This observation raised a number of important questions for us. Why, we asked, was there such a consistent disconnect? Why, if there was such an emphasis on policy from governments, NGOs and the donor community, was there such a repeated mismatch between local realities and policy positions? Our interest then focused on the social and political shaping of knowledge in policy: whose knowledge was included and whose excluded? How did science and different forms of expertise interact in the policy process? What were the politics of policy-making? And how might policy processes be changed in order to encourage a greater inclusion of otherwise excluded voices, and a reframing of policy that takes more account of the local realities of the village settings with which our earlier research had engaged.

But in order to answer these questions, we initially lacked a conceptual route map. Many different disciplinary perspectives speak to these issues – political science, anthropology, public administration, sociology, science studies and other perspectives all offer particular insights. Yet, they are all limiting in their own ways – some may offer a rather simplistic structural perspective of broader pattern, missing out the micro detail, variability and diversity. Others do the opposite. In Chapter 2 we introduce a range of conceptual perspectives. In the end we came up with an eclectic bricolage of approaches. We are not wedded to one perspective alone – for example, more structuralist political science is clearly good at outlining the broad patterns of interest group politics. Anthropology, by contrast, offers rich ethnographic examinations of micro-practice and politics, while discourse analysis is, in turn, helpful in discerning the relations of knowledge and power in the creation of policy. Our aim in this book is to bring such approaches together in order to offer a more complete picture than would have otherwise been offered by an approach constrained by a single discipline. By triangulating across conceptual spaces, and so approaching an issue or question from multiple angles, our understanding of often highly complex policy processes is, we would argue, expanded and deepened. Thus, the conceptual map offered in Chapter 2 is not an attempt at an integrated and all-encompassing synthesis, with all contradictions and overlaps neatly ironed out. Instead, it is a menu to pick from – a selection of prompts to ask useful questions.

Such a diverse conceptual starting point inevitably pushed us towards an unconventional methodological approach. By choosing a number of particular policy processes – plans, initiatives, laws, policy statements – we traced connections upwards, downwards, sideways and outwards: in other words, in whatever direction it took us. This meant mapping networks of people, ideas, objects, documents and so on, identifying how they were connected, the power relations that existed, and the history of emergence of the policy debate. Thus, an 'archaeological' approach (following Foucault) was adopted that allowed for systematic excavation, but did not constrain us to any particular boxes or categories in our search for linkages. Such tracings took us to local villages, district HQs, research laboratories and field stations, national govern-ment offices, NGO project sites, donor offices, conferences and meetings. It was, par excellence, a multi-sited approach. Our 'field work', therefore, linked Sodo-Wolayta to Harare, Bamako and Addis to London, Nairobi, Rome and Washington, DC, to conferences and workshops in various locations, as well as into the cyberspace networks created on the Internet. Such an approach must also necessarily be historical in scope, looking at how various forms of path dependency open up or constrain policy options in the present. An analysis of institutions and the practices of science and development in particular places over time also reveals how policies are embedded in particular contexts that are historically created.

BRIEF OVERVIEW OF THE BOOK

This book can be read in a number of different ways. Some may prefer to look at the beginning and end, and then select from the case studies in the middle. Others may wish to read it straight through, getting a sense of the details of the case material before reaching the conclusions. Still others may prefer initially to skip Chapter 2, which covers a range of conceptual and theoretical issues, and, consequently, a huge array of different literatures, and then return to this chapter after getting a sense of the specific empirical examples by reading the case study chapters first. The choice is yours. The next few paragraphs offer a quick summary of some of the key features of the chapters that follow, and may offer a guide on reading the book.

Chapter 2 draws on a wide range of sources from a variety of disciplinary approaches to understanding the policy process. Our aim is not to provide an exhaustive and comprehensive review, but to point to issues, themes and questions raised by the literature that may provide useful conceptual and methodological tools for investigating environmental policy processes. Understanding the knowledge–policy relationship involves clarifying exactly what policy is and how it is developed, and reflects on the particular nature of scientific knowledge that plays such a major role in environmental policy-making. Analysing the policy process also cuts to the heart of key debates in social science: why is reality framed and dealt with in certain ways? How important is political conflict over the distribution of power and resources? What is the role of individual actors in policy change? Three contrasting explanations of policy change are explored in the chapter: firstly, that policy reflects political interests; secondly, that change reflects the actions of actor networks; and, thirdly, that policy is a product of discourse. These set up the approaches adopted in the empirical examination of cases that are covered in the following chapters.

Chapter 3 turns to an examination of policy processes in an international context. The creation and selling of ideas of global environmental crisis has been a core characteristic of the post-Rio decade. Global science and global policy-making processes are central to these crises. However, framings of global environmental problems – the knowledge claims and interests that underpin them, and the plans that flow from them – are often accepted without critical examination. The idea of an African soil fertility crisis is one such case. To illustrate this, the chapter traces the history of the Soil Fertility Initiative (SFI) for Africa, a major multilateral programme. We look at the role of science in creating both a problem and potential solutions to that problem. By tracing the evolution of the SFI, the chapter documents that not as much has flowed from the initiative as initially envisaged. While bureaucracies may easily coalesce around a problem and make a big noise, translating rhetoric into concrete action is much harder. The unravelling of the SFI, the chapter suggests, can be explained as a consequence of bureaucratic politics between, and within, the key players, and also as a result of inadequate links between global and local scales. The implications for international activity – conventions, strategies, action plans and so on – are serious. Too often what claims to be global is really not global at all, but has barely concealed links to localities in the North. Accordingly, the challenge, this chapter argues, is to design more effective global processes that allow more meaningful inclusion of diverse local problem framings.

Chapter 4 is the first of the country case study chapters and focuses on Ethiopia. Policy discourses urging environmental rehabilitation and rapid agricultural intensification for food self-sufficiency are firmly entrenched in Ethiopia. This chapter examines the actor networks and key policy spaces associated with the establishment of these discourses, taking natural-resource management policies and institutionalization of the SG2000 extension programme as case studies. An emergent, and potentially challenging, participatory natural-resource management discourse is also identified. Contrasting the regions of Tigray and the Southern Nations, Nationalities and Peoples' Region (SNNPR), the chapter concludes by arguing that, with decentralization, differences between regional administrative and political cultures are key to policy processes, affecting the degree to which central policies reflect local concerns.

Chapter 5 aims to understand how crisis perspectives find their way onto the policy agenda and result in policy problems being framed in particular ways in Mali. We begin by outlining key political, economic, bureaucratic and agro-ecological factors, and by suggesting how these factors drive discussions and thinking about soils in a particular direction. The chapter then focuses on two contrasting framings of the soil fertility problem. The first we label 'productionist', where we concentrate on cotton, a crop in the Malian context for which this narrative is particularly potent. The second framing we identify as a 'land management approach'. Soil fertility in this approach cannot be isolated as a matter of inputs and outputs, but is seen in a broader environmental context. The chapter proceeds through an analysis of bureaucratic, scientific and political cultures, and processes of actor–network construction to suggest why they have achieved different degrees of influence. We then examine the SFI as an arena in which different framings of soil fertility are contested. Tracing the history of the SFI in Mali reveals much about where policies come from, and why they take particular shapes. The SFI, we argue, is organized around an influential narrative that could result in a major national policy activity. However, tensions in the actor network exist and these potentially threaten its future. Finally, the last section concludes that the policy process, and the embedded relationships that help produce particular policy framings, may be changing in quite fundamental ways as a result of new political processes that are emerging.

Chapter 6 asks why policy processes in Zimbabwe have consistently reinforced a highly technocratic approach to natural resources management, while excluding alternative perspectives and framings of problems for policy. Political contexts and interests, it is argued, shape policy discourses. While there has been continuity between the colonial and immediate post-colonial periods, in more recent times the range of actors engaged in the policy process has widened, responding to state reform, the growth of a diverse range of civil society organizations and a post-Rio international environmental agenda. Reflecting these changes, policy processes have taken on new shapes. Participation has become a key theme. The chapter takes four case studies to ask how substantive this participation is. It concludes that, while much participation is 'instrumental' and only succeeds in reiterating early narratives and technocratic approaches, policy spaces can also emerge where actor networks can be constructed that promote more fundamentally 'empowering' forms of participation in policy processes.

Chapter 7 draws the themes of the book together by looking, in particular, at the prospects for more participatory and inclusive forms of policy process. The chapter first reviews the lessons learned about contexts for environmental policy processes in Africa from the case study chapters, discussing, in turn, internationalized science policy and the three country cases. The next section then moves on to ask what spaces for engagement exist for alternative perspectives on environment and land management that go beyond the mainstream received wisdoms. By looking at a range of different spaces – from engagement with international activities, involvement in research-action pilot projects, opportunities arising from decentralization and local-level planning and organized citizen action and campaigning of different sorts – we evaluate the degree to which relations of knowledge, expertise and policy-making are being reconfigured, resulting in new forms of policy process.

2

Understanding Environmental Policy Processes: a Conceptual Map

INTRODUCTION

This chapter opens environmental policy-making up to scrutiny and offers a conceptual route map for understanding policy processes. The framework that emerges forms the basis for the analyses of the case studies reported in the subsequent chapters. Two key challenges have shaped this work: firstly, to examine how policies are created and upheld through the institutions of science, government and administration; secondly, to examine how they are contested, where they are open to incremental change and where alternative discourses are emerging and finding expression in the policy process.

To examine this we bring together perspectives from different disciplinary areas, including anthropology, science studies, political science and public policy. Anthropological perspectives emphasize the ways in which language and styles of argumentation are critical when analysing policy processes. Knowledge for policy, we argue, is produced discursively. This means it both *reflects* and *shapes* particular institutional and political practices and ways of describing the world. Discourses frame the way in which problems are thought about, linking up different issues, often in highly programmatic, narrative, cause-and-effect form. These framings guide interventions in relation to objectified problems by setting up causal links through rhetorical power, and through the marginalization of alternative perspectives as being biased, subjective and non-scientific. Often these discourses, and the institutional practices upon which they rely, are so entrenched that people are unaware of them and the way in which they shape world-views.

Our understanding of how certain types of knowledge about policy problems become dominant is also informed by literature on science and decision-making. Knowledge for policy is very often associated with the creation of iconic 'facts', which can be critical in shaping the management and control of people and resources. Insights from the field of science and technology studies help to interrogate the processes by which knowledge is generated, particularly the creation of influential facts or 'wisdoms' and their supporting data. Such perspectives highlight the ways in which particular scientific disciplines, cultures and practices become authoritative. This type of analysis reveals the centrality of social and political values to the presentation of what appears as 'rational/scientific' policy.

Policy must also be located in political and bureaucratic contexts. Specific histories of state and society interaction are significant in shaping the emergence of a given policy path in a particular setting. Policy does not move neatly from stages of agenda-setting and decision-making to implementation; policy is often contested, substantially reshaped or even initiated from a range of places or points between macro and micro levels. It is this complexity and dynamism, we argue, that may allow for the assertion of alternative story lines and practices, which, in turn, can gradually result in substantial challenges or shifts in the knowledge and practices associated with previously dominant discourses.

Through examining environmental policy processes across different settings, this book suggests that scientific and other forms of knowledge – and the interests they reflect and shape – interact in a range of different ways. Distinctions between the technical and the political become blurred, and contests occur in the process of developing scientific facts, in official decision-making fora and in the implementation of projects, programmes and policies. Policy, we suggest, can change in unexpected ways. Moments of 'policy space' (see, for example, Grindle and Thomas, 1991) emerge, allowing alternative perspectives room to challenge the power of more totalizing discourses, influential social interests and particular patterns of state formation.

WHAT IS POLICY?

In order to understand how 'received wisdoms' about environmental problems find expression as policy in the first place – to prise open the black box of policy-making – it is necessary to have some conceptualization of how policy is made and, more broadly, what policy actually is. The traditional starting point for defining policy is that policy comprises decisions taken by those with responsibility for a given policy area, and these decisions usually take the form of statements or formal positions on an issue, which are then executed by the bureaucracy.[1] Conceived of in this way, policy is a product of a linear process moving through stages of agenda-setting, decision-making and, finally, implementation.

However, in practice, policy is notoriously difficult to define. As one British civil servant commented: 'Policy is rather like the elephant – you know it when you see it but you cannot easily define it' (Cunningham, 1963, cited in Hill, 1997: 6). Rather than seeing policy as simply a single decision implemented in a linear fashion, many observers have noted that, in practice, policies generally consist of a broad course of action (or inaction, for that matter; see Smith, 1976) or a web of interrelated decisions that evolve over time during the process of implementation (Hill, 1997). Policy also needs to be seen as an inherently political process, rather than simply the instrumental execution of rational decisions.

In attempts to understand the policy process, three broad approaches can be characterized. Firstly, there is the linear model, based on assumptions of rational and instrumental behaviour on behalf of decision-takers (Simon, 1957). The focus is on the decision and the subsequent stages of implementation that follow (see, for example, Easton, 1965; Jenkins, 1978; Hogwood and Gunn, 1984). The linear schema is useful up to a point; and, very broadly, this is often what happens (Sabatier, 1986). However, there is also plenty of evidence – as the case study chapters that follow amply show – to say things do not actually work in such a tidy way. Policy comes from many directions, and implementation can be as much about agenda-setting and decision-making as execution of decisions. Roe, for example, building on Wildavsky's work on the politics of the budgetary process, argues that budgets, far from being examples of classic examples of linear policy-making, where allocations are agreed and announced at fixed points in time and then spent as planned, are, in fact, texts to be interpreted. He argues that the moment of decision is, in fact, a fiction, given the revisions and amendments to budgets and parallel fiscal processes at work (Wildavsky, 1974; Roe, 1994). A focus on policies as courses of action, part of ongoing processes of negotiation and bargaining between multiple actors over time, therefore provides a second approach to understanding policies (Dobuzinskis, 1992).

In such a view, policies may not even be associated with specific decisions. If they are, they are almost always multiple and overlapping. Lindblom, for example, famously described policy-making as the 'science of muddling through' (Lindblom, 1959) and advocated an incrementalist perspective on policy process (Braybrooke and Lindblom, 1963; Dror, 1964; Etzioni, 1967; Smith and May, 1980) that focuses on the actions of policy actors and the bureaucratic politics of the policy process. Such a perspective suggests a more 'bottom-up' view of policy (see Hjern and Porter, 1981), where the agency of different actors across multiple 'interfaces' is emphasized (see Long, 1992). Here, an analysis of practitioners and their day-to-day dealings with policy issues is key (Schön, 1983), as is an insight into the timing of 'trigger events' and the role of 'policy entrepreneurs' in pushing policy discussions in new directions (Cobb and Elder, 1972; Kingdon, 1984).

However, both these two broad approaches (see, also, reviews in Parsons, 1995; Hill, 1997; John, 1998) remain surprisingly silent on issues of power. A third approach to understanding policy processes, then, can be added which takes the relationship between knowledge, power and policy as the centre of analysis. Foucault, for instance, sees policies operating as 'political technologies', enmeshed in the relations of power between citizens, experts and political authorities (Foucault, 1991; Burchell et al, 1991). Dreyfus and Rabinow (1982: 196, cited by Shore and Wright, 1997) argue that: 'Political technologies advance by taking what is essentially a political problem, removing it from the realm of political discourse, and recasting it in the neutral language of science.'

In this view, by mobilizing a legitimizing discourse – and the associated metaphors, labels and symbols of scientific authority – support is granted to 'official' policies. Through the power of expertise, certain assumptions are normalized and subsequently internalized by individuals (Shore and Wright, 1997). In the context of environmental policies, where scientific expertise plays a major role in framing policy debates, conceptions of the world that become dominant in policy discussions are a reflection of the norms through which people are governed. By seeing policy as discourse, analytical attention is turned to the webs of power underlying the practices of different actors in the policy process, as well as the practices that are invested in policy negotiation and contest. Thus, linguistic and textual styles, classificatory systems and particular ways of speaking and acting – forms of 'governmentality' (Burchell et al, 1991; see below) – can be seen to empower some and silence others.[2]

POLITICS AND POLICY PROCESSES

These different perspectives on understanding the policy process assume different relationships between state authorities, bureaucrats, expertise and broader civil society (Torgerson, 1986). In the largely top-down, decision-oriented, linear model, a privileged role for expertise is granted and rational actions in the implementation process are assumed. Science creates a 'technocracy' (Habermas, 1973; Fischer, 1990, 1993a, 1995, 2000) and rational decisions are implemented in a clearly defined way by administrators, bureaucrats and field agents. With the process of implementation seen as unproblematic – merely a matter of good administrative management – the key focus is on agenda-setting. For most commentators, this is ideally served by a representative, liberal democratic politics, where citizens participate in elections, and science and bureaucracy are left to get on with it (Mazmanian and Sabatier, 1983).

But a more practice-oriented perspective problematizes the multiple, incremental and complex processes of policy formation and implementation to a far greater extent. While there are some who still regard such divergences from the linear model as a problem of 'implementation deficits' (Pressman and Wildavsky, 1973; Hogwood and Gunn, 1984) to be dealt with by more effective public management approaches – communication, incentives, sanctions and rewards and so on – in order to get aberrant rational actors back in line, others see the processes of negotiation and bargaining among actors with different forms and styles of expertise as central. Proponents of such a view may take a pluralist stance, where a variety of interest groups compete over policy positions (Dahl, 1961), or a more participatory approach, where citizens have a more direct role in the creation of policy (Held, 1996).

Such standard models of democracy – whether liberal, pluralist or participatory – have been critiqued by more post-structuralist perspectives on politics and policy. Such analyses adopt a more fragmented view of the state and relationships with the multiple actors of 'civil society'. Power relations operating as part of the policy process act to construct individuals as subjects with a range of identities; here, local actions are set within the context of wider 'global ethnoscapes' (Appadurai, 1996). With changing styles of governance – for example, in the context of neo-liberal reforms and decentralization – policies can be used in new ways as instruments of power (Shore and Wright,

1997), resulting in new challenges for citizen action, the negotiation of expertise and participation in the policy process.

Across this range of perspectives, different emphases on individual, everyday practices and wider structuring processes are evident. With this come contrasting views of the role of the state, the nature of scientific and other expertise, and the relationship with other actors and interests in civil society. Cutting across all perspectives are different conceptualizations of power, ranging from essentially instrumentalist views to perspectives that highlight a much more diffuse and fragmented view.[3]

In subsequent sections of this chapter, and through the empirical cases that follow, we will explore elements of these themes in more depth, with a particular focus on how science shapes environmental policy processes. In the next section, we look at the relationships between science, expertise and policy, which – given the complex and uncertain nature of many environmental problems – are central. In subsequent sections we take three different approaches to understanding policy processes. These focus, firstly, on the role of political interests; secondly, on actors, agency and practice; and, finally, on discourse in the policy process. While not completely distinct, each suggests different conceptual perspectives on the relationships between knowledge, power and policy. In the case study chapters that follow, different comb-inations of such approaches have been applied – sometimes alone, sometimes in combination – with the aim of developing a rich, multi-faceted, yet theor-etically informed, understanding of environmental policy processes in Africa.

SCIENCE, TECHNOCRACY AND EXPERTISE

While knowledge may not get established in policy in a straightforward linear fashion, it is still often assumed that what drives environmental policy-making is scientific knowledge: scientists establish the facts about environmental realities, and policy-makers come up with policy options in the light of the facts. So, in a range of policy areas, analysts in think tanks, research institutes or government ministries aim to provide rational, technical policy analysis that rises above politicization of policy issues: 'speaking truth to power' (Price, 1965; Wildavsky, 1979).[4] In separating out the role of scientific expertise in the policy process, policy formulation becomes increasingly technocratic, with science given a major role and lay publics often labelled as ignorant, or incapable of handling the scientific complexities that guide decisions.

The case for technocracy is that it is efficient to specialize in a complex society. Those with expertise, it is argued, are highly experienced in a given area; with detailed knowledge of a range of relevant cases, they are trained in the specialized collection of data and the systematic analysis of information, and, as professionals, they tackle issues with neutrality, aiming at dispas-sionate objectivity. Furthermore, if one takes a positivist view of knowledge, there is simply no need for excessive consultation over technical decisions, as any group of experts would eventually arrive at similar conclusions regarding policy (see, for example, Fischer, 1993b).

There are, however, several problems with the idea of rational, scientifically driven policy-making. Firstly, it is not always clear when a policy issue is going to be decided on technical arguments and when on other criteria, and even how these choices should be made. Do politicians use technical arguments and draft in technical experts to escape difficult issues and absolve themselves of responsibility for policy areas? Habermas notes that the 'scientistic practices' of technocracy are inherently depoliticizing (quoted by Fischer, 1993b: 166).[5] Secondly, it is also not always clear who should decide on who is a technical expert: why is this think tank neutral and objective and that one not?[6] And thirdly, what happens to democracy and public debate when issues are reified as technical and the sole preserve of experts? Does this result in disaffection with the policy process that has deleterious long-term consequences?[7]

These questions are equally prominent when one thinks about science and environmental policy-making. Work on the politics of science underlines the importance of contests over which scientists are deemed authoritative and allowed to speak on an issue; which policy questions are seen as issues for scientific deliberation and which are firmly kept within the realm of politics; and which potential biases emerge from commercial and government funding of scientific research (Ezrahi, 1990; Jasanoff, 1990; Nelkin, 1979, 1992). Clearly, the stakes in terms of resource allocation around many environmental issues are extremely high. As a result, having authoritative scientists support-ing your case can be critical. All of these contests exist alongside the scientific professions' concern to maintain their own credibility with the public as neutral mediators of reliable information.

What is unique about the claims of science, according to Latour, is that scientists attempt to shortcut the political process and access 'nature' by scientific experiment in order to bring back 'facts' (science) to speak to the world of 'values' (politics) (Latour, 1993). Rangeland ecologists, for example, deliver the facts about what is happening to pastures; climatologists explain the greenhouse effect; soil scientists offer assessments of changes in the soil fertility status of soils; and forest scientists inform us of rates of loss of primary forest cover. With 'truth speaking to power', bodies of scientific expertise then inform policy in an unproblematic manner.

Such a view has, of course, been widely criticized.[8] Weinberg (1972), for instance, identified the domain of 'trans-science', where policies are developed before scientific closure, and science and policy interact in the context of continuing uncertainty and unresolved debates. Much work on the sociology of science has highlighted how science needs to be seen as constructed knowledge, the result of competition between different interest groups (see Barnes, 1974, 1977; Bloor, 1976; Barnes and Shapin, 1979; Shapin, 1979), as well as micro-social negotiations among scientists over scientific controversies (see Latour and Woolgar, 1979).[9] For example, studies of the actual everyday practice of scientific activity have provided important insights into how certain scientific ideas gain ascendancy (Pickering, 1992). Through such work, the performative aspects of scientific activity have been emphasized in which the routinized forms of scientific practice, located in particular institutional settings, become important in creating and maintaining policy styles (Pickering, 1995) and 'epistemic cultures' (Knorr-Cetina, 1999). Expert knowledges, therefore, are not insulated from their social deployment and use, carrying with them a variety of social commitments (Irwin and Wynne, 1996). Seen in this way, 'Science. . . offers a framework which is unavoidably social as well as technical, since in public domains scientific knowledge embodies implicit models or assumptions about the social world' (Irwin and Wynne, 1996: 3). The whole process is thus bound up in the power relations underlying the conduct and organization of science, highlighting issues of funding, professional organization and institutional governance.

An important part of the scientific enterprise is seen as generating universalizable statements. This often requires the containment of uncertainties through the standardization of procedures, measurements, classifications and modelling routines, sometimes removing such uncertainties from wider discussion (Jasanoff and Wynne, 1997). For Latour, the type of firm scientific pronouncements that are seen in policy statements are no more than effective and extensive knowledge networks.[10] Scientists, he argues, create facts by closing controversies, and by black-boxing uncertainties and assumptions away from further scrutiny, while simultaneously universalizing locally specific knowledge through enlisting the support of institutionalized knowledge networks (Latour, 1987; see also Callon and Latour, 1981; Callon, 1986a, 1986b). What counts as a valid scientific experiment, and hence as acceptable evidence, is often highly political, dependent on the role of networks in establishing the validity of scientific facts.[11] A key feature of experiments is that individuals do not have to be physically present at an experiment in order to be persuaded of its validity as a result of a process of 'virtual witnessing' (Shapin and Schaffer, 1985). This occurs through the use of 'inscription devices', such as journals and conferences (Latour, 1987). What makes scientific knowledge different from other forms of knowledge, actor-network theorists argue, is that this virtual witnessing allows scientific knowledge to be globalized and, hence, perceived as rational, universal and modern. Other forms of local or indigenous knowledge are, by contrast, more context specific and lack the devices to achieve global reach, leading to the perception that it is 'traditional' and 'non-modern' (Latour, 1993; Murdoch and Clark, 1994).

As the case studies in Chapters 3–6 explore through a range of examples, scientists and policy-makers engage in complex processes of 'mutual construction' (Shackley and Wynne, 1995). Scientists contribute to the framing of issues by defining what evidence they can produce and by making claims about its significance for policy-makers. The negotiation process works both ways, however, and policy-makers also delimit areas for scientific enquiry in the process of effectively cutting off certain avenues of research, and the very possibility of the creation of certain facts. In the boundary work between science and policy, particular terms, objects, statistics, data and procedures become important (Gieryn, 1995). These may create 'anchoring devices', allowing the emergence of a tentative consensus between groups of scientists and policy players in areas where there is a great deal of uncertainty (van der Sluijs et al, 1998). For the case of land and soils management discussed in the subsequent chapters, examples abound – nutrient balance models, desertification maps, soil loss estimations and so on are all seen to be key in establishing a particular 'mutually constructed' policy position.

As emphasized throughout this book, the internationalization of the science–policy interaction has become an important feature of the contemporary scene. Since the 1992 Earth Summit in Rio, debates about desertification, biodiversity, deforestation, water management and other themes are increasingly being held in international contexts. Scientific commissions, advisory panels, international initiatives, expert consultations and large conferences are all part of the process. These are the emerging sites for the mutual construction of science and policy on an international stage, where knowledges and practices are exchanged, discourses are shaped and political actions are designed (Jasanoff and Wynne, 1997). In Chapter 3, for example, we explore a particular case of such an internationalized form of science policy through an examination of the Soil Fertility Initiative (SFI). Similarly, in other chapters cases are identified where there are strong interactions between the local and the global.

The simultaneous processes of globalization and localization create a fluid and diverse range of settings for the co-production of science and policy (see Appadurai, 1996). While global knowledge, linked to global institutions, initially appears all powerful, such framings should not be taken for granted. Rather, they are the product of the activities and strategies of concrete actors. There are a variety of actor networks, creating different images of the global, with different local roots. Some are clearly more extensive and more powerful than others; but, as the case study chapters show, things change, and new configurations of actor networks emerge that are associated with new connections between the global and the local and new constructions of knowledge about the environment. In this way, the construction of local settings is informed by different borrowings from the global discourses. Local experiences, therefore, may help to shape the accepted definition of the global. But, equally, global processes do not just impact on, and uni-directionally shape, the local; they are inevitably refracted and reinterpreted through different local settings.

In the processes of producing globalized knowledge and policy about the environment, models of various sorts play an important part. As discussed for the case of nutrient balance models in Chapter 3, or soil erosion loss modelling in Chapter 6, the simple policy prescriptions that sometimes emerge from such modelling attempts may hide a range of uncertainties from view (Wynne, 1992; Funtowicz and Ravetz, 1993). Sometimes this may be well known but conveniently ignored by both scientists and policy-makers. On other occasions, caveats may be present in scientific papers, but these may be obscured by the way in which findings are cited and taken up in policy documents, having the effect of creating an artificial sense of certainty. In other instances, scientific methodologies may themselves be problematic, with assumptions that appear to hold true under one set of circumstances failing under alternative scenarios. Mackenzie (1990) has pointed out how perceptions and admissions of uncertainty vary depending upon who you are and your relationship to the production of knowledge. Scientists directly involved in producing knowledge may admit high levels of uncertainty, whereas users who are institutionally committed to the knowledge being produced may admit far lower levels of uncertainty. By contrast, those distant from the sites of knowledge production, who are alienated from it and mistrust the institutions associated with its production, may perceive high levels of uncertainty.

When predictive models are transferred from the laboratory to real-world situations, unanticipated variables and relationships between variables may become important (Wynne, 1996). Fundamental indeterminacies, once exposed, have the effect of undermining the presumed objectivity of scientific knowledge that enters the policy process (Wynne, 1992). Such issues are particularly apparent during the creation of predictive models for looking at environmental change. When (what are, in essence) indeterminacies are presented as 'deterministic uncertainty' – elements of the model that require further work – the hope of prediction, management and control is maintained (Wynne, 1992). However, if the basic character of uncertainty in complex ecological systems is accepted, a rather different policy conclusion is the result (Holling, 1993). As with other areas of environmental change, such as climate (Shackley and Wynne, 1995), forest dynamics (Fairhead and Leach, 1996) or rangelands (Behnke et al, 1993), this equally applies – as the subsequent chapters comprehensively illustrate – to land and soil management in Africa.

In many parts of the world – and particularly in Europe and North America – the authority of formal scientific pronouncements on a range of public policy issues has increasingly been called into question by publics who lack trust in official positions. With a growing lack of faith in scientists and the policy institutions associated with science, the legitimacy and authority assumed for successfully implementing the rational linear model are being undermined. Thus, with the outbreak of 'mad cow disease' (BSE) in the UK, no matter what scientists and politicians said, the public refused to buy beef, even if deemed 'safe' (Irwin, 1995: 115–116). Similar issues pertain in the cases of the mumps, measles and rubella (MMR) vaccines and genetically modified (GM) foods in the UK. But how important are these changing relations of science and society in the African contexts discussed in this book? Is there a similar emergence of a 'risk society' (see, for example, Beck, 1992, 1997; Adam et al, 2000) in Ethiopia, Mali or Zimbabwe (see Leach et al, 2002)?

With growing public distrust of institutionalized science, publics, in some instances, have taken up their own 'citizen science', developing their own methodologies and partnerships with experts. Such challenges to conventional forms of expertise are observed in various forms across the case study sites, the implications of which are drawn together in Chapter 7. Such approaches to 'participatory technology development' (see van Veldhuizen et al, 1997) raise queries about who frames the questions for science and technology development, who does the science and how does this articulate with policy? Thus, following this line of argument, encouraging the 'public understanding of science' must not simply be seen as a process of stimulating communication of facts to an essentially ignorant, or at least disinterested, public. Instead, broader questions of institutional legitimacy and public trust arise, including the importance of encouraging a greater reflexivity in the interactions between scientific institutions and increasingly informed and environmentally aware publics (Irwin and Wynne, 1996).

A growing recognition of a wider range of knowledges and perspectives beyond the confines of science and scientists suggests new ways of interacting with lay publics. In Africa, there is an increasing consensus on the importance of so-called 'indigenous technical knowledge' (Richards, 1985; Warren et al, 1995). Local knowledge systems and farmer innovators and experimenters have been widely documented and acclaimed in the field of soils management (Reij et al, 1996; Reij and Waters-Bayer, 2001). However, very often such approaches create new reified categories, and set up 'local' knowledge in opposition to 'scientific' knowledge, ignoring the dynamics of knowledge construction and the differentiated and power-laden processes that this implies (Scoones and Thompson, 1994). Nevertheless, particular forms of knowledge – be it the 'high science' of sophisticated computer modelling of soil characteristics and dynamics or more lay understandings of soil processes based on 'indigenous technical knowledge' – need not be seen as distinct (Murdoch and Clark, 1994). Once acknowledged as having something to contribute, farmers' knowledge about land management may offer another set of inevitably partial knowledges, carrying with them, of course, their own social commitments and assumptions. With this move, the unhelpful divide between 'science' and 'lay public' or 'local knowledge' begins to break down (see Agrawal, 1995). Thus, across a variety of actors – scientists, policy-makers, lay publics – a variety of partial positions arise that are intimately bound up with the situated subject positions of the actors concerned (see, for example, Haraway, 1991; Harding, 1991). It is these plural and partial positions on environmental issues that must be negotiated in the context of wider political interests, discourses and interactions of different actors. It is to these themes which we now turn.

To sum up, knowledge – we have argued – does not get established in policy as part of a simple linear process where problems are identified and solutions are operationalized. Policy contests – which are substantially contests about knowledge – run throughout the policy process from macro to micro scales. At the same time (as examination of the relationship between science and policy suggests), neither is policy-making a gradual process of moving closer to an ideal and 'rational' approach to problems. So, how does policy change and how do different types of knowledge get established in policy? The following sections identify three ways of explaining policy change. These explanations identify, in turn, key roles for political interests, actor-oriented and practice-based approaches, and policy discourses.

POLITICAL INTERESTS AND POLICY CHANGE

The first approach we identify presents policy change primarily as the upshot of interactions between different groups with differing political interests, a position traditionally associated with political science and political economy. Knowledge in these accounts is presented as essentially subordinate to interests and politics. What different groups or categories of actors believe and do about a policy question is a reflection of their interests: if you understand policy as the consequence of political interactions, then you will understand why particular types of knowledge prevail. Assessments of the key political fault lines have changed over time. They are, alternatively, between classes, between different interest groups within society, between the state and society, and between different factions within the state, or some combination of these (Grindle and Thomas, 1991; Hill, 1997).

Interactions between state and society actors in the policy process are primary concerns of political scientists. Early attempts to explain the origins of policy focused on competition between groups within society over the allocation of resources and the formulation of rules for social and economic life – what came to be known as pluralism (Truman, 1951; Dahl, 1961). Policy to these political scientists is essentially about processes of bargaining and competition between different social groups. While some influential advocates of pluralism, such as Dahl, do not entirely ignore the state, state agencies are portrayed as only one of many competing actors around different policy issues (Hill, 1997). Groups in a pluralist polity might be organized around a whole range of variables – for example, region, ethnicity, professional and industrial sectors, and economic class.[12]

This society-centred slant on the policy process remains influential, with the earlier language of interest groups finding echoes in concerns with civil society, non-governmental organizations (NGOs) and new social movements (Offe, 1985).[13] Much of the environmental governance literature frames the difficulties within environmental policy-making in terms of the need to balance competing social interests (Hempel, 1996). As the case study analyses in this book show, it is often possible to identify core conflicts between environmental, business, consumer and local interest groups as central to the policy process.

The growth of environmental NGOs and movements in different parts of the world has received extensive commentary (see, for example, Jamison, 1996; Yearley, 1994; Wapner, 1996; Newell, 2000). An important question arises about the degree to which environmental groups are entering a new arena for policy influence that is created by the withdrawal of command-and-control state regulation, the apparent failure of formal international environmental agreements and the emergence of international trans-border dimensions of environmental change (Litfin, 1994; Paterson, 1996; Vogler and Imber, 1996).

Different types of relationship with other actors can be identified, ranging from cooperation and collaboration with governments, international agencies and the corporate sector to a more critical approach involving confrontation and direct action. A similarly varied articulation with science can be observed. On the one hand, many environmental groups base their campaigns on a basic distrust of 'high science' and the supposed negative consequences of modern technology; on the other hand, in order to make their case, they must appeal to scientific authority for universalistic statements about the consequences of environmental destruction. Thus, compromises are made, resulting in campaign strategies based on 'pragmatic epistemological flexibility' (Yearley, 1996: 183). The role of the media in the framing of issues and in developing public and political commitment to particular campaign themes is also highlighted by the literature. The environmental concerns of the media may be key to highlighting particular issues and excluding others (Burgess, 1990; Burgess and Harrison, 1998). In Chapter 7, we examine the evidence for the role of non-state actors and the media in policy change. We find that in contrast to European or North American settings – from where much of this literature derives – environmental movements are less influential in Ethiopia, Mali and Zimbabwe. And where such actors do exist, they tend to articulate a particular form of global environmental discourse.

However, contemporary political debates are seldom explained purely in pluralist terms. Following the widely cited work of Nordlinger (1981, 1987) and Skocpol (1985), there has been a renewed emphasis on the state and its agencies as key variables in policy change. Two broad approaches are identifiable: those that concentrate on the state in broad macro terms and those who look at the activities of specific components of the state. The state is not a neutral arbiter of social conflicts, but is active in shaping policy. States also vary immensely, and it is important to understand in detail why some states are strong (guiding the policy process to clearly defined ends) and why others are weak (leaving policy incoherent and more captive to limited interests in society) (Migdal, 1988).[14] As Chapter 1 has already indicated, the histories of state formation in Ethiopia, Mali and Zimbabwe are highly divergent, resulting in different forms of state authority, power and control.

The bureaucratic politics literature (see Allison, 1971; Halperin, 1971) recognizes the considerable expertise and discretion residing in the executive arm of government. This perspective is less concerned with states as macro actors, but more with the way in which policy emerges from contests between different parts of the state. As the case study chapters show, different bureaux, ministries and agencies have differing functions and histories, and are staffed by people with different types of (often technical) training. These differences in perspective and more general predilections for increasing jurisdictions and agency resources mean that policies often emerge incrementally from the micro-level trade-offs and contests within the bureaucracy. Lipsky (1979) makes clear that front-line workers (or 'street-level bureaucrats'), far from being cogs in a Weberian machine, exercise considerable agency in the policy process.[15, 16] They prioritize, interpret instructions, deal with overlapping and contradictory directives, and take the initiative in areas where there might be a policy vacuum. Even where directives are clear, street-level workers can block, deflect or ignore instructions. A focus on the practices of front-line workers – project workers, field agents, regulators, extension workers and others – is a key theme of the case study chapters that follow, highlighting how policy change often emerges from changing implementation practices.

Thus, knowledge and policy can interact dynamically at a variety of points in a process, often in the context of highly heterogeneous bureaucracies. To avoid failing to differentiate between bureaucratic contexts, the specific characteristics and histories of different administrative settings need to be understood. As we have already emphasized in Chapter 1, this involves engaging critically with the broader processes of state formation that shape political and governance institutions (Young, 1988, 1994; Sivaramakrishnan, 1995). Bureaucracies and formal systems of decision- making, understood in context, enable us to comprehend the variability of possible knowledge–policy interactions in the policy process.[17] Our discussion of the World Bank and the Food and Agriculture Organization (FAO) in Chapter 3, for instance, provides an illustration of how management and organizational issues can be crucial to performance and, ultimately, policy-making processes.[18]

These differing strands within the political science literature are brought together, to some extent, in work on policy communities, policy networks and discourse and advocacy coalitions.[19] Each policy domain needs to be looked at empirically in order to see whether the state is weak or strong, how bureaucratic interactions work and how different social forces are able to shape a policy. Policy, it is argued, emerges from the deals forged in the policy networks that constitute these 'sub-governments'. These networks vary in composition from domain to domain; but, as illustrated in each of the case study chapters, they are likely to consist of government agencies, key legis- lators, farmers' groups, business and industry representatives, consultants and policy analysts and journalists, among others.

Some of these approaches offer ways of explaining how knowledge finds its way into policy. Discourse coalitions (Hajer, 1995), for example, are alliances between a range of different actors and organizations around a common approach to a problem, often expressed as a unifying story line. These bring together many institutional and discursive practices and are given meaning around a policy project. Through these coalitions, actors 'not only try and make others see the problems according to their views, but also seek to position actors in a specific way' (Hajer, 1995: 53).

Approaches focusing on policy networks (and the various variants), then, have the advantage of moving debates beyond the oppositions of state and society that characterized earlier discussions about what drives policy change. Depending upon the policy domain, a more pluralist or a more state-centred approach may be appropriate, since states may be weak or strong in different areas. Thus, we are obliged to look at the historical context of particular state formations, the lack of homogeneity in the state and bureaucracy, and the way in which networks of political patronage and lines of affiliation have been formed over time (for examples from Africa, see Bayart, 1993; Mamdani, 1996).[20]

A policy network approach makes an explicit recognition that processes of interaction, bargaining and the construction of coalitions are important. We cannot simply read off political change from reified representations of state and society; instead, as emphasized in the set of approaches discussed in the next section, we must understand how actors – and their knowledges – interact across networks and coalitions in the process of policy change.

ACTOR-ORIENTED AND PRACTICE-BASED APPROACHES

A second set of approaches that we wish to highlight emphasizes – in a similar way to elements of the policy networks approach just discussed – the practices of individuals and groups of actors, connected in networks, alliances and coalitions of different sorts. In this view, actors involved in the policy process – whether field-level extension workers or senior officials in ministries – are seen to have a degree of discretion and choice in their actions, although their actions are perceived as occurring within socially embedded networks and cultural settings. Such an approach draws on theories of practice and agency (see, for example, Bourdieu, 1977; Giddens, 1984), and rejects the more structural analyses typical of the more conventional political science literature highlighted above, centred as it often is on aggregate pictures of interest groups and policy communities. Thus, expressions of agency through repeated practice may result in both intended and unintended outcomes; often, serendipity, contingency and chance are important elements in policy change. This makes any idea of predictable, rational and linearly planned intervention or policy-making very unlikely (Long and van der Ploeg, 1989, 1994).

Latour sees 'science in action' as a process where the 'construction of facts. . . is a collective process' (Latour, 1987: 104), where 'black boxes' (defined by Latour, 1987: 139, as hard facts, powerful theories or indisputable evidence) are created and then both transmitted and transformed through networks of different actors. According to Latour, 'the black box moves in space and becomes durable in time only through the actions of many people; if there is no one to take it up, it stops and falls apart' (Latour, 1987: 137).

Those wanting to build an argument must, therefore, enrol others in their project, ensuring that the argument does not get too dramatically transformed in the process and that recognized authorship is maintained. Latour identifies a number of different tactics. Enlisting others by appealing to their explicit interests is the most obvious; here, interests overlap to such a degree that mutual advantage is found in joining forces. In other cases, others can be enrolled if they piggy-back on the idea for differing reasons. However, there may be two contrasting problems: either indifference, where those enlisted do nothing to promote the idea, or overwhelming and sometimes misguided enthusiasm, where 'your tentative statements can be turned into claims of gigantic size' (Latour, 1987: 110). Another tactic is to reshuffle interests and goals – for instance, through the creation of new groups who are offered new objectives and a site for a new coalition around which narratives can be built.

Such networks emerge through associations of power (Law, 1986). Latour (1987: xx) argues that 'since the proof race is so expensive, only a few people, notions, institutions or professions are able to sustain it; this means that the production of facts. . . will not occur everywhere and for free, but will occur only at restricted places and at particular times'. Particular types of resource are needed to make credible claims. These may be in the form of particular types of data, graphical representations, computer models and published papers in certain journals. But access to these is not open to everyone. Financial research resources comprise one obvious limitation for many; but perhaps as important is access to the fora where power is centred, networks are built and claims established, whether around expert consultations, specialist conferences or invited contributions to journal issues. The process of mobilization (Callon, 1986b), or the spreading of a particular viewpoint, therefore, depends upon interaction with effective networks and the application of human and material resources to the endeavour.

The interaction of science and policy can therefore be seen as a process of mutual construction where – through the interaction of knowledge and power – science and society are co-produced (Jasanoff and Wynne, 1997). In other words, science is not dissociated from the social and political worlds of policy processes; the two emerge in tandem. Thus, the social commitments and values inherent in policy are deeply implicated in the construction of scientific 'facts' (Wynne, 1996; Latour, 1999). In this process the institutionalized practices of science and policy-making are a key part of the power of discourse and one of the parameters within which individuals exercise their agency. Thus, the seemingly mundane daily activities of scientists and bureaucrats engaged in preparing scientific papers or consultancy reports; the elaboration of models; participation in workshops, meetings or e-mail discussion groups; and engagement in formal and informal policy briefings are a central part of the joint production of science and policy. They exist as part of wider 'epistemic cultures' defined by the cultures of labs, offices, research stations or international agencies (Knorr-Cetina, 1981, 1999).

Such practices may be central to the activities of 'epistemic communities' of scientific experts who transcend national boundaries and, through their actions, influence the processes of policy-making within and between nation states (Haas, 1992). The epistemic communities' literature (Haas, 1990, 1992), which is more explicitly rooted in international relations theory, makes similar points. Cooperation on environmental agreements and treaties does, in fact, come about because of the strategizing of 'epistemic communities': networks of individuals sharing core – often predominantly technically informed – beliefs about the subject area. These communities fill key positions in national bureaucracies, create international negotiation processes and generally enrol important target individuals and institutions to create national and international supporting constituencies.[21]

Epistemic communities are defined as a type of knowledge elite. They share similar basic assumptions about cause-and-effect relationships, and, if presented with similar scenarios, different members of the community would reach broadly similar policy conclusions. The spaces that allow epistemic communities to achieve influence derive from the uncertainty that policy-makers face in an increasingly complex range of policy domains. Where the community can convince policy-makers that there is uncertainty, or where they can take advantage of already perceived uncertainty, they can help shape the framing of problems and suggest appropriate courses of action.[22]

Linking the worlds of science and policy are a range of key actors in the policy process, whose aim is to push policy in particular ways through the mobilization of knowledge and expertise. Such individuals and groups are usually well placed and, indeed, invest considerable efforts in creating their own networks of influence. They are also well attuned to the timing of policy: they are able to see policy spaces opening up and are able to respond to 'trigger' or 'focusing' events when they arise (Cobb and Elder, 1972; Kingdon, 1984). Such 'policy entrepreneurs' may emerge from the scientific community, from politics, from business, from the NGO sector or from the arts. In the environmental policy field, there are good examples from many realms (Hempel, 1996), including the arena of soils and land management in Africa. As the case study chapters relate, there are key influential individuals who operate at national and international levels and whose role is paramount to understanding policy change.

Actor-oriented and practice-based approaches therefore make it clear how the processes of mutual construction of science and policy are often obscured from view.[23] The putative neutrality of science and the prestige of powerful scientific institutions throw a veil over the politics of who gets funded; who is discredited as a crank; how particular scientific bodies and particular researchers have access to key government committees; and how and why and on what terms politicians invoke scientific authority. Under-standing actor networks also leads us back to original pieces of research and to the practices and processes – often battles – that led to the closure of scientific controversies, the black-boxing of uncertainties and indeterminacies, and the establishment of knowledge. Such approaches are then primarily a way of understanding the spread of knowledge. Furthermore, by emphasizing the practices and actions of multiple and interacting actors, these approaches help to break down the divisions between such aggregated categories as state, civil society, community and scientific establishment imposed by a more structural approach to interest groups and policy change.

It is, therefore, the relentlessly detailed prying apart of the linkages in the skeins and webs of knowledge which such approaches offer that enables us to understand how received wisdoms are built and, subsequently, upheld through the actions of different actors. With these tools we can explain, for example, exactly why there is a widespread consensus that soil fertility is declining at a particular rate in a particular place; why an action plan is being formulated to deal with it; and why certain technologies are deemed necessary for amelioration.

POLICY AS DISCOURSE

A third way of understanding policy change is to look at policy as discourse. Hajer defines discourse as 'a specific ensemble of ideas, concepts, and categorizations that are produced, reproduced and transformed in a particular set of practices and through which meaning is given to physical and social realities' (1995: 44).[24] In Foucauldian terms, 'ideas, concepts and categorizations' are expressions of knowledge and power (Foucault, 1980), controlling human subjects by the definitions and categories imposed upon them. Discourses are frames that define the world in certain ways; in the process, they exclude alternative interpretations (Schram, 1993; Apthorpe and Gasper, 1996; Grillo, 1997). Discourses do not emanate exclusively from particular individuals and institutions; they are larger than this – the cumulative effect of many practices. Even the discursive practices of identifiable actors are themselves reflections of other discourses.

In relating discourse to policy, two ideas stand out. Firstly, the very idea of policy itself needs to be problematized. If policy is understood as a 'political technology' (following Foucault, 1991), then policy practices involve categorizing the world into different sectors and areas for the purposes of managing and maintaining social order. It entails ordering and labelling populations in different ways, and so relates to a range of practices such as the collection of data, the regulation of social and economic life and the allocation of resources (Darier, 1996). Thus, the basic units in the policy analysis and planning vocabulary, such as policy areas or sectors (for instance, the environment), are not givens but are themselves discursively created (Apthorpe, 1996). Behind the widely unquestioned phenomenon of policy, Shore and Wright (1997: 3–4) suggest, stands the notion of governance that is not value free; it is necessary to ask who is being governed by whom and to what ends and with what effects. For this reason, Foucauldian writings on 'governmentality' emphasize the values and expressions of power concealed in the neutral language of policy (Burchell et al, 1991).

In different policy areas, the way in which issues are talked about is highly significant. Concepts have histories and they reflect types of knowledge and practice. They empower some institutions and individuals whose concerns and competencies they are associated with; simultaneously, they marginalize others (Drysek, 1997). A range of linguistic and literary concepts emphasizes the importance of styles of story-telling in policy analysis. Examples include narratives (Kaplan, 1990; Roe, 1991), tropes (Throgmorton, 1993), rhetoric (Apthorpe, 1996), and styles of argumentation (Toulmin, 1958; Majone, 1989; Fischer and Forester, 1993). It is impossible to talk about policy neutrally; rather, whatever one says carries assumptions and is, in some sense, prescriptive. The language in which it is framed is as significant as the actual content.

At times, the embedded assumptions in the way in which specific policy areas are talked about come together in particularly explicit and quite simplistic summaries of situations. Policy narratives are one example of these simplified framings. Many of the received wisdoms about African environmental issues that are discussed in this book rely on their narrative format, whether these are the 'Green Revolution' or 'environmental conservation' narratives from Ethiopia (Chapter 4), or the 'productionist' or 'land management' narrative framing of Malian policy debate (Chapter 5).[25] Knowledge finds its way into policy through the prolonged reiteration of these programmatic tales of cause and effect. Such messages are easily communicated; they make for good sound-bite political marketing, and they fit well with the demands for clarity and measurable manageability of large-scale bureaucratic organization. Given these selling points, the reasons for their persistence seem all too clear.

While making insightful links between knowledge, power and policy, some of the more extreme interpretations of a discourse perspective on policy processes, however, see science and development as somehow monolithic and integrated – simply reproducing relations of power due to historical location (Ferguson, 1990; Escobar, 1995). Such analyses fail to give credit to varied actors' consciousness, intentionality and responsibilities – in other words, their agency. The result, often in such accounts, is a presentation of simple confrontations of competing discourses – experts versus publics, developers versus local people and so on. This creates unhelpful divides between social categories and sources of knowledge. The analysis in this book, by contrast, attempts to go beyond such simple analyses to see the actual and potential interactions across blurred and contested boundaries.

CONCLUSION

The three broad (and, to some degree, overlapping) approaches to understanding policy change presented above suggest that knowledge is established in policy in different ways. Knowledge is established as:

- a reflection of structured political interests;
- a product of the agency of actors engaged in a policy area;
- part of overarching power–knowledge relations that discursively frame practice in particular ways.

How compatible are these different positions? From one point of view, not at all. The political interests' approach presents knowledge as subservient to interests. It also works at a more aggregated macro level than the actor/practice-oriented approach – what matters is the structures that shape individuals' behaviour. Without these structures, political conflict and the policy and dominant types of knowledge that emerge from conflicts make no sense. The actor- and practice-oriented position would obviously cavil at this. By exploring the micro detail of different policy and knowledge controversies, it can detail precisely why a certain statistic or methodology became influential for policy-makers. In this view, the world is, in large part, what people do, the choices they make and the agency they exercise. Finally, the third position would take a post-structuralist sceptical glance at both the other positions. Interests are socially constructed; political conflicts look different depending upon where you stand and they change as discourses shift. Likewise, actors' agency makes sense only within the context of broader narratives and frames of reference.

In the following chapters, we use these three ways of understanding policy in different combinations to offer a multi-faceted analysis of policy processes. Combining approaches helps us to explore a range of perspectives on how received wisdoms enter and become entrenched in policy. Yet – given what we understand about policy processes – how do we challenge orthodoxies and create processes that are more participatory and allow room for alternative perspectives and previously marginalized interests? Again, insights from these different conceptual lenses help us to explore who is included or excluded, and why, as well as to illuminate the prospects for more fruitful participatory engagement.

In arguing against a linear view of policy, Clay and Schaffer (1984a: 192) claim that 'the whole life of policy is a chaos of purposes and accidents'. We would not go so far. Analysis of policy processes from a variety of different conceptual lenses highlights the continuous interplay of discourse, political interests and the agency of multiple actors. While certainly non-linear, policy processes, we argue, are not simply chaotic and down to chance and accident. A combination of these different analytical perspectives highlights both complex dynamics and structural constraints, but also emphasizes opportunities for agency, action and change. Improved understandings arising from such analyses, therefore, may – as we argue in the chapters that follow – reveal opportunities to open up environmental policy debates to a greater range of perspectives.

3

Global Science, Global Policy: International Policy Processes in Africa

INTRODUCTION

This is a history of the selling of a story: a narrative of potential crises and disaster for the soil resources of Africa, a story whose conclusions lead to a particular set of actions, requiring an international response. The characters in this drama, connected in various and changing ways, are scattered across the world – in Rome, Washington and Wageningen, and a range of African capitals. They include scientists, consultants, government and aid bureaucrats, politicians and complex hybrids between these. The plot emerges over several years through the writing of august scientific papers, the production of glossy brochures and stylish websites, the creation of sound bites of information and statistics, attendance at meetings and workshops and informal conversations and lobbying. All combine to muster support and interest and sell the idea to politicians, funders and others.

As discussed in Chapter 1, global environmental crises have been a media, research and policy concern for some time. The 1992 Earth Summit in Rio spawned a range of frameworks, conventions and initiatives to respond to these crises by setting up an international architecture for problem assessment, regulation and project funding. In 1996, for example, the Convention to Combat Desertification (CCD) entered into force and joined climate change and biodiversity as one of the key global environmental issues with pledges for action across the globe, but particularly in Africa.[1] In this chapter we concentrate on the construction of land management issues in Africa as an international environmental problem and take as a case study the Soil Fertility Initiative (SFI). This was launched with much fanfare by the Food and Agriculture Organization (FAO) and the World Bank in 1996, featuring an impressive array of collaborators and supporters. Linked as it is to a variety of other initiatives similar in aim, this case offers insights into the way knowledge, power and practice interact in constructing global policy issues. [2]

The processes of construction that we describe have two aspects. The first is to do with the social and political processes surrounding the creation of globalized knowledge that claims to speak about very large areas. The second relates to the development of forms of organization that are international, offering the potential for the global management of environmental issues. We argue that the two processes are critically inter-linked. We suggest that this examination of the framing of problems by science, in interaction with bureaucracy, helps to explain the persistence, and to illuminate the contingency, of some frequently unquestioned, but urgent, policy problems.

The chapter is organized as follows. The first section picks up on themes introduced in Chapter 1 and looks at narratives about a soil fertility crisis in Africa. We then look in more detail at the practices of science and scientists in representing the soil fertility problem. The following section emphasizes the importance of looking at the activities of individuals and suggests that it is the actions of key protagonists that are critical to the way in which an issue is discussed and is set up as a problem requiring action. The subsequent section examines the importance of the bureaucratic context within which scientists interact and networks of actors engage. The chapter concludes by arguing that, in the future, there may increasingly be challenges to the type of global frameworks and framings of global problems described in the chapter. We suggest what some of these might be and the implications for global science and policy initiatives.

CREATING A STORY LINE: THE EMERGENCE OF A SOIL FERTILITY NARRATIVE FOR AFRICA

Soil fertility, as a policy problem, does not emerge randomly or in intellectual isolation. It should be seen as an assumption linked to a set of deeply held beliefs about rural development, food security and agricultural development in Africa. These narratives are entrenched as intellectual and practical organizing principles. Why do they matter? They are important because, as firmly rooted world-views, they shape judgements and behaviour. Sets of assumptions and premises are key. While the logic that flows from them may be good, it is nevertheless the case that if the first premise is flawed, then whole courses of action, plans, programmes and policies can arise that are, at root, misconceived.

Two key narratives underlie the argument that there is a soil fertility crisis. The first of these can be cast as a 'food-gap' narrative. In this Malthusian view, population growth rates are contrasted with anticipated growth in cereal production, and one is subtracted from the other to leave scenarios of alarming and unsustainable aggregate food deficits in the future. The influential *World Food Prospects Report* produced by the International Food Policy Research Institute (IFPRI) warns that 'the world's farmers will have to produce 40 per cent more grain in 2020, most of which will have to come from yield increases. . . however, growth in farmers' cereal yields is slowing' (Pinstrup-Andersen et al, 1999). A paper in the IFPRI *2020 Vision* series argues that present trends in agricultural, economic and population growth will result in

Africa needing to import 27 million tonnes of cereals in 2020, as opposed to 9 million at present (Badiane and Delgado, 1995: 2; Agcaoili and Rosegrant, 1994: 1).[3] In 1996 a World Food Summit was organized by the FAO precisely to bring attention to this issue. Publicity for the summit warned strongly against complacency, arguing that the world will need to feed an extra 3 billion people by 2030, requiring a 75 per cent increase in food supplies (FAO, 1996).[4] Ismail Serageldin (2000), then chair of the Consultative Group on International Agricultural Research (CGIAR), warned:

> *The world's population is expected to exceed 8 billion by 2025, an increase of 2 billion in the next 25 years. . . there will be more mouths to feed in complex circumstances. Norman Borlaug calculates that 'to meet projected food demands, by 2025 the average yield of all cereals must be 80 per cent higher than the average yield in 1990'. These increases must come primarily from increasing biological yields, not from area expansion and more irrigation.*

This story line is associated with a range of key players in the international food, agriculture and natural resources debates. In addition to those linked to the CGIAR, it is also frequently heard emanating from agricultural economists in the World Bank as the intellectual underpinning for investment plans designed to promote agricultural growth. Targets of various sorts based on such analyses are favourites for the bilateral aid agencies.[5] Non-governmental organizations (NGOs) also make use of this sort of argument to justify their interventions. For example, the influential Sasakawa Global 2000 (SG2000), the brainchild of Norman Borlaug, 'father of the Green Revolution', is now a key player in the agricultural sector of many African countries (including Ethiopia – see Chapter 4).[6] The food-gap story line also frequently gets media headlines in the well-publicized announcements of Lester Brown and the World Watch Institute, and their annual *State of the World* reports.[7]

A second important narrative proclaims a crisis of environmental degradation. This pessimistic view of population and environment interactions has dominated thinking about the environment since the Club of Rome reports in the 1970s (Meadows et al, 1972).[8] This perspective is – as with the food-gap narrative – Malthusian in flavour. A *2020 Vision* briefing by researchers from the International Fertilizer Development Center (IFDC) begins: 'as the region's [Africa] population continues to grow rapidly, outpacing the growth rate in other regions of the world, its agricultural land is becoming increasingly degraded' (Henao and Baanante, 1999).[9] This view is articulated particularly clearly in the work of Kevin Cleaver of the World Bank. Together with Schreiber, he presents negative trends in agriculture, population and natural resource management coming together in an alarming 'nexus', which in itself sets off further rounds of poverty increase and environmental degradation (Cleaver and Schreiber, 1995).[10]

These arguments are invoked as part of the rationale for action in the concept note for the SFI prepared by the World Bank. Shortened fallows and expansion of farming into marginal areas, it is argued, lead inexorably to degradation of resources. To quote:

> The nexus of rapid population growth and high population densities, low productive agriculture and depletion of natural resources has created negative synergies that exacerbate existing conditions of soil nutrient mining and underdevelopment, thus creating a vicious circle of poverty and food insecurity (World Bank, 1996: 4).

It is argued that these issues are so serious that:

> Without restoration of soil fertility, Africa faces the prospect of serious food imbalances and widespread malnutrition and likelihood of eventual famine (World Bank, 1996:1).

Indeed, for some, addressing issues of soil fertility is absolutely fundamental to the unlocking of Africa's developmental potentials. The International Crops Research Institute for Semi-Arid Tropics (ICRISAT) website quotes Henk Breman, now of IFDC:

> Over the years stupendous efforts have been made to bring the Green Revolution to Africa. Yet, the magic that has worked in Asia and elsewhere in the world has somehow eluded Africa. Many theories have been proposed, but the one that is gaining ground is in a way the most revolutionary, because it doesn't agree completely with what most people think is the biggest limiting factor. In fact, one can say, 'fertilization is irrigation', stated Dr Breman, because it has been found that soil improvement increases the water use efficiency of crops and leads to higher recovery of applied nutrients.[11]

The point made by Breman is key to understanding the bite of soil fertility narratives. It is argued, in the context of the larger food and environmental crises, that soil fertility is not just one component problem. Instead, it is actually the lynch pin, the factor that, if addressed, will result in the much sought-after transformation (see Chapter 5 for a further discussion in the Malian context). According to one eminent international research scientist we talked to: 'looking at soil fertility can transform agriculture and get us out of the food security trap – the same as with HYVs [high-yielding varieties] in Asia'. Sanchez et al make the argument that 'per capita food production will continue to decline unless soil fertility is effectively addressed' (Sanchez et al, 1997: 13).[12] Likewise, Christian Pieri of the Agriculture and Natural Resources Department at the World Bank, a board member of IFDC, author of a central text on African soil fertility (Pieri, 1989), and another key figure in the history of the SFI, comments: 'Donors are well aware of the fact that within the chain – food security, agricultural development, protection of the global environment – the main link is soil fertility maintenance.'[13]

Likewise, the answer to the land degradation crisis does not lie with traditional approaches. As a senior international scientist argued: 'Land degradation concentrates on soil erosion. . . but economists don't know the limits of soil erosion plots. . . and they miss the boat. Soil fertility is now more important than soil erosion.' We have, then, a narrative in which the soil fertility problem is located within wider views of food and land degradation crises, but with a critical twist where it is presented as actually pivotal rather than subsidiary.

Having set a broad scene and then located the key to the crisis, the narrative then moves from diagnosis to prescription. A key part of the solution is that action is needed – and that this entails some form of international mobilization:

> During the next 10–20 years, if West African governments and the international community adopt a 'business-as-usual' attitude, it would not be far-fetched to predict that there would be gross migration from the drier countries bordering the Sahara desert to the more humid countries farther south. This would probably be followed by mass starvation (IFDC, 1996: 5).

What action is needed from the international community to avoid 'mass starvation'? Exactly what benefits are proposed to flow from coordinated international action? The then vice-president of the Environmentally Sustainable Development Department of the World Bank, Ismail Serageldin, made the case for the SFI at its launch in November 1996, saying:

> We therefore welcome the Soil Fertility Initiative as a new form of collaboration among international institutions to promote collective dialogue, reach consensus on critical issues, avoid duplication of effort, share information and formulate effective strategies to increase the productive capacity of soils, especially in regions where inadequate plant nutrition management threatens food security.

Soil fertility is seen by some as the key entry point to a range of policy areas. While the starting point may be the narrow technical issue of soil fertility management, the implications for policy are wide. In an introduction to the SFI on the IFDC website, it is argued that:

> African governments have to wake up to the urgency of the problem. . . the Initiative seeks primarily to convince governments of African countries to create a favourable climate – in terms of land reforms, credit availability and input accessibility – that will allow farmers to adopt sound resource management practices.[14]

We have argued that the food gap and population–environment nexus are two powerful development narratives, and that the particular narratives surrounding soil fertility management in Africa both add something and bring the two narratives together. We have suggested, too, that these narratives emerge out of the international development arena and that one of the key things they do is to provide a rationale for further action by those located in that milieu – those charged with the jobs of 'waking up' and 'convincing'.

So, what type of action is proposed? In our discussions, most informants suggested a range of activities that embrace some combination of policy reform, institutional change, technology transfer and scaling-up of support for local initiatives and efficient local practices. However, specific emphases do emerge. Concerns with the food gap frequently lead to advocacy of greater use of inorganic fertilizers. Numerous policy documents cite the low levels of fertilizer use per hectare in comparison with Northern countries or other countries in the South, such as India or China, as a matter of great concern.[15] For some, this offers the potential for an African Green Revolution – a transformation of agriculture through intensification and the adoption of modern technologies – akin to the dramatic changes in Asia during the 1960s and 1970s.[16]

Others concentrate less on fertilizers, specifically, but rather on developing new combinations of fertilizers and organic sources of nutrients. As a senior figure in one international research institute proclaimed:

> *Soil fertility is a natural resource. . . ions are ions – plants are neutral about nutrition. . . the old paradigm is dead; now it's integrated organic and inorganic solutions, rather than the extremes: all fertilizers or pure organics.*

The relative emphases placed on different narratives can become critical as they reflect different perceptions about the degree to which 'external' resources and technologies are essential for resolving the crisis of African soils.[17]

But whatever the relative emphases, a new project emerges, as well as a new concept to guide development agendas: the recapitalization of soils. One scientist commented: 'Soil capital is shrinking. You get lower returns from the same amount of nutrients. Only with capital do inputs lead to higher outputs.' The metaphor of 'capital' is frequently a central part of the narrative form, whether used by protagonists arguing for organic build-up or renewal through inorganic applications. This, in turn, links to other key terms used, including notions of soil 'mining' and imbalances in nutrient 'budgets'. Through the use of metaphors from economics, accounting and mining, the message comes across loud and clear. You can carry on with current practice up to a point, but without replenishment the moment of reckoning will eventually arrive, and this, according to some, is perilously close. This, then, provides the justification for a major recapitalization initiative to restore and enhance soil productivity.

The argument for a global response rests on more sophisticated arguments about soil capital being an international public good, requiring international action, and deserving of Global Environmental Facility funds (Izac, 1997).

According to an International Centre for Research in Agroforestry (ICRAF) researcher:

> *For soil fertility replenishment, the costs are beyond the individual farmer. You have to think about future generations. If it's degraded today, then there will be less for tomorrow. So we need cost sharing. Subsidy is a bad word, but who should pay the cost? He's doing it [investing in land husbandry] for the benefit of future generations.*

Of course, not everyone involved with the SFI is committed to exactly the same diagnosis and prescription. One FAO manager, for example, was quite sceptical about the approach adopted by some and argued, for example, that 'an exclusive focus on yields is very misplaced. The issue is mitigating risk, not maximizing yield.' However, whatever the caveats expressed by particular individuals, a broad story line about soil fertility is discernible in the SFI literature and in related academic and other publications. It emerged forcefully during interviews with key figures involved in the initiative. It is precisely the simplicity and the starkness of the narrative, we would argue, that explains its purchase and the very effective creation of soil fertility as a global issue requiring global management.

The subsequent sections of this chapter attempt to explain how this happened, examining the issue as emerging from particular scientific practices, individual actions and bureaucratic settings. We begin by examining the scientific creation of soil fertility as a policy problem.

CONSTRUCTING FACTS: THE EMERGENCE OF A SCIENTIFIC CASE

This section explores how science and scientific practices have, firstly, contributed to the framing of a soil fertility crisis and, secondly, have also helped to provide potential solutions. We begin by examining how science has contributed to the framing of the problem. The introductory chapter of a widely circulated special publication of the *Bulletin of the American Soil Science Society* on soil fertility announces:

> *The magnitude of nutrient depletion in Africa's land is enormous. Calculations from Smaling's seminal work indicate that an average of 660 kilogrammes of nitrogen per hectare per year (kg N ha per year), 75 kilogrammes of phosphorus per hectare per year (kg P ha per year) and 450 kilogrammes of potassium per hectare per year (kg K per ha per year) during the last 30 years has been lost from about 200 million ha of cultivated land in 37 African countries, excluding South Africa (Sanchez et al, 1997: 4).[18]*

The concept note for the SFI makes use of similar figures, as we shall see, and also provides statements on the degree of African land degradation:

> It is estimated that 320 million hectares of vegetated lands have been degraded over the past several decades in SSA [sub-Saharan Africa]. In terms of magnitude, this estimate is larger than the 213 million ha of presently cultivated lands in SSA. Presently, about 26 per cent of the dryland areas suffer from varying degrees of soil degradation (World Bank, 1996: 2).

These alarming statistics are cited in many places in the literature on natural resources, land and soils in Africa.[19] The nutrient budget figures derive – as the quotation notes – from 'Smaling's seminal work' for the FAO (Stoorvogel and Smaling, 1990).[20] The land degradation data derives from global assessment of the status of human-induced soil degradation (GLASOD) maps that are produced by the International Soil Reference and Information Centre (ISRIC) (Oldeman and Hakkeling, 1990). Both pieces of work have helped to shape the soil fertility narrative set out above in significant ways. No international publication on soil fertility issues would be complete without some reference to either (or usually both).[21] Soil maps with large areas in red (indicating nutrient deficits or land degradation) sit on the walls of policy-makers – as we observed during many of our discussions. The dramatic picture presented often goes completely unquestioned: it is assumed that the data, and associated maps, offer scientifically rigorous and precise knowledge about the world.

Yet, in both cases they represent, in fact, highly contingent knowledge claims, as the authors were at pains to point out to us. There is sometimes bewilderment about how data achieves such grand status. One of the soil scientists working on one of these studies commented: 'When we wrote it we added umpteen footnotes and qualifications, which seemed to get lost as the figures were taken up.' The aggregated Africa-wide nutrient balance figures were based on extrapolations from a limited amount of work carried out in small areas of a few African countries. With such heroic assumptions required, they were seen, at the time, as only rough estimates.[22] Smaling et al (1997: 50–52) comment on the nutrient balance studies:

> The studies were often done at the mini-plot level, the results of which cannot be linearly scaled up to the watershed. . . The sub-continental scale and uneven data implicitly brought about a considerable amount of generalization, simplification and aggregation.[23]

The GLASOD study was based on estimates from scientists in a wider range of countries using measurements of top-soil loss. Again, there are the same methodological problems of extrapolation, and much of the constitutive data is of the 'best-guess' variety.[24] In a discussion of the soil maps, a lead researcher on the ISRIC work commented:

Previous soil maps were beautiful wallpaper, but they weren't used. People want relevant things. Soils in themselves are not a sexy subject. GLASOD was a wake-up call, but definitely not a product of the highest scientific standards. It was the best available at the time.

Despite the recognition of limitations in these studies by their creators, such works can, and do, achieve an unchallenged status.[25] They get used as evidence in documents seeking to raise funds and support for projects and programmes, and are quoted in newspapers to substantiate a particular case or to create opinion. On occasion, the figures change and details as to their original provenance are lost.[26]

When figures have a respected organization's name attached to them, it can add to perceptions of their trustworthiness. FAO statistics, in particular – whether on forests, agricultural production or the status of soils – can create this aura for some. A consultant working with the SFI, apparently unaware of the widespread critique of FAO yearbook statistics, put it quite straight-forwardly: 'The FAO says 83 per cent of land is degraded. Surely we must take the FAO seriously?'

So, we can see how this type of data can suddenly find a life of its own and become authoritative through association with particular organizations. But why does this type of data come about in the first place? Firstly, there is a demand issue. As a World Bank staff member, working on the SFI, argued – reflecting on the difficulty of making the case to his superiors: 'We need more data and more ammunition.' In various interviews, in a range of organizations and at a range of different scales, it was put to us that figures – particularly aggregated national or international data, percentage assessments or dollar values – can help when it comes to persuading and making a case. In one instance, someone even commented that it did not really matter if the data used in a presentation was spurious since the chances were that nobody would notice and he would 'win' the argument.

Of course, part of the appeal of this type of quantitative information lies in the fact that it is well adapted for the needs of those making policy decisions, especially those who want information that is translatable into the language of economic planning. Both the soil maps and nutrient balance information were created at the behest of global bureaucracies: the ISRIC data for the United Nations Conference on Environment and Development (UNCED) conference, and the nutrient balance studies for the FAO. As one of those working in the field put it: 'They appeal to those who want to turn soil maps into productivity maps.' It is a small step to add monetary values to the figures. Thus, based on the Africa-wide nutrient balance analysis, IFDC researchers show how estimated net annual losses of nutrients across sub-Saharan Africa 'represents a total loss of US$1.5 billion per year in terms of the costs of nutrients as fertilizers' (Henao and Baanante, 1999: 2). Similar translations into annual loss of farm income are made for Mali in a study that has again been widely cited by policy-makers (Van der Pol, 1992).[27]

Such unequivocal statements are often required for policy-making. As a scientist in the World Bank commented: 'Nutrient balances raise awareness. They are a red lamp.' By selling a simple message you create an audience; you may acquire funding commitments, and this, it is argued, creates the required space to work on the details, uncertainties and complexities. One researcher noted in similar vein: 'The role of nutrient balances is large-scale awareness; at a smaller scale there is more sensitivity and accuracy.' As an international soil scientist observed:

Nutrient budgets were successful because they were simple; the message was simple. . . you can't take money out of the bank without putting something in. The principle of mining is understood by everybody. Mining leads to lower yields, that's clear. But in the details it's not so simple.

However, it is too simple to say that this globalized knowledge effectively arrives from a more or less explicit process of trading between those who perceive themselves to be, alternatively, in the worlds of policy or science. It also arises from specific institutional locales and practices and therefore carries sets of commitments reflective of a particular social and political order.

So, from where has the knowledge that informs globalized discourses on soil fertility emerged? What is striking when one looks at international science is the dominance of Dutch soil science (see, also, Chapter 5). Many of the key figures are Dutch – de Wit, Breman, Smaling – and the two key studies highlighted above were the work of Dutch scientists, all based at Wageningen. One researcher noted: 'The Dutch have always been good on a particular kind of applied science.' Others argued that Dutch soil and land survey approaches, the production ecology school founded by de Wit, and the Dutch mineral book-keeping tradition have shaped current approaches in significant ways. Donor support from the Netherlands is also evident for fertilizer importation, rock phosphate programmes in West Africa, technical support for soil management projects in Kenya and Mali, and the IFDC in Togo. In various ways, as we shall see, each of these has played key parts in the African soil fertility story. Thus, what may, at first, appear to be global science and policy is rooted in much more local, historically embedded practices.

DEALING WITH COMPLEXITY AND UNCERTAINTY: THE ANATOMY OF A SCIENTIFIC DISPUTE

Through the language of 'balancing the books', of inputs and outputs, drawing down capital stocks, creating deficits and so on, discursive commonalities between the worlds of science, planning and policy-making are created. Sanchez et al (1997: 11) argue that 'there is an exact congruence between the concepts of capital stocks and service flows in economics and that of nutrient pools and fluxes in soil science'.[28] However, in making these discursive linkages, important complexities and uncertainties are often hidden from view, and ambiguities are introduced. One scientist commented: 'People say you never get a straight answer from a scientist. Next year, they say, and next year never comes. They are right.' Nor does such data lead uncontroversially to a strategy for action. Another scientist observed: 'Nutrient budgets don't tell you what should be done. NPK [nitrogen, phosphorus and potassium] may be being mined, but that doesn't mean there is a deficit or it's limiting yields. It may be that soil organic matter is the problem.'

The 'black-boxing' of uncertainties – where key assumptions are removed from further discussion (see Latour, 1987; see, also, Chapter 2) – is part of regular scientific practice. According to an ICRAF soil scientist: 'Closure depends on the magnitude of the question. It comes down to how comfortable you are making strong statements. And it depends on your audience – whether it's an academic journal or the annual report of the institute.' But, critically, closure allows you to do other things: 'We need the bigger picture, then we go down to villages and farms.' But ambiguities and uncertainties are not just the stuff of aggregate models with multiple assumptions. Scientists not only produce contingent knowledge when they address the 'bigger picture', but also when they produce technologies and recommendations and 'go down to villages and farms'.

In some commentators' eyes, the SFI grew out of plans during the mid-1990s for a Rock Phosphate Initiative (RPI), a plan to recapitalize soils through massive one-off applications of phosphate rock (World Bank et al, 1994). This raised a range of technical issues centred on the relative importance of phosphorus or nitrogen as nutrients, and posed questions surrounding the balance between mineral and organic applications, as well as economic feasibility issues. Attempts to integrate rock phosphate applications and more organic approaches also emerged, prompting new work on improved fallows and green manuring by ICRAF and partners using a range of 'wonder plants', such as *Tithonia* and *Sesbania* (among others). The benefits of this apparent win–win technical solution was presented in a discussion with a senior researcher in ICRAF:

> *N is biological – it can be taken care of through improved fallow. So, the old argument that such nutrients are too bulky to transport disappears. You can get 100–200kg of N per hectare, an amount any European farmer would respect; labour may be a problem, of course. P won't work biologically – TSP [triple superphosphate fertilizer] is OK, but why not use local rock phosphate; some is very high quality. Minjingu melts in the soil, it's lovely, the best you can get. . . an investment of 250kg of PR [phosphate rock] once every five or ten years is best. Little by little is just not as good. . . now we need to convince the donors to invest.*

However, there are substantial doubts within the soil science community about the efficacy of large-scale applications of phosphorus, and the soundness of the science used to justify such an approach. One scientist complained of the lack of 'scientifically sound reasons to advocate large inputs of rock P. We need real data on the real effects of rock P and soluble P,' he said. In an attempt to resolve some of this debate, experiments were run looking at different dose rates. To many, the results of these trials were inconclusive; but a decision was eventually made to proceed with pilot work in western Kenya.

What was key to this decision was that well-positioned scientists within the organization were convinced of the case and were able to carry the argument, despite the doubts of other colleagues. An important factor here was that a country task manager with a technical background in the World Bank was himself convinced and saw the opportunity of developing a funded project. He commented to us that, despite the uncertainties, there was no fundamental problem. Uncertainties could be dealt with as they went along:

> How to make rock phosphate more soluble is the key issue in ICRAF. They are reluctant to release it before they are sure. I say, we should look for a solution while we are expanding. Scientists want to know why; but if the results don't do any harm, then so what. This is development!

Another ICRAF scientist argued the case for an adaptive approach, where recommendations are refined in the light of ongoing results:

> We need to understand why things do and don't work. . . we get feedback from development saying what the needs are, and then science tries to provide the information. . . for example, with the west Kenya pilot project. Scientists create options, what sort of things might be suitable for different conditions. . . For example, Mucuna in some places will work, in some it won't, and in some it will be terrible.

But others would not accept this logic, arguing that moving along iteratively was all very well in principle, but if there were fundamental doubts among peers about the wisdom of the path advocated, then substantial investments could be very misplaced:

> You have to think about the costs to the tax payer. The experiments only ran for two years and, really, you needed much longer. Other things could have explained the response. The best use of public money for soil fertility is to build roads. Farmers will do it themselves if there are markets and good infrastructure.

Organizational – and, particularly, funding – imperatives often drive the agenda. Magic bullets and big ideas have much appeal. While the whole approach of looking for a single solution was regularly scorned by our informants, the rationale for such an approach was also widely appreciated. One scientist, while sceptical of the technical merits of rock phosphate recapitalization, noted: 'I don't believe in one-off recapitalization. It's logistically impractical, for one thing. . . but modest things get no money.'

Thus, while there are often uncertainties and disputes around the scientific efficacy of particular solutions, there are also debates about the principles upon which decisions to move ahead should be taken. For some, you do nothing until you are sure; for others, you move ahead cautiously; and for still others, scientific recommendations need to be examined from a broader perspective that addresses social and political factors and possible consequences, as well as economic opportunity costs. Values, risks and uncertainties, though not often directly addressed, are key parts of science, in practice. Science, therefore, begins to look much more contingent, and much more bound up with institutional practices and organizational or political realities. What actually happens – whether a problem definition, or an offered solution, moves to a position of influence – can amount to whether well-located actors take things up and put their weight behind them. Examples include individuals in key organizations who publicize data, for example, or a project manager who decides to move ahead and invest in a technology. The centrality of these networks of actors to the development of the SFI is the theme of the next section.

EXTENDING THE IDEAS: THE CREATION OF ACTOR NETWORKS

For some scientists we spoke to, science was assumed to influence policy in a rather linear fashion. Knowledge was produced and then offered to policy-makers who decide on appropriate courses of action: 'We develop expertise and let policy-makers know the costs and benefits over 20-year projections – consequences of different policies – enabling policy-makers to make comparisons of different scenarios.'

This view is, however, problematic. It may be part of the story, but there is also reason to believe that scientists interact with policy-makers in many different ways, and at many junctures. In this process, dominant narratives are created and maintained. Looked at this way, policy should not be understood as part of a process of 'speaking truth to power', as some models of policy-making assume.[29] As this section argues, policies emerge, instead, through the interacting situated practices of scientists and policy-makers and through the mutual construction of story lines and the building of networks and coalitions.

The creation of actor networks can be understood as a process of building ever-thickening webs that run between the supposedly distinct realms of science and policy, creating hybrids of 'fact' and 'value', and so shaping knowledge in action (Latour, 1993, 1999; see Chapter 2). Examining the building of such networks is essential to understanding the development of soil fertility as a global policy problem, and the development and subsequent fate of the SFI. Evidence for these networks can be found in the references people make to each other in conversations, in publications, in reference lists that suggest a shared vision, or a commitment to certain norms.

Networks are built through a variety of overlapping means: periods of shared study; being taught by the same people; working in the same organizations; attending conferences, workshops and seminars; being on advisory committees; working on joint projects; cooperating on funding proposals; serving on funding committees and journal editorial boards; acting as referees; and so on. These often overlooked social practices – which are frequently seen as rather irrelevant to the seemingly more substantive issues of making decisions or doing research – are actually highly constitutive in building a paradigm or a discipline (see Latour and Woolgar, 1979; Knorr-Cetina, 1999; see, also, Chapter 2).

Thus, for example, many prominent technical scientists engaged in international work in soil science have studied together at Wageningen in the Netherlands, Montpellier in France, Reading or Wye in the UK, and Cornell in the US, carrying with them particular commitments to styles of science, as well as networks of contacts. Professional meetings are also a key part of international networking. For instance, the World Congress of Soil Science or meetings of the Soil Science Society of America may be critical events where networks are formed, extended and reinforced.[30] Certain journals – such as the *Soil Science Society of America Journal* – may also be key routes for exchange, as well as certain e-mail discussion groups or web-based interactions. Funding sources also often bind groups of people together. For example, the investments by the Rockefeller Foundation in Eastern and Southern Africa have been important in linking national agricultural research scientists with international actors, based in universities or the CGIAR system.[31]

Through these networks, norms of good and bad practice are reinforced, research agendas are set and orthodoxies or conventional wisdoms are reiterated; very often, dissenting opinions or unconventional views are also suppressed. Such networks also work to advance the interests of an overall field. Hence, even while people may look askance at the Smaling and Stoorvogel data in one respect, they also see it as a good thing, more generally, because raising the profile of soil science and, particularly, of soil fertility is important, and perhaps can also benefit everybody in the field.

To reach further and to extend to other spheres, networks require actors who are protagonists, or 'policy entrepreneurs', as they are labelled in the literature (Kingdon, 1984; see Chapter 2). To those who know the field, it is clear that there are several characters in the soil fertility world who have plenty of charisma, vision and a good strategic sense. As one FAO informant wryly labelled them, they are 'the zealots'. These figures can play crucial roles in publicizing an issue, succinctly defining the urgency of a problem and offering the possibility of solutions that are within reach. In a world of complexity, where multiple issues compete for attention, this ability to distil a clear, simple and pressing narrative should not be underestimated.

Henk Breman's ability to suggest, strikingly, during the 1980s that the problem of the Sahel was one primarily of fertility, rather than, as was conventionally assumed, lack of water, is an example of a sound-bite approach that was immensely challenging because of its sheer directness. And it came along with a solution, again graphically communicated: publicity posters of bags of fertilizer being dropped from a plane over the Sahel (see, also, Chapter 5).[32] This ability to communicate should not be underestimated; and imaginative figures committed to having an impact in the public domain have been central to highlighting soil fertility issues in the international arena. Champions are important. As one senior researcher commented: 'Professor de Wit started all this in the 1970s. These were his ideas. I wish I'd worked with him. I love that man.'

These 'policy entrepreneurs' clearly communicate and publicize effectively – but not only that. They are also often excellent strategic players who know how to persuade, or even to cajole, where to exert leverage, when the time is right to make a push, and exactly who to target and how, in order to extend influence. Latour (1987) refers to these processes as 'enrolling', extending the power and reach of an actor network by bringing more individuals into its ambit. Strategizing is key, using connections to push a point, identifying people who can, in turn, use their links to others.

CREATING A GLOBAL NETWORK: THE ORIGINS OF THE SOIL FERTILITY INITIATIVE

These processes of network extension were key to the launch of the SFI and the initial splash that it made. One informant explained how he saw the development of the SFI:

> *The SFI started here. Three years ago we took policy-makers to the field and that's when it really took off. A key player was Bob Blake [Ambassador Robert Blake, chair of the Committee on Agricultural Sustainability for Developing Countries, an influential NGO lobby group based in Washington, DC]. He is an old friend; he said, when you've got something, call me. He came to Zambia three months later and saw [the improved fallow experiments] and raised holy hell. He saw Wolfensohn [president of the World Bank], and we got the concept note of the SFI.*

Blake returned to Washington and wrote an impassioned and detailed 20-page letter to Wolfensohn.[33] Wolfensohn called in a range of advisors to help draft a reply.[34] Shortly afterwards, at a critical stage in the World Bank's rethinking of its rural development strategy and support for Africa, Wolfensohn started adding soil fertility as a key issue to his speeches. In his 13 October 1995 reply to Blake, he observed:

> *Your letter provides many valuable insights and solutions aimed at revitalizing agriculture in African countries by restoring soil fertility and increasing agricultural productivity. Based on our experience in the region, we agree with your assessment that continuous mining of soil*

nutrients throughout Africa has contributed to lower crop productivity and slow agricultural growth. Without restoration of soil fertility, Africa faces the prospect of serious food imbalances and widespread malnutrition. It is therefore important that African countries implement actions involving stakeholders at both the local and national levels.

The capturing of some key players of the Washington policy elite was certainly seen as indicating a significant expansion of the soil-fertility actor network. Meanwhile, other more junior officials in the World Bank had similarly been working to raise the issue, and had produced notes documenting the alarming nature of the soil fertility problem, and using the studies and figures discussed above (World Bank, 1996). These things were key to what one World Bank staff member called the 'first phase' of the SFI: 'The first phase was to put the issue on the agenda and it worked quite well. Johnson, the environmentally and socially sustainable development vice-president, came on board, and then "the Pope" – Wolfensohn.'

The World Food Summit likewise provided an excellent opportunity for those with a vision concerning global action on soil fertility. Officials in the FAO suggested that they had also played a key role in lobbying the World Bank: 'We [in FAO] managed to convince the technical people in the Bank that our solutions were sufficiently sophisticated'.[35] Links were then made to Diouf, the director of the FAO, and a formal launch took place at this high-profile international summit. With the launch, a glossy brochure was put out with a Foreword by Serageldin of the World Bank, and with individual sheets for key organizations deemed part of the formal initiative, including ICRAF, the International Fertilizer Industry Association (IFA), IFDC, the World Bank, FAO, IFPRI and the US Agency for International Development (USAID) (FAO et al, 1996). Each gave details as to why they were committed to soil fertility and what they were doing. The effect was to give the impression that a global actor network had been created, incorporating a United Nations (UN) body, CGIAR centres, the major international development bank, a key bilateral donor and the fertilizer industry.

In 1997, a year after the World Food Summit, there was a major inter-national meeting on the SFI in Lomé which again brought together all of the key players and also potential new partners – largely bilateral donors. A very impressive actor network of global reach had been constructed. Facts were extended, a new global policy problem was created, important people were interested and had lent their voices, and a new architecture appeared to address the problem.

LINKING THE GLOBAL AND THE LOCAL

But these tactics of building networks and enrolling actors were not only being used to construct an international coalition, and a formal soil fertility initiative. They were also being used to build critical networks in particular countries, linking global processes to the local. A researcher in ICRAF presented his interpretation as to how concern about soil fertility took off in Kenya:

> *We took the Dutch ambassador and the assistant minister of foreign affairs to the field to see what was going on. . . On the way back, he was travelling next to the minister of finance and one of our 'troops' was in the back seat, and he overheard him say, 'you have phosphate', and it caught his interest. Now it's in the Ministry of Agriculture.*

Again, persuasion, contacts, making opportunities and showing people things – processes of construction – were key. The use of the word 'troops' also suggests the degree to which the researcher views his work as a type of campaign. He went on to indicate how the process went further when a newly enrolled member of the network caught something of the vision and went about engaging other important players:

> *Cyrus [Cyrus Ndiritu, then Kenyan Agricultural Research Institute (KARI) director] saw one trial. 'I don't need to say anything else', he said, 'now this is a Kenyan problem, we'll take the leadership'. Within two months there were seminars in the Ministry of Finance. Cyrus gave a bouquet of Tithonia flowers and explained. Kenyans really campaign – soil conservation is still authorized from the president's office. KARI is now a donor to ICRAF. They put their money where their mouth is.*

Having concrete pilot projects, backed by local advocates, has been an important strategy in many of the NGO attempts to influence policy in this field. Perhaps the most successful in this regard has been the Sasakawa Global 2000 (SG2000) programme. In many respects, this organization is peculiar in that it has access to exceptionally well-connected people. Two of the most key players are ex-US President Jimmy Carter and Norman Borlaug, the Nobel Laureate who was a significant player during the 1960s Green Revolution in Asia. Through these connections, links between the global and the national are made. Thus, direct access to senior officials in the World Bank and to African presidents is no problem. For example, President Meles Zenawi of Ethiopia (see Chapter 4) has been a strong supporter of the programme, as has Ed Jaycox, former World Bank vice-president, both appearing on publicity videos for the NGO (Sasakawa Africa Association, 1996). While many do not necessarily agree with all that SG2000 do, no one questions their effectiveness at influencing policy in a number of countries. As one commentator put it: 'SG2000 are effective lobbyists, pushing and kicking; they come and knock on the door.'

While talk often remains at a rhetorical level, much is made these days of the need to demonstrate a 'demand-led' approach to development, with local 'stakeholders' and building development programmes built on the basis of 'partnership' and 'participation'. Enrolling farmers in the actor network is therefore an important part of the strategy. Across Africa, farmers are involved in development projects that are used as pilots to make a broader policy point. Whether it is the *Tithonia* and *Sesbania* growers working with ICRAF in eastern Zambia or the farmers of Ethiopia applying the SG2000 fertilizer/seed package in Ethiopia, all are important to the wider actor network. The visits of Wolfensohn to Zambia or Meles Zenawi to Shashemanene (in Ethiopia) have been seen to be key in significant policy shifts within the World Bank and the Ethiopian government, respectively. The then director general of ICRAF was at pains to point out how their highly technical work on soils and agro-forestry was based upon local demand: 'Soil fertility came up as an issue. Farmers told us soil fertility is a problem. We transfer farmers' participatory diagnosis into hard science.' But who are these farmers? It is important for the stability of the actor network to have farmers who are 'on-message'. There is nothing worse than a ministerial visit where the 'wrong' message comes across. Farmers and pilot project sites are thus often carefully selected so that success can be guaranteed. Participation in terms of the technologies to be tested or the management techniques to be applied is usually highly constrained.

Of course, actor networks need maintenance. You can enrol senior influential people for a period, but it is not necessarily easy to maintain their interest or their support in an effective way. Likewise, you can build a coalition of the type listed in the SFI publicity brochure; but you also have to encourage actors to come together and be committed to a core project. Too much dissent or excessive compromise can only dilute the message and dissipate the network. Finally, any global actor network needs links to localities – to the national level and below. A global initiative with no roots may be hard to sustain. Actor networks around international organizations must therefore move across many scales. Key figures in the institution live in a hybrid world of science and policy, and in a world that blurs the lines between scientific experiment and practical application; but they must also assist in localizing a global discourse and in globalizing local discourses.[36]

BUREAUCRATIC POLITICS: INTER- AND INTRA-ORGANIZATIONAL DYNAMICS

Having identified the centrality of actor networks to an understanding of the creation of a soil fertility problem, the globalization of particular forms of scientific knowledge and concomitant forms of organization, and the importance of an understanding of scientific practice, we move to locate science and actor networks in bureaucratic contexts.

We have seen how scientists have to deal with the tensions of balancing the need for compelling messages with awareness of the limitations of transmitting messages that obscure complexity and uncertainty. We have also seen the importance of constructing actor networks, and the critical role of individuals in getting the SFI off the ground in the first place. All of this takes place against a backdrop of inter- and intra-organizational dynamics.

Understanding these bureaucratic settings is key to comprehending how a platform for a global initiative was constructed, and how this moved from conception and launch to planning. It is also crucial in understanding how, later, the initiative, in many respects, changed shape altogether.

It is worth recalling what exactly the rationale was for a major international initiative. The case was put in a document produced by the FAO Investment Centre in 1996, called 'Recapitalizing Africa's Soils', the second major paper produced for the SFI. De Alwis, the report's author, argued that:

> *There is a strong case for heightening the awareness and focus on soil management/ regeneration issues, particularly in Africa. . . Given the wide range of national and international research institutions concerned with soil management and fertility issues, as well as the bilateral and multilateral donors, NGOs, international agencies and industry institutions involved, a process of collaboration needs to be fostered. The [World] Bank and the FAO are well placed to foster such collaboration with a view to identifying opportunities for investment and policy initiatives, as well as for catalysing studies, analyses and development assistance directed to upgrading soil productivity and restoring soil health (De Alwis, 1996: 23).*

In other words, numerous people were doing things, and bringing individuals together might make the whole bigger than the sum of its parts. As a commentator in the World Bank put it: 'The SFI was a kind of flag.' However, this rather bright view of the virtues of cooperation is only one part of the story. Another commentator suggested that there were other factors at work: 'There are agendas, of course: institutional survival. . . bureaucratic agendas are key.'

What, exactly, might these agendas have been? Broadly, several are discernible. For some organizations with a very specific soils management focus, there is a clear imperative to raise the profile of soil fertility and, importantly, to ensure that it has a certain complexion. Others have redefined part of their core mission as being about soil fertility. Others have joined in because organizations' global mandates require international initiatives and soil fertility stood the chance of becoming the basis for one.[37] For still others, soil fertility was never going to become a defining issue central to their organization. In these cases, though, through the work of highly committed internal protagonists, a focus on soil fertility in work on agricultural and natural resource management issues in Africa fulfilled a certain organizational need for rallying points and flagship themes.

In this section we look at a number of the key organizational players linked to the SFI. We begin with organizations with very specific objectives. The IFDC, for example, has – as part of its mandate – the promotion and improvement of fertilizer use, and the Africa wing, based in Togo, of this US-based international organization has a strong interest in Africa-wide initiatives.[38] A close alliance with industry players was necessary for the IFDC, given its focused interest in fertilizer-supply issues. This was particularly evident through the Paris-based IFA, a body which represents industry interests and, at least in the early stages, was very much linked with SFI efforts.[39]

Fertilizer use in Africa is obviously tiny when viewed globally, and even smaller than it once was, given the removal of subsidies as part of structural adjustment programmes. However, it is now viewed by some as a significantly expanding market, albeit from a small base. This is particularly so given the fact that many previously key markets are now be shrinking for reasons such as subsidy withdrawal and environmental regulation. A sense was expressed by some individuals whom we spoke to in the industry that, with logistical and infrastructural improvements – and even comparatively simple marketing innovations, such as selling fertilizer in smaller packs and with a more diverse range of combinations of nutrients on offer – scope for significant expansion might exist in some places.

Discussions also revealed that agrochemical trans-nationals such as Norsk Hydro had been busy acquiring shares in the limited number of national companies that exist on the continent, were involved with discussions about the development of new fertilizer factories linked to the SFI, and generally were expressing a strategic interest in the continent, or at least in particular parts of it. Evidence of this can also be seen in the development of an Agribusiness Forum for Africa, coordinated by SG2000, and involving seed companies such as Novartis, Cargill and Monsanto, and fertilizer producers such as Hydrochem. Given the World Bank's long-running interest in fertilizer-supply projects, it is no surprise that they, too, have been involved (see Chapter 4).

For a CGIAR centre such as ICRAF, there is also an institutional mandate. Under the directorship of Pedro Sanchez, author of key texts on soil fertility, it was possible to identify a shift in the focus of the organization, or a clearer articulation of the selling points of agro-forestry – which is where improved soil fertility comes in.[40] In recent years, all CGIAR organizations have been under financial pressure as donor commitments have declined. This, in turn, puts them under pressure to make the case for their relevance at the international level. Clearly, where one can define one's work as central to a potentially big international theme, there is a strong attraction.

The same pressures apply to the FAO.[41] There is substantial debate within the development community, and further afield, as to what, exactly, the role of the UN technical agencies should be and, for some, whether they should exist at all (Imber, 1996). From our discussions there currently seems to be something of an impasse. People are really not sure what the value is of these still very large bodies, despite restructuring in recent years. But, equally, many are reluctant to be seen to openly articulate a line associated with isolationist US senators – namely, some form of dissolution.

We asked a senior regional FAO official what exactly he saw as the comparative advantage of the FAO. He went quiet and fidgeted for an awkward length of time; finally, he said: 'I know what I'd like to answer to that question.' His frustration was echoed by the rather jaded comments of a range of similar individuals in Rome and elsewhere, who had come into the organization often two or three decades earlier when there was a definite role for their technical skills. Now, these individuals have a more devolved role, where transfer of technology paradigms are broadly discredited. The sense – to outsiders, at least – of trying to find something to do, or just shuffling paper until retirement, is palpable.

The only growing part of FAO is the relatively new Sustainable Development Department. Charged with doing strategic thinking and being more policy focused, this department exists in tension with the older technical departments, such as Agriculture, as many made clear to us. One official noted: 'The Sustainable Development Department and the Agriculture Department are conflicting. . . it's a case of who shouts loudest.' A close external observer commented on the resentment that this 'shiny' new department had generated: 'They are viewed as interlopers by the old guard.' There is a sense that 'FAO will finally be reduced to an information centre talking and thinking about strategies'. This division between talking and managing things is crucial. Organizations can either spend or loan money, manage projects, and offer tailored technical advice, or they can live in the world of words and ideas: 'development guff', as a manager in the World Bank put it to us, observing the same tension in his own organization.

In the FAO, the technical sections appear to be losing out, and the role of the FAO in the SFI can be understood in this light. The Agriculture Department and, in this case, the Land and Plant Nutrition Management Service within the large Land and Water Division, incorporating the former fertilizer section, has many technical people whose skills need to be used.[42] Likewise, the FAO's Investment Centre requires projects, and staff are particularly reliant on consultancy operations commissioned through trust fund arrangements with the World Bank. Although these groups can move into the strategic ideas stratosphere, and there is an element of this to the SFI, they ultimately need technical projects with an international dimension – hence, the critical appeal of the SFI to particular parts of the FAO looking for a role.

By contrast, the World Bank – not even large sections of it, as with the FAO – does not have a significant bureaucratic interest in the SFI. Particular individuals may be extremely interested, especially when restructuring threatens jobs and empires. For example, in the mid-1990s, when the Africa region section was being overhauled, one insider recalled: 'Jobs were on the line at the World Bank. . . so the memo [from Wolfensohn] gave an opportunity to X.' However, as an issue of institutional survival or expansion, it is not essential other than as one of many mobilizing themes articulated to the larger development community.

In a later section we will return to the World Bank and the FAO, looking in more detail at their internal bureaucratic procedures and ways of working in order to gain insights on the progress (or otherwise) of the SFI. At this point, however, it is useful to explain the progress and mutations of the SFI in terms of the institutional machinations of bureaucratic politics and the associated shifts in actor networks.

Institutional Mandates, Bureaucratic Politics and the Soil Fertility Initiative

The SFI began, as we have shown, with some lobbying of key people and the preparation of some concept notes and technical papers, which publicized work in soil science on the magnitude of the problem. In the meantime, scientists and economists in different organizations had been looking at rock phosphate as one solution to the perceived crisis of African soils. There was an international launch at the World Food Summit in 1996 and, in the following year, a gathering of a network of interested people in Lomé. Up to this point – with such influential scientific and bureaucratic support – it looked like the SFI would run as a major international initiative. However, by the next international meeting in Rome in 1998, when donors were assembled in an attempt to get significant financial pledges, things appeared to falter. By late 1999, talk was far less grand and something far smaller was being discussed.[43] As someone commented when we explained this research: 'Your introduction and conclusion must be that the SFI is going nowhere.' So, what happened? One comment made after the Rome meeting was that there had been a significant shift in thinking away from the 'phosphate and inorganic fertilizer large-scale input agenda' towards 'locally driven, farmer-initiated and funded interventions reflecting local needs and recognizing both diversity and complexity'.

Certainly, while enthusiasm for massive rock phosphate applications continues in particular places – such as Kenya, Burkina Faso and Mali – the sense that this is the 'big solution', as some early discussions suggested and the early proposal for a Rock Phosphate Initiative (RPI) revealed, has diminished significantly. There has even been some backtracking, suggesting that it was never seen as a large-scale magic bullet anyway. In the period between 1996 and 1998, the scientific black boxes around rock phosphate were reopened. As a technical person in FAO argued:

> SFI started as RPI, but that was not practical and was technically unsound. The idea that you throw on rock phosphate as a once-and-for-all public investment is extremely naïve.

The publication of a key paper by internationally renowned soil scientists advocating a more circumspect approach to mass phosphate application was, it was claimed, 'suppressed'. But, despite this, a year or so later (and in the interim through informal e-mail circulation) an outlet in another book on soil fertility was found (Giller et al, 1998). The apparent closure on the scientific debate (see above) was, in the end, premature, as alternative actor networks were formed, bringing key uncertainties back under scrutiny. Although, initially, actor networks embraced important people such as Wolfensohn, in the final analysis it was not possible to convert this early commitment into sustained support. Therefore, the actor networks became unstable. 'There are many who could have thrown their weight behind it but haven't,' was the view of one researcher.

However, this instability needs further probing. There was instability in the science and, as we have suggested, in the actor networks, but also crucially within the bureaucratic settings where such networks operate. There are three key points to this. Firstly, there are, and were, important 'attitudinal differences' (to quote another informant) between organizations. Secondly, internal organizational cultures, missions and dynamics have also been key. And thirdly, global initiatives can only exist divorced from 'localities' up to a point. The nature of their interactions with smaller scales is two-way and ends up affecting the shape that something takes: the global impacts on, and shapes, the local; but the local can also significantly redirect and recreate the global.

Inter-organizational dynamics take many forms. One view expressed is that 'there is one bag of money and we all have to compete'. There is something to this view, but it is only part of the story. Industry does not compete for money in the same way that ICRAF does, and while elements of the World Bank require donor funding, their interactions with donors are rather different from those of the IFDC. More salient is that organizations move in different ways and are concerned with different things – 'organizations will do what they want to do'.

The fertilizer issue is key in this regard. At one level, there is absolutely no contradiction between organic and inorganic approaches. Very few people argue exclusively for one or the other. It would be misrepresenting the IFA, the IFDC or SG2000 – all well-known strong supporters of increasing inorganic fertilizer use – to say that they argue only for fertilizers. SG2000 conduct trials on nitrogen-fixing plants, and the IFDC and IFA make much in their literature of 'integrated plant nutrition solutions'. Indeed, there is a strong argument (put to us by a number of industry players) that the best way to sell more fertilizer in Africa is to develop other technologies to go with it.[44] In the end, it is a matter of emphasis. When it comes to the crunch, such emphases matter, as competition may develop, compromises may become difficult to forge, and ultimately, actor networks may unravel.

The sense of a difference in emphasis is clearly very real to key participants in the initiative. A senior CGIAR researcher commented: 'The problem with soil fertility is that it gets equated to fertilizers and then, in the next breath, to nitrogen. . . then it becomes nitrogen fertilizer economic policy.'[45] Another researcher complained about the role of the IFDC:

> IFDC pay lip service, but they are really just working on national fertilizer action plans, using rock phosphate of low quality. IFDC are trying, but they can't do it because they have no organic approach. . . the driving force behind Burkina phosphate is not a technical person.

For others, the SFI has generally become much less fertilizer oriented. Many in the FAO expressed the view that they had been working on a far more organic-led approach, and the fertilizer push, often associated with FAO technical advice, was part of history. The role of the bilateral donors in failing to come up with the required funds to push the SFI in the way that it was envisaged by some was clearly crucial. Worries were expressed that the SFI was too linked to an inorganic fertilizer agenda. Many such donors are guided by 'sustainable agriculture' strategies and policies, which are, in turn, informed by work on 'farmer first' approaches and low external-input sustainable agriculture.[46] Through the influence of advocates of a more integrated approach to soil fertility management, it became increasingly difficult to hold the position that a 'big bang' 'mega-bucks' soil fertility initiative was the answer. While such approaches are appealing to many donors in terms of the potential for rapid high-profile disbursement of aid money, the qualms about the technical, economic and social consequences were increasingly evident as the debate began to open out. Some of the early supporters of the SFI appear to have distanced themselves from it. For example, recent issues of the IFA newsletter have virtually not mentioned the SFI.

The global framing of the soil fertility debate remains contested terrain, making it difficult for a tight, coherent and focused actor network to be maintained. Many of the key players have got on with what they were doing, either ignoring the global, laying claim to it or criticizing the shape it is taking. Here, the national refraction of global issues may be key, with the fertilizer industry apparently retracting, consciously or not, from an open global positioning to getting on with particularly promising avenues in particular places. Others have focused geographically, with the IFDC, for example, continuing their work in West Africa, while ICRAF continue to work in Eastern and parts of Southern Africa. In each case, the global may have had its place, but the actor networks constituted at the national and regional level are, in the end, more instrumental.

However, despite this, relationships between organizations remain important. For some in ICRAF – the organization who, as we saw above, claimed a key role in raising the issue strategically – these issues are important. There is a sense of being marginalized from something that might have offered the possibility of doing more than just activities in limited places: 'I said to X. . . you are the father of soil fertility; why aren't you on the scientific advisory committee of the SFI – well, he rang up and eventually got on it.' Another senior researcher vented his frustration with the SFI: 'I can't go to Rome. They didn't tell me. They should get out of their bureaucracies in Washington and Rome and come and see what we have been doing. The next meeting should be in Kenya! I've told Bob Blake to rattle the cage against bureaucratic inertia.'

This gripe about Washington and Rome, though not an unusual development jibe, is pertinent. Someone else commented, again raising eyes to the heavens: 'The FAO and World Bank own the SFI – we don't know what is going on.' Inter-organizational competition between the FAO and the World Bank has, in many commentators' eyes, been a significant stumbling block. As we have discussed, significant sections of the FAO need the SFI – the declining technical departments require a new role, and the Investment Centre requires consultancy funding for technical support missions. Given the funding squeeze at the FAO (or, in some people's view, mismanagement combined with diversion of funds to special projects and new high-profile departments), these FAO players also need the World Bank and, in particular, the trust funds it holds. Thus, a key factor in explaining the grinding to a halt or trans-formation of the SFI is the internal workings of these organizations, a subject to which we now turn.

Internal workings: constraints and opportunities

We begin with the FAO. The FAO, it can be argued, has a systemic problem – everybody knows that there are some excellent people inside, and even a few very good approaches, but the overall perception – and, indeed, much of the reality – is of a cumbersome bureaucracy beset with politics. Take the acclaimed work on integrated pest management (IPM) through farmer field schools. One person in the land division commented: 'IPM began as a clandestine group. . . there are now 60,000 farmer field schools, and FAO had to claim their part; but going public could be the kiss of death.'

The sense that many people are political appointments was made repeatedly. People complained of sycophancy, secrecy and plain wasted experience: 'the Diouf line'; 'assistant director generals just go along to take their instructions from Diouf'; 'what will your man do for us? How many projects?'; 'having a sensible discussion is hard. A lot of people are watched'; 'people say: "I have been here for 25 years; no one has ever asked me what I think."' Recording these comments may seem harsh, but they do help to explain how some of the internal dynamics within the FAO may have contributed to some of the inertia around the SFI. In addition, they are expressed quite openly by people within the organization. As someone else within commented, again in relation to the SFI: 'Bilateral X won't get involved while [FAO official] Y is involved.' There are a lot internal politics that prevent effective action both inside the organization and in cooperation with those outside.

Turning to the World Bank, internal dynamics are, again, central, but in a different, though equally systemic, way. As with the FAO, there are schisms in the Bank – particular individuals wield considerable influence, and there are clearly certain task managers who, for example, see fertilizers as the solution to everything, while others advocate more multi-faceted approaches.[47] Spend long enough talking to World Bank staff and you will hear most contemporary development wisdoms articulated. This is, however, something of a red herring; what really matters in the Bank are its structures, rather than what particular individuals think. As Brechin argues: 'To understand the World Bank and its operations, one must view it first as a bank' (1997: 31).

The World Bank can be understood as a matrix (Wade, 1997). There are 'vertical people', country directors and task managers who identify projects and loan money, and there are 'horizontal people' in thematic groups, cross-sectoral departments or 'families'. These latter people deal in ideas and strategies, and are responsible for most of the impressive sectoral or thematic publications that emanate from the Bank which have such an impact on wider development debates. While this 'development guff', as our informant amusedly referred to it, undoubtedly matters in contributing to – or preventing – paradigm shifts in development thinking, there are no significant structural mechanisms to translate this into an impact on the core Bank activity: lending money.[48] As Brechin argues:

> *Getting its loan portfolio out as quickly and efficiently as possible has been a major Bank objective that colours its internal operating procedures. . . the need to move money has tended to bias the Bank's lending activities to larger loan projects and to those that require less staff time to prepare and supervise (1997: 33).*[49]

For a task manager, preparing projects and securing loans is all. The incentive system for such staff rests on this, and promotions may be linked to the amount of money lent (Brechin, 1997: 34). As a number of task managers commented to us, they really do not have the time to buy in 'quality-assurance' time from the centre. They go through the hoops of the required environmental or social appraisals, but rely, in preference, on their own network of consultants who are both usually cheaper than World Bank staff from the centre and will provide more reliably the sort of information to support their loan strategy. In the early days, when the SFI appeared to be gearing up for big investments of rock phosphate or fertilizer, this had much appeal. Large disbursements seemed to be on the horizon, concentrating on a theme that fitted the new World Bank rhetoric of poverty-focused, environmentally friendly investments. It is not surprising, then, that some of the SFI 'successes', as far as the Bank has been concerned, have been linked to ongoing fertilizer-supply projects. To the cynical observer, the SFI offered a great opportunity to dress up what had been going on before in new clothes with a glossy international appeal. However, as the big investment option began to retreat and alternative, rather less grandiose options were proposed (by those in the World Bank's ideas centre and by others), the appeal of the SFI certainly began to fade.

One official in the World Bank lamented: 'The bottleneck is the country directors: they make decisions on the basis of macro-numbers, not people. They don't link human faces to decisions – rational Cartesian thinking. The farmer in Segou or Sikasso is just not in the picture.' A similar point was made by another staff member in the cross-cutting Rural Development Department:

> *Country directors are the kings in the Bank. 95 per cent are hard-nosed economists. They must choose between roads, AIDS, education, etc. Unless they understand that you are investing in soil productivity increase, then you get nowhere. Things have to be like a Coca-Cola machine. With soil fertility, one dollar now yields two to three dollars later on. They need it to be immediate.*

Another individual complained that technical people – irrigation specialists, soil scientists, agronomists – were simply not being replaced in the World Bank, other than with yet more economists.[50]

Since many of the strongest advocates of soil fertility in the World Bank are on the 'quality' or 'horizontal' side, we have one reason for the limited amount of SFI activity. As internal advocates in the Bank, they can produce many impressive publications, convene a range of high-profile workshops and even get the World Bank president to proclaim on their behalf. However, in terms of leverage on the core activity of the bank – loaning money – they have little purchase. Raising an issue such as soil fertility, therefore, requires intense internal lobbying, most effectively articulated in the language of costs and benefits: 'Country directors are the most important target to reach. To do that you have to make links between soil poverty, economic growth and human poverty.' Constructing these internal actor networks between the horizontal and vertical structures of the World Bank is hard to do: 'Task managers in a tight budget situation bypass you, saying, "Sorry, we've no budget to bring you on board for quality enhancement."' Interestingly, the only soil fertility action plan financed so far by the World Bank is for Kenya, where there is a task manager who is, unusually, not an economist and has a background in soils and is committed to the broader SFI agenda.[51]

SFI advocates have therefore increasingly had to rely on others outside of the World Bank to see through their vision. The link with the FAO is key here. Action plans were produced with the FAO for 13 countries out of the World Bank joint agreement fund with the FAO; but this was not enough. To quote a World Bank official: 'The problem is that action plans are there and there is no money forthcoming.'[52] Without support from task managers within the World Bank, they must rely on bilateral support to see through the plans developed. And this, as we have seen, has been fraught with problems.

Linking the global and the local

The complex jockeying for position and competition over ideas and funds, both between and within organizations operating at the global level, explains much of the fate of the SFI over the past few years. But the story is not complete without some reflection on the interaction of this global manoeuvring, particularly on national and local contexts. International initiatives do not exist in complete isolation from smaller scales; rather, there are always threads running from one to the other – localizing the global and globalizing the local. Local contexts affect, whether implicitly or explicitly, the shape of initiatives from conception through to their later stages. Take, for example, the Convention to Combat Desertification (CCD). While widely perceived as existing only in the organizational stratosphere, many would argue that this initiative exists partly as a result of lobbying on behalf of African governments at the Earth Summit in Rio. Its current shape depends heavily upon local contexts and continued interactions with the global secretariat (Toulmin, 1995).

As we have argued, the global is contested and exists with many stamps upon it. Despite the globalized representations of science and policy, close scrutiny highlights a set of footprints leading to particular localities – whether to field sites in Kenya and Mali, or laboratories and offices in Nairobi or Wageningen. The global, whatever the appearance, is never able to detach itself from its moorings to specific locales; it can just do more or less effective jobs at hiding them away.

This is the case with the SFI. One informant reflected: 'Where did the SFI begin? In Washington. That's the problem with it.' Another told of the chaos at the 1996 launch of the SFI, at the World Food Summit in Rome, as staff ran around trying to find 'black faces for the photo shoot'. So, although this global initiative was rooted, from the start, in Western capitals, links to Africa, however dubiously, were quickly made. African bureaucracies are, in a sense, much like those that have a global stamp: they need funding, projects, initiatives to plan, and frameworks to discuss. It was relatively easy to find some common cause. As one official in the World Bank commented: 'A trade union spirit drives the SFI, linking national and international bureaucrats; we are all in the same trade union.' He went on: 'It's a supply driven system – it's true that initiatives are driven from the outside. When you offer cookies and peanuts – of course, people join in.'

People join in and, in the process, they begin to negotiate as their more complicated bureaucratic and political settings come in to play, much as we have presented with the SFI core group. More actors means more complexity, and the difficulties of holding the network together become even more challenging. In the process, new actor networks are created that reflect particular parts of the global arena that are well connected to certain localities. With donors having favoured countries for aid disbursements and the international agencies wanting to link actions to ongoing programmes, the connections to the national level have been fragmentary. As a World Bank official noted: 'We can only work on a country-to-country basis – there is no general line.'[53] This has produced considerable frustration from some international players: 'After Togo, soil fertility action plans have become "cookbooks" reflecting different interests.'

What happens in particular places also reflects the interests of those who are funding the activities. In some places, where organizations such as the IFDC or ICRAF have been working for some time, the initiative has their stamp upon it. In others, bilateral aid agencies are essential for new funding. Rather despairingly, one FAO official committed to the SFI observed: 'Without money, people in the 14 countries won't commit themselves to the work. Unless the bilaterals come on strong, this just won't be a huge thing.' In others, it depends upon the interests and predilections of World Bank task managers who may link the SFI to an existing loan portfolio. In all of these places, there are negotiations reflecting interests and contexts. In some places, the SFI is on hold, or has been terminated because actor networks could not be constructed between international and national players.

These interactions between the international and the national are often as important, then, as interactions within, or between, parts of the international system in creating, upholding or reframing globalized knowledge and the frameworks that are created with it.[54] Uncertainties concerning science are opened up in some places and not in others. In some places, globalized science and the soil fertility crisis narrative very much shape debate and planning; in others, there may be more renegotiation in order to reflect local knowledge, local interests and local complexity. New actor networks form around these elements as the original core weakens in some places and extends itself in others. In other words, while at first sight the dominance of global discourses seems all powerful, this remains so only if the institutional commitments and practices required can be maintained in local spaces. An incredibly tight, focused actor network stretching from the global to the local is, therefore, essential. In the case of the SFI, this could not be sustained. As the science was unpacked, key players failed to join up, and local contexts became impossible to ignore. The standardized global narrative began to dissipate and with it the actor networks associated with the SFI launch. Six years on, the SFI is made up of a rather weakly linked, rather disparate, constellation of fairly diverse interest and positions – a far cry from the original vision.

CONCLUSION

So, what can we conclude from this story? The SFI can be seen as part of a broader pattern, typical of the post-Earth Summit era, where globalized narratives of environmental change influence particular courses of action at the local level. While there are clear peculiarities to the SFI case, some basic comparisons with, for example, the CCD, sustainable development strategies or environmental action plans show that a characteristic policy process is evident. The interactions of science, actor networks and bureaucratic politics across scales from the global to the local result in a range of actions typified by action plans, technical interventions and community-based projects. These are not minor undertakings – significant investments of donor and government resources, both financial and human, are committed to such activities every year. It is difficult to assess what has been spent on the SFI as the activities have been too diffuse – spread, as we have seen, between a range of organizations and country actions. However, it is not insignificant. The question arises: is this an appropriate allocation of resources? What lessons can we draw from the SFI experience? What implications are there for the post-Johannesburg approach to international environmental governance and policy processes?

Three conclusions are possible. The first is that, fine, the SFI started off as a bit alarmist and oversimplified the problem. However, because of this, people are now more aware of the issue – a 'flag' was raised, a 'red lamp' was lit and, as a result, some funds were committed. Through debate and inter-action some of the more extreme claims were dismissed and some of the more fanciful project ideas were rejected. The result is a set of more-or-less sensible activities, in places where there is commitment. The pragmatists' line concedes that things are not perfect, but what more can you expect from the development business? This is just how things work.

A second view offers a rather pessimistic perspective. Plenty of money and time has been wasted, with little result. At least no damage was done, but little was achieved, either. This is yet another example of the post-Earth Summit syndrome', of how bureaucratic imperatives to create action plans around global problems are both diversionary and wasteful. The only achievements that the SFI could boast in a summary paper were national action plans, the ICRAF work, the soil fertility management unit supported by IFDC in Burkina Faso, and the Rockefeller-funded SoilFertNet in Zimbabwe and Malawi (World Bank, 1999). Except for the action plans, all these things occurred before, or independently of, the SFI. One judgement would be that this is not very impressive. What is perhaps most problematic is that relatively scarce trained people have been diverted from doing useful things and have been whisked up into the international circuit – into the seemingly never-ending process of engagement with conventions, initiatives, plans and programmes conjured up in response to the global environment and development debate. This was a point acknowledged by an official in the World Bank: 'In Benin, we discovered there were more networks than scientists – this leads to no time to do their own jobs.' In Zimbabwe, commentators referred to the 'per diem hunting' practices of government officials, and how, at certain times, no senior officials are present in the ministry at all because of attendance at international meetings of various sorts (see Chapter 6). The World Bank official admitted: 'It takes others away from good work going on in country.'

A third view takes a more fundamentally critical stance. Through the creation of powerful actor networks of scientists and policy actors in a range of organizations, a problematic narrative was constructed. This had some success in some places, and has thus forced an agenda on unsuspecting people. Because it is insufficiently nuanced, and lacks local definition and ownership, this is potentially damaging since alternative framings of the issue were not countenanced. The comment of a task manager about work in Mali reflected this view: 'In nowhere are we starting from zero – much is known already. We don't need detailed research. We know that there is acidification in the cotton zone, erosion in the sandy areas and salinization in the Office [du Niger].' As this quote highlights, for all the talk of the SFI as participatory, there is not much room to redefine the question or challenge some of the key assumptions (see Chapter 5). Clearly, where the problem being addressed is misconceived, this can have high opportunity costs in terms of the use of scarce public funds.

So, what do we conclude from our reflections on the SFI process, and global policy processes more generally? As will almost certainly be clear by now, we locate ourselves at the more critical end of the spectrum. However, as one pragmatist commented to us: 'It's easy for you researchers to be critical. But we all know the problems. Until you can come up with something better, then what are we expected to do?' Fair point. By offering a critique, we do not want to suggest that all of those involved are not aware of some of the failings we have highlighted. As we have indicated at various points in the chapter, scientists are acutely aware of the limitations of their work, and are often aghast at the uses to which it is put. Equally, those operating in large bureaucracies confront the obstacles we have referred to on a daily basis and have necessarily developed all sorts of ways of coping with them. In the same way, the 'policy entrepreneurs' who are vocal champions of particular views know that only certain things get listened to, and respond accordingly, again being fully aware of the limitations of sound bite-style advocacy.

In other words, there is no large-scale conspiracy going on, orchestrated by bad people with malevolent intent. By teasing out the complexities of the policy process, our intention has been – by making the often implicit practices and processes of policy more explicit – to encourage a more open and informed discussion about how to improve things. It is widely accepted that the current situation is far from ideal. As a senior director in a UN organization observed:

> We've got to rethink what we do at the international level. We operate in a world which is out of touch. We have dozens of projects all over Africa, but most are disasters. This is not the way to go. We've got to find ways of linking what is really going on, on the ground, with the wider debates. By and large, the convention processes have not done this. We need to find new ways.

So, what lessons have we learned that might provide insights into these 'new ways' of doing things? A number of themes stand out. Firstly, the scientific 'facts' upon which global initiatives are based are often plagued by uncertainties. As we saw in relation to the debate about rock phosphate and organic alternatives, there is often little consensus even within the mainstream scientific community. Add in the often-excluded perspectives from resource users themselves, and such uncertainties grow further. This, of course, is to be expected; but too often policy processes assume a rather linear mapping of uncontested technical scientific information onto policy solutions. If the local priorities, values and contexts where such solutions are expected to be applied are taken more firmly into account, a diverse range of problem framings and potential solutions is almost inevitable. Accommodating such diversity within the current architecture of policy-making is, as we have seen, problematic.

This chapter has highlighted the need to recognize the limitations of bureaucratic procedures. As we have seen, with particular mandates, organizational structures and incentive systems, policy outcomes are necessarily constrained. No matter how much rhetorical play is made of local perspectives and participatory processes, there are clear limits. Therefore, if the rhetorical ideals are to be realized, a long, hard look at the organizational arrangements for policy-making will be required. While there clearly is a role for international organizations, this may – as many informants we spoke to acknowledged – need to be redefined. Where complex, non-linear policy processes are at work, and where contests of knowledge, politics and power are key, processes of convening, channelling and facilitating will be vital. Yet the current arrangements are clearly inadequate, set as they are within a linear vision of policy-making that is based upon assumptions about unproblematic scientific framings and upon largely instrumental, top-down implementation procedures. The post-Summit flood of conventions, initiatives, programmes and action plans clearly, in many ways, reinforces this and therefore does not meet the demands of a flexible, adaptive and grounded policy process.

Yet, as we have seen, global agendas are far from monolithic. Particular narratives and discourses are often based on relatively fragile, clearly mutable, actor networks. There is frequently also an iterative shaping of agendas through interaction with local settings. But there remains a tension between the 'stratospheric' realms of the global debate and engagement with local settings which very often limits the scope for local voices to be heard. New, more inclusive, forms of deliberation in such global policy debates are clearly required that allow for a diversity of perspectives to engage, opening up the 'black boxes' of mainstream science and bringing in different actors who can help reframe the questions and develop a greater diversity of solutions. Creating the framework for such engagement remains a major challenge for all international initiatives, including the SFI.

4

Knowledge, Power and Politics: the Environmental Policy-making Process in Ethiopia

INTRODUCTION

This chapter is concerned with how policies surrounding agriculture, natural resources and the environment get established in the Ethiopian context. Our analysis sees policy-making as a diverse, diffuse and complicated activity, where sometimes competing, sometimes overlapping, policy positions are presented by a range of different groupings of actors, including scientists, administrators, non-governmental organization (NGO) personnel, government officials, rural people and politicians. Policies, we argue, are culturally embedded, and understanding how national and sub-national political and administrative histories and practices shape policy processes is key. Policies can be seen to rise and fall in prominence as a result of the interplay between context-specific circumstance and the changing effectiveness of different networks of actors in the policy debate. Our analysis of environmental policy debates, therefore, suggests a very different type of process to the conventional simple, linear and technical model (see Chapter 2).

Our focus is the range of debates that have emerged in Ethiopia over the last decades surrounding three core questions regularly posed by policy analysts. Firstly, what can be done to increase food production in a country prone to substantial food deficits and with a rapidly increasing population? Secondly, what can be done to ameliorate the progressive degradation of natural resources? And thirdly, what can be done to promote effective participatory management of natural resources by rural communities? Linked to these questions, three broad policy discourses can be identified. These are a Green Revolution discourse, an environmental rehabilitation discourse, and an emergent participatory natural-resource management discourse.

These three discourses are intertwined within the contemporary policy debate in Ethiopia; but it is also the case that they start from different premises and therefore can provoke serious conflicts over policy in terms of decisions, laws, programmes and actual implementation practice. For example, conflicts may arise over strategies for environmental rehabilitation, with some arguing that large, mass-mobilization schemes are the only way in which to address the long-term challenge of combating soil erosion. Others feel that increasing farmers' incentives to invest on their own land is more important. Similarly, some regard the promotion of Green Revolution technologies in the marginal areas of the country as the only way of boosting food production and solving the recurrent food crisis. On the other hand, others think that more integrated, low external-input solutions based on the principles of conservation agriculture are more appropriate ways of dealing with the dual problems of environmental degradation and food shortage in the longer term. These are all controversial issues in debates about environment and rural development in Ethiopia. The aim of this chapter, however, is not to provide a technical analysis of these policy debates, nor a comprehensive review of their historical origins. Rather, the objective is to identify the types of knowledge about natural resources from which these policy conflicts emerge, and to explore how particular positions get established in (and others excluded from) the policy debate, and how, once established, such positions are challenged and transformed.

In the following sections, we will examine the nature and evolution of these policy debates in some detail. Using some of the concepts introduced in Chapter 2, we examine the way in which policy discourses, actor networks and policy space interact to support particular policy positions. In this chapter we argue that actor networks take advantage of different degrees of policy space in order to establish and uphold different discourses about agriculture and natural resource management in Ethiopia. The chapter is organized as follows. Firstly, the basic characteristics and recent history of the Green Revolution and environmental rehabilitation discourses are laid out, highlighting how arguments are framed; the role of science and expertise; and what key circumstances, contexts or personal influences have been important in establishing the discourse in the Ethiopian policy debate at particular times. Next, the chapter examines how these discourses became established and subsequently transformed through an examination of the multiple actor networks linked to different policy positions. An analysis of the evolution of these policy debates highlights the importance of mainstream policy arising at key moments, allowing particular policies to become dominant. The emergence of discourses surrounding agriculture and natural resource management are not monolithic, and are subject to change. In this regard, the influence on conventional wisdoms of an emerging participation discourse is explored in the following sections, with the analysis highlighting, in particular, the increasingly apparent regional differences in the way actor networks are formed and policy space created. The concluding section reflects on the changing nature of the environmental policy process in Ethiopia.

A SHORT HISTORY OF THE AGRICULTURE AND NATURAL-RESOURCES POLICY DEBATE IN ETHIOPIA

While this chapter does not attempt to provide a comprehensive guide to recent Ethiopian history, or to debates about Ethiopian political culture, it is necessary to set the following discussion of policy change in context. In 1974, Emperor Haile Selassie was overthrown in a coup by the Derg, who established a Marxist military government led by Mengistu Haile Mariam. This Soviet-supported regime carried out a radical land reform, ending the landlordism associated with the imperial system. Agriculture was closely managed through state control of prices, input supply and marketing. Parallel to this, the regime sought to transform rural life through large-scale plans for resettlement and villagization. Some liberalization followed during the late 1980s, as Soviet support collapsed. The long-running insurgencies in Eritrea and Tigray in the north of the country intensified during this period, and the Derg were eventually toppled in 1991. Following a period of transitional government, elections were held consolidating the power of the Ethiopian People's Revolutionary Democratic Front (EPRDF), a coalition dominated by the Tigrayan People's Liberation Front (TPLF). A new constitution enshrined the principles of democracy and 'ethnic federalism', and the country was administratively restructured around ethnically based regions, which were to reflect the ethnic complexity of Ethiopia and counter long traditions of centralized government.

Despite these apparently profound changes – from imperial, to Marxist-military, to democratic regime – there are many continuities, as many individuals have commented.[1] The first of these is that the country has been repeatedly affected by famines, with particularly marked crises during 1973–1974, 1984–1985, 1991 and 2002–2003. These have had political repercussions and have made concern over food production and food self-sufficiency the preoccupation of all regimes. Secondly, a number of characteristics of the Ethiopian state have remained remarkably persistent over time. These include a tendency towards authoritarianism, hierarchy, centralized rule and lack of transparency. For Levine (1965), deference to hierarchy and equivocation, rather than directness of speech, are hallmarks of Abyssinian (Tigrayan and Amhara, but not all Ethiopian) culture. These (clearly not universal) traits have, arguably, translated into bureaucratic cultures that are antithetical to bottom-up or decentralized practices and to reflexivity and learning. These points should be borne in mind when trying to understand why top-down approaches to agricultural extension and natural resource management have been so prevalent.

It is also significant that Ethiopia has always been dominated by the Abyssinian north. Southern regions have never been politically dominant and, indeed, were largely only incorporated into the Ethiopian state at the same time as the European 'scramble for Africa'.[2] With the exception of several small kingdoms, the south does not have the long traditions of state organization of the Abyssinian north. As part of Ethiopia, these areas have consistently lacked resources and administrative capacity. This regional diversity, we shall argue, along with the broader points mentioned above has important implications for the political embedding and transformation of discourse.

A GREEN REVOLUTION IN ETHIOPIA?

The challenges of national food production have long been a policy concern in Ethiopia. One of the central aims of the large-scale integrated rural development projects that dominated the Ethiopian rural development scene from the late 1960s was increasing yields through the supply of new crop varieties and inorganic fertilizers. The Chilalo Agricultural Development Unit (CADU) project was the first and most prominent of these efforts. Started with much fanfare in 1967, it ran with Swedish support for eight years (Dejene, 1990; Cohen, 1987).

This was followed by similar programmes, such as the Wolaita Agricultural Development Unit (WADU), which ran until the early 1980s with support from the World Bank. Extensive research efforts, starting in the mid-1960s, by the Ethiopian (then Imperial) Institute of Agricultural Research and the United Nations Food and Agriculture Organization (FAO) focused on testing fertilizers with a range of key crops in different parts of the country. The result was a Minimum Package Programme that was launched by the government in 1971. In various guises, a package approach, linking the supply of external inputs (seeds and fertilizer) to a credit programme, has been the centrepiece of the Ministry of Agriculture's extension programme since then.[3]

The narrative associated with this policy stance is very familiar, drawing on the arguments used in support of the Green Revolution in Asia. Growing populations and declining per capita food production, it is argued, will result in major food gaps that must be filled by boosting aggregate food-grain production. Off-the-shelf modern technologies are available, it is stated, which could achieve this if only they were properly extended to the farming population. Resistance to change, however, is due to traditional agricultural practices, inappropriate tenure and a lack of a commercial outlook. A radical transformation of existing farming systems is, therefore, required, the argument goes.

Over the years, such a position has been put forward, in particular, by the technical scientific elite, who demonstrate on their research stations and in their laboratories the real potentials of adopting such a modern, efficient approach to farming in Ethiopia. This argument is supported by economists looking at the agricultural sector, who, making use of available macro-data, demonstrate the likelihood of growing and significant food gaps, and the economic costs of filling these.

Since the fall of the Derg regime and the take-over by the EPRDF in 1991, these arguments have been reinforced by strong political statements about the need for food self-sufficiency in the country. The arrival of the Sasakawa Global 2000 (SG2000) programme in the country in 1993 was a particularly significant moment. Having been accorded a very high profile by political leaders, and supported by an extensive media campaign, the programme became highly influential within the upper echelons of government and was well known among the general population. With its expansion as part of the new extension policy (the national extension intensification programme) in 1995, the SG2000 seed fertilizer credit package became firmly established at the centre of the new government's approach to agricultural development across the country, reinforcing the long line of such approaches in Ethiopia. The speed at which the programme has grown is remarkable: 32,046 farmers in 1995, to 600,632 in 1997 and 2.5 million in 1998. Over 4 million farmers were involved by 2001, backed up by over 5000 extension management training plots in 67 districts (Howard et al, 1998; SAA, 2001).

An 'aggressive technology transfer' approach (see Borlaug and Dowswell, 1995), typified by SG2000, has become central to a number of key policy documents, most notably the government's Food Security Strategy (FDRE, 1996:16).[4] Also, since 1991, the World Bank has invested extensively in technology transfer in the seed and fertilizer sectors through two major projects.[5]

ENVIRONMENTAL CRISIS, ENVIRONMENTAL REHABILITATION

Alongside the policy debate around food security and agricultural production, there has been a recurrent concern about the natural resource base upon which agriculture depends. Soils, in particular, have featured prominently. Again, the generalized Malthusian narrative is very familiar. With growing populations, resource depletion is accelerating, it is argued, resulting in widespread deforestation, overgrazing, biodiversity loss, soil erosion and soil fertility decline. With continued environmental degradation, the argument continues, agricultural production will decline, food deficits will increase and poverty and starvation will result. In order to prevent such calamity, the familiar collection of natural resource projects is suggested as solutions – woodlots, hillside closures, terracing, bunding and so on.

While this summary is, of course, a caricature, many policy statements from government, NGOs and donors alike carry a similar message. The environmental policy of Ethiopia (FDRE, 1997), for instance, states:

> Renewable natural resources. . . have now deteriorated to a low level of productivity. . . In 1990, accelerated soil erosion caused a progressive annual loss in grain production estimated at about 40,000 tonnes, which unless arrested will reach about 170,000 tonnes by 2010. . . In economic terms, soil erosion in 1990 was estimated to have cost (in 1985 prices) nearly Birr 40 million in lost agricultural production (FDRE, 1997: 1).

In our interviews, a similar story line was regularly told. For example, a senior manager in the Ethiopian Environmental Protection Agency (EPA) commented: 'Land degradation and soil conservation are the number one environmental problems in Ethiopia.' These positions are echoed at regional level. Thus, the 'Regional Conservation Strategy' prepared for the Southern Nations, Nationalities and Peoples' Region (SNNPR) comments:

Nowadays, environmental issues have attracted the attention of the public. Dense forests which were once filled by various tree species are now filled by sand dunes. . . Furthermore, the loss of vegetative cover has, in turn, led to the destruction of wild animals and the loss of organic chemicals, which play an important role in maintaining the fertility of the soil. These phenomena, coupled with population pressure and overgrazing, have finally become the main sources of the environmental degradation we presently observe (SNNPR, 2000, Chapter 11, Section 13).

Similarly, the standard solutions are listed in the targets for the 'Five-Year Plan of Tigray National Regional State' (Berhane, 1995). They include: construction of stone/soil bunds to conserve about 696,000 hectares; biological conservation measures on bunds of over 105 kilometres; gully treatment measures on 4500 kilometres; and the planting of 435 million forest seedlings.

Sources of authority for such a narrative are drawn from natural scientists and, particularly, from the extensive work carried out on soils and soil erosion in Ethiopia. In interviews, two key sources of information are regularly mentioned: firstly, the results of the Soil Conservation Research Project (SCRP), a national network of research sites collecting data on soil erosion established by Hans Hurni in 1981; and, secondly, the report of the Ethiopian Highland Reclamation Study (EHRS), published in several volumes in 1986 by the FAO (FAO, 1986).[6,7] A range of key data and statements were produced from this research and have entered policy debates. Soil loss figures extrapolated from SCRP plot data are regularly quoted as evidence of major soil loss. For example, the EHRS report and the *National Conservation Strategy Phase I* report (Wood and Ståhl, 1989), each significant and influential statements on the state of the Ethiopian environment, both make use of this data.[8] In addition, a suite of standard technical solutions was widely promoted through the Ministry of Agriculture and Natural Resources following the publication of the manual for development agents in 1986 (Hurni, 1986).

Following the major famine of 1984 and the publication of the EHRS report, which explicitly linked the famine to natural resource degradation, the construction of physical soil conservation measures became central to the widespread food-for-work efforts supported by the World Food Programme and others (Maxwell and Belshaw, 1990). For some, this became the perfect win–win solution to the food crisis in Ethiopia – food aid could be supplied to fill the gap, at the same time as soil-erosion control measures were built that would, in the long term, increase food production sustainability (Maxwell, 1993).

Thus, since the late 1960s – from the Haile Selassie era through the Derg regime, to the present government – two dominant narratives have influenced the agriculture and natural resource debate in Ethiopia. Each has been associated with particular events, linked to particular scientific studies and supported by different interest groups and (sometimes) different government ministries or external donors. However, despite the contrasts between the Green Revolution and environmental rehabilitation discourses, in many respects they are quite similar as they are both derived from a Malthusian diagnosis of over-population and impending crisis. Over the last 30 years, they have offered different, yet complementary, solutions, with elements of each discourse being prominent in policy debates at different times. A Green Revolution approach, for example, dominated discussions during the 1970s, and, with SG2000, a similar policy stance returned during the 1990s. Environmental issues rose to prominence in the 1980s with concerns over soil erosion, and have been kept on the policy agenda into the 1990s – in part through continued international debate surrounding the 1992 Earth Summit conference in Rio, and follow-up initiatives such as the Convention to Combat Desertification (CCD), signed by the Ethiopian government in 1994.

A number of important questions about the policy process arise from this brief review. How did these discourses get established within the Ethiopian policy apparatus? Which actors in what networks were involved? What were the links to international debates? What were the key events and circumstances resulting in shifts in policy? What bureaucratic and political factors influenced policy change? It is to these questions that we now turn.

THE ESTABLISHMENT OF POLICY DEBATES IN ETHIOPIA: ACTOR NETWORKS AND POLICY SPACE

The Green Revolution debate: the case of Sasakawa Global 2000

The post-1991 re-emergence of a strong Green Revolution discourse can be traced to a number of factors. As already discussed, since the late 1960s, the agricultural bureaucracy and scientific establishment has had a general orientation towards Green Revolution approaches, reinforced by personal influences derived from educational and training experiences. Despite major changes in personnel since 1991, these have been key contextual referents in terms of the construction of recent policy space. However, specific circumstances have also been important in promoting the Green Revolution position. These include the arrival of a government that strongly prioritized food self-sufficiency as a policy issue, bringing with it a long commitment to such a stance from the days of the liberation war. The very personal commitment of Prime Minister Meles Zenawi has been important. Informants noted how the famine of 1984–1985 'left a deep scar' and galvanized his commitment. Someone recalled a conversation with him where he reportedly said: 'If I live long enough to prevent famine in Ethiopia, I will have achieved something.'

The new government and the prime minister, in particular, have invested substantial political capital in promising to 'cross the divide' to food self-sufficiency, and were therefore highly responsive to the proposals of the Sasakawa Global 2000 (SG2000) programme. This NGO had a clear vision: what was needed were new varieties combined with a consistent application of fertilizer. It was articulated most forcefully by the key advisor, Nobel Laureate Norman Borlaug, but also by the team in Ethiopia, which included Marco Quiñones, who had experience in Mexico and elsewhere in Africa, and Takele Gebre, a former head of extension in the Ministry of Agriculture. Quiñones commented to us:

> *The number one issue in agriculture is soil fertility. Farmers have been mining the soil of plant nutrients for hundreds of years. No matter what you do with agronomy or breeding, you won't get much from the soils without applying fertilizers. We are keen on fertilizers. We are impatient; we don't want to wait.*

In 1993 the work started with a series of demonstration plots in the south of the country. The NGO provided the backing and offered incentives to farmers to join the programme. It also guaranteed to cover the risk of failure of any plot in the first seasons. Working with local varieties produced as part of the Institute of Agricultural Research's breeding programme, the demonstrations showed the potentials of increasing yield with the addition of fertilizer. One observer recalled the early enthusiasm: 'Government thought it would solve the food problem in Ethiopia. SG 2000 reinforced this view. It looked simple: add fertilizer and improve production by 300 per cent.'

The relatively plentiful rainfall in the years up to 1995 allowed for the successful demonstration of the potential for improved yields under the new package programme in a wide range of demonstration sites across the country. The year 1995 – described by one commentator as the 'lotto year' – was particularly significant; due to the success of the harvest in some parts of the country, the government was able to announce that it was actually exporting food.

According to many observers, an essential moment in establishing a strong actor network around this issue was a visit to a SG2000 demonstration site by the prime minister (then president of the transitional government of Ethiopia), Meles Zenawi, in September 1994, accompanied by Norman Borlaug and ex-president of the US, Jimmy Carter. One commentator we interviewed noted:

> *Food self-sufficiency at any cost is the number one priority for the present government. . . SG2000 came in with off-the-shelf packages, and maize yields increased ten-fold. It was sellable. They found it extremely attractive. Carter came and saw before the harvest. Now it's the government's pet project. On the radio, morning and afternoon, it's extension, extension, extension. But if it fails it will be bad. Moving from famine to exporting food is very important politically.*

The SG2000 programme became incorporated within the official National Extension Policy and became an inviolable policy priority for the government. In 1996, the task force set up by the prime minister – chaired by the minister of agriculture and with SG2000, a key member – recommended the massive expansion of the pilot programme, combining the package and demonstration programme of SG2000 with elements of a training and visit (T&V) extension approach. Since then, the number of extension demonstration plots has expanded from 161 in 1993 to 3,793,757 in 2000 (Ibrahim Mohammed and Temene Terfa, 2001). With this, there has been a commitment to increasing the number of front-line extension staff by several fold, as well as major efforts in securing fertilizer imports. As the centrepiece of the government's agricultural and food security policy, this became highly politicized. In the early years, space for critical discussion in public was drastically curtailed. Sceptics were quickly sidelined or were transferred. Most remained compliant and quiet, at least in public. To quote an official in a bilateral donor agency: 'It's the one policy we can't do anything about.'

The World Bank is a key participant in the actor network associated with the post-1991 Green Revolution policy position. Earlier support for the Minimum Package Projects and substantial investment in the seed and fertilizer sector made the World Bank an obvious ally. A World Bank consultant who was an original author of the government's 1996 Food Security Strategy emphasized the importance of a technological strategy involving elements of the SG 2000 approach (FDRE, 1996). Similarly, in a 1998 World Bank report on agricultural growth in Ethiopia, the same consultant again makes explicit reference to the SG 2000 initiative:

> The most important way to increase food availability in Ethiopia is to increase yields, which for cereals are among the lowest in the world. A 'package' programme supported by Sasakawa Global 2000 initiative, in which improved cultivation practices, seeds and fertilizers are used by farmers, has demonstrated the possibilities for substantial yield increases in three basic food crops (World Bank, 1998c).

Close ties between the SG 2000 network and influential elements in the World Bank are further suggested by contributions made by Edward Jaycox (former World Bank vice-president for Africa) in the SG2000 promotional film *Ethiopia: My Hope, My Future*. SG 2000's ties with the Ethiopian government can be traced through many workshops, reports and interviews. For example, the editorial in a SG2000 newsletter observes:

> The government of Meles Zenawi deserves due credit for identifying agriculture as the engine of change, for seizing the opportunity of the SG 2000 initiative, and for launching an expanded and ambitious agri-cultural extension agenda, and backing it up with significant resource commitment and unreserved attention (Sasakawa Africa Association, 1998: 2).

How did the network become so influential? When we asked a representative in a bilateral donor agency to explain the influence of SG 2000, he observed:

Firstly, it's the Carter link and then there are the technologists – Borlaug himself, Bob Havener, John Coulter. They've all retired from the CG system [Consultative Group on International Agricultural Research] and have now arrived back as consultants through the revolving door.

Most commentators concur that this combination of top-level political support and the mobilization of internationally credible scientific expertise, together with support from the World Bank, have been highly successful in creating a strong and effective actor network.

In explaining their strategy, SG 2000 staff first put it down to luck and good fortune, but then went on to explain how links were made:

We have been very fortunate that government has listened to us. You have to be lucky. Timing was important. . . You have to work on both sides. Farmers can show how it works. Then you have to go up there – if you can get to the PM, that's what counts. The minister of agriculture can easily be overruled by finance or planning. You have to focus on the highest level, and show him that it really works. If the PM doesn't see anything on the ground, how will he accept us?

More recently, the actor network has expanded yet further, with a new emphasis on enrolling actors in the private sector, and linking this to donor interest in supporting public–private partnerships. For instance, the Agribusiness Forum held its first meeting in 1997. This was convened by Prime Minister Meles Zenawi and SG2000 country director Marco Quiñones, and chaired by Jimmy Carter. The meeting 'brought together key ministers and senior advisors concerned with economic development, foreign investment and agriculture; senior representatives of the World Bank; the US; SG 2000; and five major multinational companies involved in agri-businesses in Ethiopia – Cargill, Monsanto, Novartis, Pioneer Hi-Bred International, and Hydro-Agri'. The aim was 'to develop stronger partnerships among public, private and non-governmental organizations to promote the delivery to farmers of productivity-enhancing new production technology' and to look at 'what organizations such as the World Bank, USAID [US Agency for International Development] and European development agencies could do to promote increased private investment in the region' (Sasakawa Africa Association 1998: 12–14).

With the strong commitment to a fertilizer-led Green Revolution, the importance of ensuring adequate fertilizer supplies became a major policy priority, with fertilizer sales rising from 290,000 tonnes in 1999 to 460,000 tonnes in 2000 (SAA, 2001). As a senior UN agency official noted: 'There is an urgency about fertilizer. There is political commitment at the highest level. When there is a lack of fertilizer, government quickly responds.' Significantly, a range of interests comes together around fertilizer supply. And most of these are members of the important Fertilizer Committee, established by the FAO in 1992 and taken over by the former National Fertilizer Industry Association

(NFIA) in 1997, which plans fertilizer needs and negotiates aid and import-ation deals. A key player, again, is the World Bank, which has had a long commitment to a fertilizer-supply programme, linked with the FAO and the national fertilizer sector project. Other donors have committed considerable resources to fertilizer aid over the years, allowing government to import without spending valuable foreign currency. International private-sector suppliers, too, are keen to enter what is perceived to be a growing market, and emerging local fertilizer companies also see benefits. Although notionally privatized, many observers note their monopolistic structure on a regional basis and their close ties to political interests. Ensuring that fertilizer is a high priority, in other words, suits almost everyone, it seems – government, as fertilizers are central to the key political agenda of food security; quasi-privatized supply companies, as fertilizers guarantee business and reaffirm political patronage links; international companies, as fertilizers fuel a growing input-supply market; the World Bank, as the fertilizer-supply project is seen to be an easy-to-administer form of loan disbursement (see Chapter 3 for further discussion of the World Bank's approach); and other donors, as fert-ilizer aid is, again, seen to be an easy form of aid support. It is not surprising, then, that the Green Revolution discourse has taken such a hold. But, as already mentioned, it is not the only policy perspective around. The environ-mental debate and, particularly, the problem of soil erosion have generated a similar amount of discussion over the years.

The environmental debate: the case of soil conservation

Policy space for the environmental rehabilitation discourse was strongest during the years following the 1984 famine. Although before this there had been a history of food-for-work conservation measures, especially following the 1973 famine, these really took off from the mid-1980s. As already noted, the EHRS was highly influential and, undoubtedly, crucial to the establishment of a donor, government and NGO actor network pressing for a high-profile environmental rehabilitation campaign. For instance, one informant who had been involved in senior positions within government and from outside since this time confirmed the importance of this study: 'The Ethiopian Highlands Reclamation Study has been very influential throughout my career. I refer to it time and again. Also, the Soil Conservation Research Project.' Similarly, a document for the World Bank-led Soil Fertility Initiative produced by consultants from the FAO Investment Centre comments: 'Although it [the EHRS] is more than ten years' old, the study represents the most compre-hensive examination of the many aspects of problems of soil conservation' (World Bank 1998a: 8).

Over the last ten years, a number of critical commentators have questioned the assumptions used in this and related studies on environmental issues in Ethiopia (see, for example, Hoben, 1996; McCann, 1995, 1998; Herweg, 1993; Bojö and Cassells, 1995; Alemayehu et al, 2001; Eyasu, 1998). Yet, despite rather fundamental questions being raised about the accuracy of the data used to support the environmental crisis narrative and its response – the environmental-rehabilitation policy approach – the central policy argument has remained. When discussing this issue, a senior official working on environmental issues with the government admitted the flaws in the data, but insisted that the basic arguments for the policy stance are not undermined:

> We use the earlier narratives again and again, although there is a lack of scientific research substantiating these. For example, there are figures claiming that 40 per cent of the country was covered by forest and now it's 2.7 per cent. We are building policy on that. But now people are saying that it is not the case; forest cover was as scant then as now. Again, data on per hectare loss of soil needs substantiating. But, in general terms, the trends are there.

Despite challenges, then, the dominant environmental crisis narrative has remained resilient and at the centre of the policy discussion in Ethiopia since the mid-1980s.[9] We have to look beyond the technical arguments about soil loss or deforestation rates to broader political questions, and to the nature and extent of the actor networks associated with the environmental rehabilitation discourse, in order to see how, in the face of increasing and apparently convincing contradictory evidence, the dominant policy stance has been so strongly maintained.

In the 1980s and into the 1990s, the continued threat of famine offered a particularly opportune policy space through which the environmental discourse was established at the centre of rural development policy. During the 1980s, a strong and influential actor network emerged involving sections of government, a range of international NGOs who arrived in the country *en masse* during and after 1984, and donors keen to off-load food aid and under pressure from international and domestic constituencies to do something about the environment. For Western donors, providing food aid to a Marxist government was politically difficult, and the ability to link relief to addressing an environmental crisis was a fortuitous opening, providing a politically acceptable solution (Hoben, 1996). For the UN organization set up to administer food aid – the World Food Programme (WFP) – the stakes were high due to the politics of food aid. Programme 2488 turned out to be one of the largest food-aid programmes in history. A consultant working in Ethiopia during this period put it to us that 'the future of the WFP depended on the success of Programme 2488'.

During this period, huge conservation works were constructed using food-for-work programmes, and the Ministry of Agriculture and Natural Resources proudly publicized its achievements in terms of the numbers of terraces and bunds built, and the area of hillsides closed, declaring a strong 'conservation agriculture' policy position, with strategies of environmental rehabilitation at its centre (Hultin, 1989; Ståhl, 1992). Terraces were a clear symbol of the presence and authority of the state in rural areas. They should also be seen as part of the concurrent villagization and resettlement policies: ostensibly, technical interventions re-ordering rural social space and livelihoods.

In the years following the 1984 famine, the environmental rehabilitation discourse and actor network remained well established, with many soil conservation initiatives being carried out with donor support. Then, during the final years of the Derg regime, this was reinforced through the establishment of a National Conservation Secretariat, with plans to develop a National Conservation Strategy (NCS). The Phase One document certainly reflects the core concern of addressing an environmental crisis, and makes extensive use of the earlier work of the SCRP and the EHRS to highlight soil erosion and soil fertility decline as particularly pressing environmental issues:

> *Improved management is vital, given the present trends in environmental degradation. These suggest that soil loss on arable land exceeds formation by a factor of six, and that wood is being used at twice the replacement rate. Unless major changes in the management of natural resources occur, complete deforestation will occur by 2025, and the land unable to support agriculture because of soil erosion will increase to some 10 million hectares by 2010. During the next 30 years, it is predicted that crop yields will decline by 1–3 per cent per annum and droughts will have more severe impacts. With the population set to double in less than 25 years, these trends could well intensify (Wood and Ståhl, 1989: 3).*

With support from the World Conservation Union (IUCN) and a series of external consultants, the NCS process became well established in the country. Phase One ran between 1989 and 1990 and aimed to identify key issues, with IUCN advice and assistance. Phase Two developed a five-volume strategy, including policy and institutional frameworks and action-and-investment plans. Initially, the NCS was located in the Office of the National Committee for Central Planning; it later moved to the short-lived Ministry of Natural Resources, Development and Environmental Protection (Kifle Lemma et al, 1998: 28). The status of environmental issues on the Ethiopian policy agenda was raised with the high-profile process leading up to and following the United Nations Conference on Environment and Development (UNCED) in Rio in 1992. In response to this, an Environmental Protection Agency (EPA) was created in 1994 (although this was a down-grading of the full ministry that was established to coincide with the Rio conference). The EPA is a parastatal organization that reports directly to the prime minister's office, and has been the focal point for developing the new environmental policy; it now houses both the NCS secretariat and the office for follow-up work associated with the CCD.[10]

Although the close association between soil conservation and food aid has declined through the 1990s, the prominence of the soil conservation debate remains. This is reflected in a wide range of documents, from the national and regional conservation strategies, to the federal government's environmental policy, to the Food Security Strategy.[11] Since the 1980s, though, both the policy space and, to some degree, the actor networks associated with the soil conservation and environment debate have changed. During the 1980s, the threat of famine and the political circumstances in which donors found themselves created a particular opportunity for the establishment of a soil conservation agenda. By the 1990s, circumstances had changed and new spaces had opened up. This was the result of a combination of changes in political conditions and the explosion of an international debate on the environment during the 1990s, and, with this, there was an increasing interest in environmental issues on the part of donors.

Through this period, the actor network associated with the environmental debate has reconfigured, to some extent. There are, of course, elements of continuity – the continued importance of the SCRP and, particularly, Hans Hurni's influence, along with the EHRS report, which has already been mentioned. The NGOs have remained interested in soil conservation; but today, soil conservation is less linked to food relief and more to a rehabilitation and development agenda. In government, soil conservation remains a significant element of agricultural policy, and a soil conservation 'package' has been developed as part of the extension policy.[12] However, with the restructuring of government departments, a soil and water conservation team now works within the Natural Resources Department, arguably making it less prominent in the main-line ministry. Some also argue that the creation of the EPA as a separate parastatal, without direct-line functions and with a limited budget, has weakened the influence of conservationists in the Ministry of Agriculture. They cite the prominence of the Green Revolution stance, and the SG2000 programme, in particular, as examples of how the ministry has abandoned its conservation agriculture stance, which – they argue – was the hallmark of the 1980s. But, as will be discussed below, with regionalization following the EPRDF take-over in 1991, different patterns are evident in different parts of the country. Today, it is often the policy space and actor networks at a regional level which are key in explaining the ascendancy or decline of a particular policy position.

UNDERSTANDING POLICY CHANGE: THE CASE OF THE EMERGING PARTICIPATION AGENDA

So far, we have explored how the two dominant policy discourses – Green Revolution and environmental rehabilitation – and their associated actor networks became established in the Ethiopian policy debate. Policy positions are not monolithic and static, however, nor are actor networks immutable and constant. Things change. New policy spaces emerge and new actor networks are formed, making use of new knowledges in order to create new narratives and discourses about policy issues. This section examines how certain policies have changed through an exploration of the emergence of what can be termed a participatory agricultural and natural-resource management discourse.

Those arguing for such a position situate a discussion of agricultural production and environmental conservation within an understanding of rural livelihoods, arguing that technical solutions to either food shortage or environmental degradation have not worked. They argue, instead, that solutions must be based on a detailed understanding of local contexts, drawing on indigenous knowledge and technical practices (see Corbeels et al, 2000). Integrated solutions are favoured, including a focus on linking agricultural production with conservation and encouraging the management of watersheds through community involvement. Top-down solutions and large campaign-style approaches are, therefore, rejected in favour of more participatory solutions, involving local consultation and village-level planning.

During the last few years, in particular, arguments of this sort have become increasingly influential. This section attempts to trace the influence of this emerging discourse on agricultural and natural-resource management policy debates in Ethiopia, identifying how and why the previously dominant discourses have come under scrutiny, and examining how old actor networks have unravelled and new ones have formed.

Shifts in environmental thinking, for instance, can easily be found in documents from different periods. Compare, for example, the difference in tone between these extracts – one from the EHRS and the other from the NCS ten years later:

> *Each PA [Peasant Association] should have 70 hectares re-afforested with eucalyptus, and a further 10 hectares with other species, totalling 1.6 million hectares by 2010. . . to provide breathing space for reclamation. . . considerably more than 150,000 persons will need to be resettled or preferably migrate annually (Constable and Belshaw, 1985: 21).*

> *Given the reported reluctance of some farmers to construct physical conservation works in some areas, through a programme of farmer participatory research, [it is possible to] determine for specific agro-ecological zones the relative efficiencies and economic advantages of physical and biological soil conservation systems to determine the biological or physical measures most suitable for conservation (National Conservation Strategy Secretariat, 1994: 58).*[13]

Similarly, a more participatory stance has recently been advocated by the Ministry of Agriculture with the launch of its Participatory Agricultural Demonstration and Extension Training System (PADETES):

> *Unlike the top-down extension method of the past, demonstration in PADETES is designed to ensure farmers' participation. The farmers are involved in all stages of activities, from planning to evaluation* (Ethiopian Herald, *10 April 1998: 8).*[14]

During the early 1990s, in particular, elements of the environmental rehabilitation discourse began to change, with a softening of approach and an
increasing emphasis on consultation and participation. A number of events
contributed to this. During the overthrow of the Derg, and in the period soon
afterwards, the extensive destruction of conservation measures, perceived as
top-down and inappropriate, was seen as a sign of major public discontent
with the previous policy (Dessalegn, 1994). In discussions, senior officials
involved in promoting the environmental rehabilitation policy under the Derg
regime admitted that they were shocked at the extent and vehemence of this
reaction.

The change in the environmental debate was reflected upon in an interview
with a senior manager in the EPA. There is a distinctive view that command
and control is no longer an option for environmental policy:

> *The outcome of policy cannot be an institution that looks after the
> environment by implementing activities – it will clash and won't work.
> The EPA has a low-level profile, so it is not threatening. With the
> environment, the only way it can work is through consensus. Enterprises
> should be regulated by law; for everything else, it is a question of
> awareness-raising and consensus-building.*

The CCD illustrates this again. While still framing the problem in terms of
mounting land degradation and impending crisis, officials associated with the
CCD make much of process and participation when talking about their work.
The aim is clearly not to replicate the large-scale rehabilitation programmes of
the 1980s; rather, the talk is of 'awareness-raising' and building projects from
the 'bottom up'. A senior manager within the EPA commented:

> *It is an iterative process: technocrats have systems for dealing with
> information that peasants don't have; but there is also information that
> peasants have that they don't. So, we try to maximize participation. It is
> important that local land users go along with what others want to do,
> because you can't have police looking at the backs of each peasant farmer
> in the country.*

Changing patterns of aid in the 1990s also curtailed much of the policy space
previously associated with an environmental rehabilitation position. A former
senior official in the Ministry of Natural Resources noted in 1999 the shift away
from a conservation approach towards a more productionist stance, associated
with the Green Revolution position:

> *Much less soil conservation is done today because, by and large, food aid
> has been cut off. Instead, there has been a shift to being fanatical about
> dams and small-scale irrigation regardless of feasibility. . . it's an
> obsession.*

This is reflected in comments made by members of the donor community. One bilateral donor official commented:

> *Soil erosion is still there at the top of the agenda. But it is more modest, now that it is clear that the WFP [World Food Programme] soil conservation programmes achieved little. . . Now, we must link this to agriculture and growing food, as part of the regional food security strategies.*

During the 1990s, then, while still recognized as important, the top-down soil conservation approaches of the 1980s lost credibility, and the debate shifted towards a more participatory approach to natural resource management. Yet, as discussed earlier, at exactly the same time, a top-down, technicist and productionist stance, framed in terms of 'aggressive technology transfer', was promoted for the agricultural sector. By all accounts, during the early years of this programme, there was not much room for participation and debate.

However, as with the environmental rehabilitation discourse, challenges have increasingly emerged for the Green Revolution stance. Following the successful harvests and subsequent export of grain in 1995, the results of demonstration trials and the level of credit repayment have not been as high as expected in many parts of the country (Howard et al, 1998). While the advocates of the programme continued to quote the impressive statistics of 1995, and the evident success stories of the higher potential zones, the story, elsewhere, was clearly less rosy. Over a number of years rumours and discontent accumulated. Given the political profile of the project in the country, public criticism was rare; but doubts began to take hold. By 1998, however, some officials in the Ministry of Agriculture were beginning to qualify the SG2000 success story with a range of caveats. For example, one senior official described their direction thus:

> *We want to go for a more sustainable approach – not necessarily maximum yield, but optimum. We want an integrative extension system, with multipurpose extension agents. We are now adding soil conservation – both physical and biological – agro-forestry and watershed management to our crop package. It's a land husbandry management approach. We are doing pilots now in three regions, based on sound land-use planning at household and village level. We want something concrete to convince the policy-makers in the PM's office, as we did with the crop package five years ago.*

As part of this reassessment, a number of additions to the Green Revolution position were being added. A convergence with the emerging participatory, consultative approach to environmental issues can be detected. As a section director of the Ethiopian Agricultural Research Organization put it: 'Whether you like it or not, participation is the order of the day.' In discussions with both regional and federal officials, a new emphasis on efforts to boost agricultural production in the context of integrated watershed management can be seen, alongside a stated commitment to involve farmers in agricultural development activities, including an appreciation of their own knowledge and technology. In addition to the main crop package (which still remains the dominant formula for extension on the ground), a variety of different packages have been added, especially those suited to more marginal dryland areas. So, in addition to the maize/fertilizer option, bee-keeping, soil conservation, fodder management and so on have been added, although the degree to which these are actually implemented is unclear.

Given the forcefulness and apparent belligerence of the Green Revolution approach only a few years before, this emerging new style is perhaps surprising. In addition to the widespread failure in many areas of the SG2000 package, what other factors have contributed to the fracturing of the hard-line Green Revolution discourse and the emergence of a more participatory stance that converges with the environmental management debate? To answer this, it is important to ask what networks are being built around participatory approaches? What influence are these having? And, in turn, what policy spaces are emerging?

In relation to both mainstream discourses, there are some key events that have provided opportunities for challenging the dominant positions, allowing new policy spaces to open up and new actor networks to be formed. The emergence of the participatory policy stance, in relation to both agriculture and environment, can be traced, in part, to such events. Clearly, the overthrow of the Derg and the arrival of a new government, offering the prospects of peace, security and democracy, helped to strengthen the adoption of participation arguments in some quarters. At the same time, growing awareness of successful participatory NGO projects, the organization of national and regional meetings on participatory approaches, and the initiation of extensive training and networking in Ethiopia combined with the increased emphasis on participation in the international development literature and the need to couch applications to donors in a participatory language.

Undoubtedly, too, acts of 'foot-dragging' or overt resistance by farmers, such as low-credit repayment rates, as well as the destruction of conservation measures are key and under-explored parts of the story. Front-line extension workers (development agents) also have tactics for avoiding, or at least circumventing, the complex bureaucratic system for implementing the package approach. With such a huge expansion in extension staff and the vast increase in the package quotas in all areas, there are limits to supervision. While the quota system and other job evaluation criteria push extensionists to expand the programme, a variety of tactics to offset this have been devised.

A clear actor network articulating an alternative participatory approach in Ethiopia is, however, not obvious. A number of NGOs and their coalitions have been important, as have the funding of various training and capacity-building projects by donors. But NGOs are closely supervised by government in Ethiopia, and the space for alternatives is limited. For many, NGOs just do standard projects – 'just woodlots and soil conservation', according to one informant – that are often very similar to those implemented by government. For some, 'participation is digging a ditch, preferably without being paid!'. The mobility of staff between government, NGOs and donor agencies and projects has perhaps facilitated the flow of ideas; but this has made the process diffuse and difficult to track.

As with our earlier discussion of the establishment of other discourses, a similar set of practical actions are evident – workshops, field days, demonstrations and case studies have all been important opportunities for enrolling new actors into networks. A number of NGO workers, committed to a participatory approach, commented that getting sceptics in government to really experience field realities through exposure visits or training was really instrumental in creating a constituency. Links to international actors have also been important. Donor support to experimental participatory projects has been significant, as have collaborative links to international research activities.[15] Such links in the actor network have been important, commentators argue, in establishing credibility in a setting where the mainstream has been unconvinced and suspicious.

In terms of influencing policy-makers, an NGO director articulated a specific strategy: 'We don't go for politicians. We go for individuals who can influence politicians.' The distinction between 'political' and 'technical' people is important. The strategy is to win senior technical people over to your worldview, and then leave them to make the arguments with 'politicians' where high-level political issues impinge, and where NGOs are on difficult terrain. These technical people can also work within the bureaucracy where policies are implemented to change culture and practice. As one senior planner in the Ministry of Economic Development and Cooperation noted: 'It's very difficult to influence policy if you are in an NGO or a community.' Within the highly influential planning ministry, he admitted:

> We have no mechanisms for public consultation. And, internally, we have no formal system. Currently, we do it on a personal level. We go to different sections and say, 'Look guys. . . we want to do this.' If we cannot resolve it there, we take it to the minister and, finally, to the PM's office. It is more of a consensus.

Gaining access to such circuits of decision-making is, not surprisingly, difficult. At the centre, documents circulate 'permanently in draft form', without a clear process of decision-taking laid out. Discussions take place between different well-placed and politically connected groups and, finally, things are referred to the influential advisors in the PM's office. As one cynical observer commented:

> Participation and consultation has a different meaning among higher officials. You are certainly allowed to discuss the government's policies – to discuss them, not to change them.

But, despite such observations, previously secure policy positions are potentially vulnerable to challenge, adaptation and change. Tight, well-integrated actor networks, drawing on particular discourses about environment and development, may unravel if contexts and circumstances change. In the case of the emergence of a participatory perspective on natural resource management, this has been a fairly gradual process. In-roads to the dominant position have been made through new networks of NGOs working together with colleagues within government and with the support of a variety of international actors, from the research and donor communities. But, as we have seen, a number of key events helped to precipitate such change. With such changed contexts, the presentation of alternative perspectives gains more purchase: new 'facts' are built, supported by new networks of actors and reinforced by the practical witnessing of other field realities. However, such changes may occur only in certain areas; others may be off limits. Discussions of land tenure policy are a case in point.[16] A senior policy advisor in government observed:

> *Land tenure – don't touch it. You can consult, if you like; but the minister will say it is not possible. With the land issue, it's ideology rather than economics. If you control the land you control the people. That's why it's important politically. No change in policy is possible, whatever the World Bank and the donors say.*

Policy change is thus not straightforward, based on a rational choices between alternative options. Instead, any understanding of policy change requires an examination of the complex interactions between knowledge, power and political process. Such interactions are, of course, dependent on contexts; in the Ethiopian setting, the regional context is an increasingly significant factor. A discussion of the contrasts in policy process in two different regions, then, will be the subject of the next section.

REGIONALIZATION AND POLICY-MAKING: THE CONTRASTING CASES OF TIGRAY AND THE SNNPR

Following regionalization, the relationship between national and regional policy debates has become increasingly significant. In many areas, the federal level has become less important, and it is in the regions that policy agendas are set, decisions taken and projects implemented. A bilateral aid official commented: 'No one knows what the federal ministries' role is now. They have no exact function.' Indeed, he commented that [in 1999] they had no working relations with the federal level and that they had only visited the Ministry of Agriculture once on a courtesy visit. Another donor official made a similar point when asked how they tried to influence policy: 'Forget the federal level – go down to the regional level.'

In this section, we explore the contrasting cases of Tigray and the Southern Nations, Nationalities and Peoples' Region (SNNPR), looking at how regional players, both within government and outside, have responded to, interpreted and acted upon the wider discourses discussed in the earlier sections of this chapter. What is clear from this analysis is that the regional context increasingly matters – in some cases, offering more room for manoeuvre, and the opportunity to reinterpret and transform policies coming from the centre for the local context. In other cases, by contrast, political and bureaucratic constraints appear to limit such opportunities, resulting in less flexibility and fewer attempts at local adaptation of centrally derived policies.

Tigray is a case where there appears to have been considerable reorientation of federal policies. In discussions with a range of officials in the late 1990s, a number of significant events were mentioned that have suggested substantial shifts of agricultural and natural resource policies originating at the centre. In Tigray, much of the debate had revolved around the SG2000 project and the new extension policy. The failure of many of the demonstrations during 1996 was witnessed, during field visits, by bureau officials, members of the regional council, NGO project staff and others. On these occasions, informants told us, farmers spoke out and highlighted the pros and cons of the approach with great clarity. Exposure to experiences further afield has also been influential in suggesting new approaches. Both a senior official in the Bureau of Agriculture and a senior administrator in Mekelle University College talked enthusiastically of a field trip with regional- and federal-level officials to India and China, in order to look at alternative approaches to watershed management. They also spoke of a subsequent meeting where these issues were discussed with senior federal ministry officials. According to the bureau official, the integrated watershed approach:

> . . . taught us to be integrated and interdisciplinary – to develop water-harvesting systems and to find ways of linking feed, fuel and soil fertility, and to put far less emphasis on terraces.

New perspectives on a more integrated, conservation-farming approach for the non-irrigated areas of Tigray, based on principles of watershed management, have therefore emerged. A local actor network has been built around a collaborative research project, linking the University College with the Institute of Agricultural Research and the Tigray Bureau of Agriculture, which explicitly sets out to test alternatives to the SG2000 approach. One of the participants in this research observed:

> With SG2000, high rainfall years encouraged unwarranted optimism, whereas with low rainfall such packages are high risk. In our research, we want to look at three woredas on a watershed basis. . . to see how farmers can go with alternatives to Global 2000. . . . There could be alternatives, a multitude of alternatives.

There appears to have been a major re-evaluation within Tigray as a result of these experiences. An agriculture bureau official recalled:

We have good experience from the Derg time, when everything was about high-potential areas. What we have realized is that equity is crucial – if households are dependant on others, then that is not good. . . We don't believe those areas are degraded and agriculture is over. We have seen great potential in drought-prone areas.

However, this picture of dynamic debate, local research and the emergence of distinct regional policy discourses, associated with strong, well-established actor networks, is not evident everywhere in Ethiopia. In the SNNPR, for example, informants gave a rather different picture. Here, despite plenty of off-the-record criticism, there is little open debate about the nature of agricultural or natural resource policy. A rather draconian, top-down stance is often seen, with apparently little room for the participatory approaches noted elsewhere. One observer commented in 1999: 'At the moment, SG2000 farmers are put in prison for being unable to repay credit when the rains fail.' In contrast to the situation in Tigray, the agricultural bureaucracy appears to operate with a much more rigid style, where:

Woredas compete with each other to say so many farmers have voluntarily joined in [the SG2000 programme]. They are actually under pressure to force farmers. The woreda *council puts pressure on the* woreda *Bureau of Agriculture and they pressurize DAs [development agents].*

An administrator within the Sustainable Agriculture and Environmental Rehabilitation Commission discussed interventions at the local level in the following terms:

Before we start we discuss – we elaborate why irrigation is the major solution. This and other issues will be briefed to them [the peasants]. Then, they accept the necessity of their participation. After negotiation, we have our own structure to mobilize the community. At the grassroots level, [there are] regional coordinating committees – others will participate in activities. First we convince them, then they accept, then we mobilize them. There is a labour mobilization department here.

What are the explanations for these apparently stark differences in outlook and approach to policy? In discussions of the regional characteristics of the policy process, informants highlighted a number of factors that, they argued, influenced the way things worked in different places. A number of interrelated issues were regularly mentioned in these conversations.

The regional political context is clearly highly significant. In Tigray, a certain self-confidence is evident that is reflected in the eagerness to present a distinct Tigrayan position. The political space to do this is, of course, depends on the close connections between regional political actors – both politicians and influential bureaucrats – and the ruling party. A number of members of the regional council and bureau chiefs, for instance, are members of the EPRDF ruling council, and were previously key players in the TPLF. In the SNNPR, by contrast, such connections are largely absent. The regional council and government bureaucracy is made up of representatives of a wide range of ethnic groupings, from across an enormously diverse region. Although appointees of the central government and party exist, they do not necessarily have privileged access to the federal level, nor do they have the necessary political connections. Indeed, a distinct lack of confidence is exhibited, reflecting perhaps an insecure and uncertain political positioning.

Young (1998: 198), in a recent review of the regionalization experience in Ethiopia, comments on the dilemmas of both imposed governance in SNNPR and the inherently weak capacity for policy-making and administration as follows:

> *The first administrations [after 1991] were military dominated and made up solely of Tigrayans; only later were southern Ethiopians, captured during the war, given political training and quickly made to assume administrative and 'elected' positions. It is indicative of the TPLF's need to control the political process that it did not build alliances with the few southern parties which existed at the time and, instead, has carried out a campaign of harassment against them. The result is that, unlike their counterparts in Tigray, cadres selected to administer the south typically have low levels of education, frequently appear to be motivated by opportunism and, not surprisingly, have questionable legitimacy among their constituents. Weak leadership gives rise to accusations of theft, bribery and incompetence, and these charges are given at least some credence by the frequent changes and short tenures in office of many leading officials in the region.*

The impact of mechanisms adopted for bureaucratic control – and, in particular, the *gim gima* evaluation system – were also pointed to by informants as a key factor differentiating regional experience. The *gim gima* evaluation system evolved during the liberation war by the TPLF as a way of encouraging both discipline and transparency. Since 1991, this approach has been incorporated within the government bureaucratic system. Every official is subject to a six-monthly review, when any person may outline their criticisms of performance in a public hearing.[17] Advocates of the system argue that it encourages openness, reduces corruption and increases people's motivation and performance. Critics point to the political control of the system and the way in which hearings are far from transparent, and often involve serious intimidation. Such critics also point to the way in which the system encourages conformity and reduces the incentives to innovate and challenge the status quo.[18] In Tigray, the *gim gima* system is based on a tradition stretching back over 20 years, and has become well established and reasonably widely accepted (although criticism is still evident). In such a setting, more of the positive elements of the system may be seen.

By contrast, in other regions, this is perceived as an imposed system, and one that is associated with intimidation and political control. In such settings, more of the negative elements are evident, with the consequence that, due to fear of negative evaluation, criticism and debate of policy is stifled, and bureaucratic inertia and a lack of local initiative are often the result. But, yet again, in practice, there is flexibility within bureaucratic imperatives. As one observer noted: 'At the level of implementation, we can see differences at the local level, even though policies are still made at the centre, with the regions only allowed to adapt at the margins.' With the closely monitored quota system for the package programme – a central policy par excellence – one extensionist from the SNNPR commented with a smile: 'We are inventing our own ways of getting the quota filled.'

Another issue that many point to is the contrasting levels of staff capacity within government across regions. Under the regionalization policy, government bureaux and departments are encouraged to employ people from that region. For some regions, where long exposure to higher education and other training opportunities has been available, the recruitment of competent staff is not a problem. Despite the war in the 1980s, many Tigrayans received such education; by contrast in the SNNPR, far fewer were able to take advantage of such opportunities during the Derg regime and earlier, with the result that the technical capacity for policy development and implementation differs widely across the two regions.

Finally, informants note that differing experiences of participation and local governance may also be important in explaining the contrasts across regions. In the SNNPR, ever since the invasion by Emperor Menelik during the late 1800s, the area has been ruled by the centre, first, by the imperial regime, and then by the Derg. Many argue, too, that, despite the talk of regionalization and local autonomy, the current government has similar centrist tendencies. Given these historical precedents, and such perceptions of the current regime, there has been little experience of local forms of governance based on participation and 'bottom-up' processes. Indeed, exactly the opposite has occurred. One church-based NGO staff member commented on their involvement in regional policy processes:

> We are on regional committees, task forces and so on. But officials from government have a dual face. In the meeting they disagree with our points, but afterwards they say we agree. There's no transparency. We don't know who the responsible and accountable persons are in the regions. The people who matter are hidden. People behind the screen are deciding on policy.

Those 'behind the screen' are assumed to be associated with the central government in Addis, keeping an eye on the regions. But, as another commentator pointed out, in the SNNPR, 'the majority of government officials are from Protestant groups. In public, they keep to their policies. But when you go down to the local areas, they close their eyes.' In other words, in practice there are ways and means – often through local interaction, or religious or ethnic affiliation – of building informal networks for policy change around processes of implementation.

In Tigray, by contrast, people comment with evident pride on the tradition of people's participation developed during the liberation war. The history of the TPLF working closely with local populations in liberated areas appears to have left its mark on society, which means that the new regional government wants to combine firm government and mobilization with sensitivity to local concerns. One observer noted the importance of:

> . . . a sense of continued dialogue, which is taken up as a culture by the people. If there is a good initiative by the community, then the will and commitment is there. . . All policy ideas have to be discussed at the grassroots level. Ideas from the top have to be discussed and endorsed. This is policy formulation.

A confidence about the potential to make local policy is stated, something which was not apparent in commentaries within the SNNPR. An official in the Bureau of Agriculture argued:

> We don't accept whatever package comes down. It has to be appropriate. Ideas can come down from this bureau or that bureau, and also from representatives of farmers. After these debates, a consensus is taken. The bureau sums up and a package is decided. . . if further study is needed. . . an ad-hoc task force may be set up to produce findings and recommendations.

Officials argue that a participatory approach is central to their style. But this does not take a liberal, populist form; there are greater resonances with the early Maoist 'mass line' approach, a connection which dates back to the ideological beginnings of the TPLF during the 1970s (Young, 1997). Informants describe such a participatory model as a process where the government 'listens' through the baito system, 'takes a consensus', makes a decision and then conscientizes and mobilizes the people around the issue.[19]

Regional context, therefore, appears to be particularly important in understanding policy processes in Ethiopia. As we have shown, a range of factors contribute to the differences, including political histories and settings, mechanisms of bureaucratic control, levels of capacity in government, and commitments to participatory forms of governance. Exploring such contextual factors, and their relationship with the centre, is therefore essential in making sense of policy-making.

Conclusion

As the previous sections have highlighted, the policy process – linked to agriculture, natural resources and environment in Ethiopia – is undoubtedly complex. Policy conflicts are not resolved, it seems, as a result of simple technical and rational choices between different alternatives. Policy is the stuff of politics and people, and of knowledge and power. The rise or fall of different policy emphases depends upon the successful (or otherwise) enrolment of actors – scientists, donors, politicians, NGO staff, farmers and others – and the creation of networks that are able to make use of a policy space, emerging as a result of particular contexts, circumstances and timings. Policies can be seen to be embedded in local settings – in the political histories of different regions, in the cultures of regional bureaucracies and administrations, and dependent upon the histories of educational advantage and disadvantage, as well as rooted in ideologies and practices of governance and participation.

Policies, it seems, often have a certain inertia: particular ideas and practices stick, despite concerted challenges to basic concepts and ways of working. If actor networks are tightly formed and impenetrable, and contexts and circumstances are not conducive to change, no amount of rational argument will budge a policy from its pedestal. However, as we have noted, things do change once distinct and well-guarded policy positions begin to fall apart, and other arguments become incorporated, softening the stance and, through this process, enlarging the associated actor network. Key events may allow this to happen, creating new policy spaces and new opportunities for challenge and open debate. The result is often the partial unravelling of old actor networks and the creation of new ones around alternative policy discourses, which, previously, featured only on the fringes of mainstream policy discussion.

5

Environmental Policy-making in Mali: Science, Bureaucracy and Soil Fertility Narratives

INTRODUCTION

That there is an 'environmental crisis' in Mali, and that something should be done about it, is often taken for granted in policy circles. This chapter aims to understand, firstly, how such crisis perspectives find their way onto the policy agenda; and, secondly, why problems get framed in particular ways, laying emphasis on some aspects and glossing over or ignoring others. The chapter focuses on two contrasting framings of a soil fertility problem. The first we label 'productionist'. Here, the important thing about soils is their role as a key variable in agricultural production. Soil fertility is cast, in a reductionist sense, as part of an equation where the final output is crop yield. Rural people are identified as producers, and the job of policy is to maintain or increase agricultural output. In exploring this framing, we concentrate on cotton, a crop in the Malian context for which this productionist narrative is particularly potent. The second framing we identify as a 'land management approach'. Here, the processes of agricultural production are not unimportant, but they are, critically, set within broader land-use and environmental management contexts. Thus, soils are understood not only in relation to agriculture, but also, more importantly, in relation to overarching questions about the sustainability of management of given areas of land. Soils go alongside trees and water resources and are looked at more systemically as a component of a wider agenda of land management issues: for example, desertification, deforestation, overgrazing, soil erosion and water resource depletion. Land is seen here to have a range of functions: producing crops, nurturing animals, supporting forest products and services and maintaining watershed functions. Soil fertility, in this approach, cannot be isolated as a matter of inputs and outputs, but is placed within its broader environmental context.

This chapter, then, proceeds by identifying particular framings of soil fertility in Mali; through an analysis of bureaucratic, scientific and political cultures, and processes of actor-network construction, it suggests why they have achieved different degrees of influence (see Chapter 2 for a discussion of the conceptual approaches used). Understanding framings contextually in this way, in turn, helps to suggest how and why they may be subjected to challenge, and where nascent alternative framings may find their own paths within the policy process.

The chapter is structured as follows. We begin by outlining key political, economic, bureaucratic and agro-ecological factors for Mali, and by suggesting why they cause soils to be talked about and dealt with in particular ways. The two sections that follow examine the emergence of two dominant and contrasting framings of the soil fertility issue. With two distinct approaches to soil fertility set out and located within a bureaucratic and political context, the chapter moves to a case study. We examine the Soil Fertility Initiative (SFI) as an arena in which different framings of soil fertility are contested in Mali (see Chapter 3).

Tracing the history of the SFI in Mali reveals much about where policies come from, and why they take particular shapes. The SFI, we argue, is organized around an influential narrative that could result in a major national policy activity. However, despite the existence of essential webs of bureaucratic and political support, tensions in the actor network exist and these potentially threaten its future. These reflections point to the fact that policy always exists in dynamic, changing and, to some degree, open-ended contexts. A final section explores why this is very much the case in Mali. Patterns of political influence may be changing, bureaucracies may be subject to new pressures and, in this shifting landscape, new actor networks may form as earlier ones unravel or weaken. As a result, policy may come to be framed in very different ways, reflecting new agendas, interests and discursive practices. The policy process, we conclude, and the embedded relationships that help to produce particular policy framings, may be changing in quite fundamental ways.

CONTEXTS FOR POLICY PROCESSES IN MALI

Policy framings are embedded within particular contexts: political, institutional, economic and agro-ecological. Malian circumstances need to be understood in order to grasp why soil fertility has emerged in particular ways, and to make some judgement about the directions these might take in the future (see, also, Chapter 1).

Soils are a highly important resource in Mali, given that a large part of the economy, over half its exports, and a large percentage of livelihoods are reliant on soil-dependent agriculture and pastoralism. The country also falls into several distinct agro-ecological zones, and soils assume a different importance in each of these. The north of the country is desert and large parts of the country are semi-arid. In these areas, dryland farming and pastoralism are practised with limited interference from the state (Brock and Coulibaly, 1999). In addition to these areas, there are two very distinct zones that concentrate on the production of particular cash crops. The Office du Niger is an irrigated rice scheme, which has received substantial state and donor support (World

Bank, 1996). The area in the south of the country, known as Mali-Sud, is another enclave and the centre of cotton production (Toulmin et al, 2000). This area is managed by the Compagnie Malienne pour le Développement des Fibres Textiles (CMDT), an organization that runs the production, marketing and processing of cotton, alongside the provision of rural development services on behalf of the state in these areas. What is meant by the state and how it operates, in practice, is quite different in each of these areas.

Mali is a particularly poor country, the 12th poorest in the world, with a gross domestic product (GDP) of US$240 per capita (Toulmin et al, 2000: 11), and is reliant on foreign aid for 86 per cent of its government budget.[1] The importance of foreign aid gives donors a strong role in influencing the policies of the country. Environmental issues post-1992 Earth Summit in Rio have been strongly pushed by donors, and have also be seen by the Malian government as offering important funding opportunities. Reflecting its low GDP, the country does not have a strongly diversified economic structure at the macro level. It relies for export earnings on a few key commodities, of which cotton is the principal one, providing over 50 per cent of export receipts. Any sector on which a country is so reliant is necessarily of high political importance. This dependence on cotton is also a reflection of the colonial legacy, as France, the former colonial power, invested strongly in the development of the sector during the pre-war years.

In the past – as with many African countries – the state played a strong role in guiding the development of the economy, setting prices and controlling the marketing of agricultural commodities. This has changed substantially, however, with Mali experiencing structural adjustment from the early 1980s onwards and substantial liberalization of the economy, including privatization, removal of subsidies and liberalization of prices and marketing structures (Brock and Coulibaly, 1999). The major exception to this has been the persistence of cotton production as a tightly controlled production and marketing system run by the CMDT: a form of organization referred to as the cotton *filière* (Degnbol, 1999).[2] Financially, the country is part of the West African franc-zone, linked to the French franc. This zone experienced a substantial devaluation of 50 per cent in 1994, which had a significant impact on the competitiveness of Malian exports, but equally on the costs of imports (Dembélé et al, 2001: 78).

Finally, in thinking about different development narratives in a Malian context, it is important to register that the country has experienced very substantial political change and, indeed, continues to do so. After independence from the French in 1960, Mali was ruled by authoritarian regimes of differing socialist or military hue. This changed substantially following popular upheaval, *les évennements*, in 1991. The military government was overthrown and a transitional regime and elections followed (Ventgroff, 1993). Mali has since been heralded as a new-style African regime, experiencing fairly successful multi-partyism.[3] The push for democracy during the early 1990s was complemented by the appearance of numerous civil-society organizations, and agitation by different sections of the population. In the CMDT area, for example, unrest among cotton farmers resulted in the recognition of a cotton farmers' union (Bingen, 1996: 26). The rural population also challenged the state in other ways. With the beginnings of the democratic process, demands were made for a move away from the previous highly centralized system of governance. Decentralization laws were passed during the early 1990s, and these were followed by the establishment of a decentralization mission. The process has taken some time; but villages have been organized into communes, which replace earlier *arrondissements*, and elections were held for commune councils in May 1999. Some powers – both legislative and budgetary – have been transferred to local councils; but whether this will result in effective local governance may take some time to become clear.

Soil fertility debates in Mali thus take place in a particular context. This is a poor country where donors play an influential role; a country dependent on agriculture and, particularly, on one commodity – cotton; a country that has liberalized economically, but at the same time has kept this key sector under fairly tight control; and, finally, a country where new voices are entering the political arena, and where, gradually, there may be new mechanisms for the articulation of previously excluded interests and pressures. It is against this background that we set the two identified framings of soil fertility. We begin with the productionist soil fertility narrative, setting this within the politics and organization of the cotton sector.

A PRODUCTIONIST NARRATIVE

This section begins by illustrating the productionist framing of soil fertility and goes on to show how it has found expression in the policy process over time. The bureaucratic and political context within which production is articulated is emphasized, as well as the way in which scientific research has shaped these contexts.

Interviewing different actors engaged in the policy process, a Malthusian narrative was frequently articulated. Population pressure was seen as central to a growing soil fertility crisis. A senior researcher in the Institut d'Economie Rurale (IER, the main government research organization for agriculture in Mali), for example, argued that:

> *Soil fertility is declining because of extensive practices, fertilizer use is low, also use of organic manure – particularly for cotton and the Office du Niger. For millet and sorghum, no fertilizer or manure are used, so degradation is widespread. In the past, there was plenty of fallow; people farmed for two to three years, then went on to another field. This is not possible now that all areas are occupied by fields. Traditional fertilizer was fallow. Now we need other methods.*

A similar style of argument is made in an overview study of the state of soil fertility in Mali. This report makes reference to key studies that document alarming declines in soil fertility:

> *In addition to population growth (of both humans and livestock), the severity of the climate. . . and socioeconomic constraints have resulted in a constant degradation of natural resources over many years (Pieri, 1989; van der Pol, 1990, 1991). Moreover, studies at the regional level (Mali-Sud) show that agricultural systems currently export 25kg per hectare annually of nitrogen and 20kg per hectare annually of potassium. The losses from erosion and volatilization are in the order of 40 per cent of the total exports. The balance of phosphorous is negative, especially outside the cotton zones (translated from Gakou et al, 1996:1).*

La politique cotonnière

This second quote highlights evidence of negative nutrient balances. These are argued to be especially prominent in the cotton zone. Cotton, as was noted earlier, is central to the economy and politics of Mali. The organizational and political setting within which cotton production takes place generates a particular shape of policy process into which a productionist soil fertility narrative fits in a particular way.

We have suggested that bureaucratic and political contexts are key to understanding why scientific debates have certain impacts. To understand this for soil fertility, it is necessary to look more closely at the characteristics of the cotton zone, the area where talk of a soil fertility crisis appears to have most purchase. The cotton zone is run as a special area by the CMDT. The French began to tightly organize the production, processing and marketing of cotton in 1924, at a time when the French textile industry was swamped by American cotton exports (Roberts, 1996). Significantly, a large-scale commercial farm model was rejected after substantial debate and cotton production proceeded on the basis of smallholder agriculture (Roberts, 1995: 223). Cotton has continued to have great strategic importance until today, and organizing smallholder producers to deliver supplies of cotton has been a key challenge. The French introduced a particular style of organization, known as the *filière*. This entails a very tightly integrated and managed system covering all aspects of the life of cotton – from provision and choice of inputs, to guidance in crop management, to supply of credit, to purchase and marketing of outputs, to processing and export. A senior CMDT official observed:

> *Professionals associated with cotton production are clear about what you must do to produce cotton – research, production, processing, transport, ginning, marketing. Our integrated* filière *allows fluidity of information and a certain flexibility and adaptability. This gives the best results.*

As Gillham notes: 'Cotton is a crop that has to be "tamed" from A to Z to achieve its optimum production potential' (Gillham, 1995, quoted in Bingen, 1998: 275). This 'taming' is linked to particular forms of political and bureaucratic organization. The development of scientific research on cotton was also essential in providing support to this system.

The French continued to run the cotton *filière* after independence, until 1974, when it was nationalized. The CMDT has dominated ever since, but with strong French influence.[4] The CMDT is 60 per cent owned by the Malian state, and 40 per cent by the Compagnie Française pour le Développement des Fibres Textiles (CFDT), 64 per cent of which is owned by the French government. The CFDT, with its African affiliates, is among the top nine international cotton merchants.[5] In addition to the integrated production chain aspect, the *filière* concept in Mali carries with it a second set of ideas and practices. These are that the CMDT is also responsible for social development in the Mali-Sud region. In fact, this goes beyond the provision of health centres and literacy training, to the provision of infrastructure, such as roads, and some commitment to environmental management. The CMDT has, then, a dual mandate as a commercial company (it is a parastatal but functions as a company) and as a rural development agency.

Again, this *filière* notion has high symbolic importance. The *filière* can be understood as a type of political technology (see Chapter 2). The tight control of production and the provision of services, all framed in neutral technical and developmental vocabularies, actually serve to construct rural people in the Mali-Sud region as cotton farmers. A CMDT publicity brochure highlights how the technical organization of cotton production is mapped onto a particular social and political configuration: 'The *filière* is composed of the Malian state, the CMDT and the producers. . . The notion of the *filière* defends the interests of its members'(CMDT, undated). Looked at this way, it can be argued that these historically inherited mechanisms serve a distinct political purpose – namely, to ensure the continuity of cotton production for the state and the company. Other mechanisms that support this include the nature of credit arrangements for the provision of fertilizer and other inputs, a system, some argue, which keeps farmers in debt so that they have to go on growing cotton (CMDT official, pers comm).

During the 1980s, input supply and credit management were reconfigured, with responsibility handed to local organizations of farmers, known as *associations villageoises* (AVs). These organizations, some argue, effectively pushed policing and surveillance roles into the villages themselves, with farmers assuming a greater role in maintaining the functioning of the *filière*, and with AV leaders serving as exemplary 'pilot farmers' (Bingen, 1998). The creation of the 'cotton farming subject' is further reinforced through functional cotton-oriented literacy training.

The political importance of cotton is further illustrated if one looks at the publicity surrounding the achievements of the *filière*. Publicity routinely announces that '*coton est le clé du développement* [cotton is the key to development]' for Mali (*Jeune Afrique Economie*, 1998). Becoming the largest producer of cotton in sub-Saharan Africa, and in Africa after Egypt, has high symbolic importance. Similarly, domestic achievements, such as passing the annual production target of 500,000 tonnes, provide valuable political capital to the ruling party, as well as the CMDT, to which it is closely connected.[6] The Malian media gave substantial coverage, for example, to the '*fête du coton*' attended by the then Prime Minister Alpha Oumar Konare in 1998.

Substantial effort is put into maintaining the existing system of cotton production, and into broadcasting the achievements of the CMDT. This is all understandable in terms of the interests of the national economy, combined with an abiding coincidence of economic interests with those of the French.[7] The CMDT supports the state at key moments, covering budgetary shortfalls with loans (*'grace à la CMDT, nos fonctionaires sont payées* [thanks to the CMDT, our state employees are paid]' is a well-worn refrain). There are close links between the ruling party and the senior officials in the CMDT, and there is widespread speculation that this may extend to the extraction of financial benefits (three vice-presidents of the CMDT were removed for corruption in 1999). Added to this, the 2300 officials of the CMDT receive substantially higher wages and benefits than other state employees.

RESEARCH STYLES: THE LEGACY OF FRENCH COLONIAL SCIENCE

A production-centred crop focus is central to making a productionist case for soil-fertility policy intervention. This way of seeing things reflects an historically embedded type of science, linked to the training and organization of farmers to produce output of ever greater quality. As Bingen (1998: 279) observes:

> With the CMDT/CFDT, this involves breeding for fibre length, colour, strength, fineness, uniformity; during production and harvest, it also involves controlling for maturity and the incidence of impurities – one reason the CMDT/CFDT has consistently adhered to a rigidly controlled programme of agricultural encadrement.

The development of tropical agronomy was closely linked to the extraction of an economic surplus from colonial possessions. As the French completed their subjugation of Mali (then the French Sudan) at the end of the 19th century, the colonial Governor De Trentinian invited the botanist Auguste Chevalier to investigate cotton varieties. These were taken to buyers in Le Havre, with the aim of securing a market and assuring the viability of the colony. A particular type of science arrived in Mali as the French set about expanding the production of cotton.[8] French scientific research was substantially restructured after World War I, when the emphasis was laid strongly on developing the colonies economically, particularly following the policy laid out by Sarraut of '*la mise en valeur des colonies françaises* [the productive development of the French colonies]'.[9] Bonneuil documents this political aspect to knowledge creation in his history of the rise of the science of agronomy in French colonies during the 1920s. The science of finding ways to improve the production of particular cash crops replaced the earlier emphasis of colonial science in the documentation of flora in colonial museums of natural history (Bonneuil, 1991; Bonneuil and Kleiche, 1993). Expatriate scientists arrived with the aim of applying scientific knowledge to serve the economic needs of the colonial power. The focus of research was very specific – dealing with pests and improving varieties, and targeted at crops of strategic importance.

This tradition continues to the present. As Collion (1995: 3) notes:

> *IER has been highly successful in the area of cotton research. The fact that cotton is market-secure and a highly valued cash crop has played a major role in the successful introduction of technology in this area. However, there is little doubt that the way cotton research was designed and funded, in close collaboration with and by the user, the CMDT, also contributed greatly to the success of the programme.*

While the number of expatriate researchers working in Mali may have declined in recent years, with the emphasis now more on short-term consultancies, French funding of crop research and technical inputs from French institutes continues. Bingen (1998: 270) notes the importance of:

> *[o]ver 50 years of French investment in cotton research throughout West and Central Africa. This French international research network, backed by central laboratories in France, is widely recognized for its contribution to the development of new cotton varieties, cultivation techniques and plant protection practices.*

This legacy continues in the present; the research that is carried out by the national agricultural research institute depends, obviously, on what organizations are willing to pay for. The CMDT and the French continue to invest substantially in research to improve cotton production and in the training of Malians in the French agricultural university in Montpellier. Thus, public research efforts of the IER are deeply intertwined with – and financially dependent upon – the quasi-private interests of the CMDT.

There is clear expression by many that this type of research, linked to particular forms of administration and social organization, has been responsible for a revolution in cotton output. According to Pieri (1989: 65):

> *The various cotton companies. . . (CMDT in Mali). . . organized the market right through from producer to consumer. This, with the research effort by IRCT [the cotton and textiles department of CIRAD] and partners, greatly increased cotton yield and total production in the zone between the 700 and 1400 millimetre isohyets.*[10]

Some commentators put it to us that what research can be done in the cotton areas is highly political. A senior donor representative said that he wanted to do strategic research to produce compelling indicators of land degradation in Mali-Sud, 'but the French consistently block us'.[11] In other words, research must facilitate production of cotton, and science that produces knowledge along the lines that 'cotton is terrible for soils' is marginalized. We have, then, science and policy shaping and influencing each other iteratively, in processes of mutual construction, rather than one speaking to and exclusively guiding the other.

There are a few additional facets of the French legacy that bear mentioning at this point. Firstly, it is often commented that in France, and to some extent in French-influenced political systems, there is dominance by a small elite with shared values, educational background and so on. This elite can be quite impenetrable. It is also, according to Suleiman (1974), dedicated to the state in a way that goes beyond the narrow and ephemeral concerns of party politics.

Secondly, scientists and technically trained personnel have high status, and it is almost expected that key public roles will be filled by people from these backgrounds. In Mali, ministers are surrounded by a close circle of *conseiller techniques* (technical advisors) who offer technical advice. Compared to Anglophone African countries, where the 'technical' is the preserve of the permanent secretaries and their staff, with ministers in a more obviously political role – and, generally, without a technical background relating to their portfolio – in Mali, ministers are more likely to be technically informed and, indeed, often emerge from the ranks of the *conseillers*. Added to the smallness of the technocratic/political elite, this means that scientific ideas can, potentially, very easily circulate into influential arenas. Classmate connections and career paths run through the system, from research scientists to the directorate, the cabinet and to ministerial levels.

This can result in a rather technocratic style of policy-making, where science and policy interact in a rather restricted sense: particular types of scientists with particular training and connections dominate, while those without that background, but nevertheless with valid concerns, are kept out. As one long-term expatriate development worker put it: 'In Mali, the principle of *cousinage* operates. Everyone knows everyone else. It's a small place. The idea of competitive tendering for anything is absurd.' The technical approach tends towards a relatively narrow and non-dynamic approach. One informant commented: 'The French are always narrow; they do three things in this area – animal production, say – and three in that, but they never connect them up!'

THE INFLUENCE OF DUTCH RESEARCH

We have seen, then, the importance of a French approach and style of directing scientific endeavour, and the importance of locating this in a particular pattern of bureaucratic and state formation. Other influences need to be recognized however, in order to understand why soil fertility has achieved such prominence. Over the last 20 years, Dutch foreign aid has played a substantial role in the agriculture and natural resource management sector. As with French research, there is also an identifiable Dutch style. The hallmarks of this are an emphasis on systems ecology and modelling techniques associated with the Department of Theoretical Ecology at Wageningen Agricultural University and key figures in the history of that department, such as de Wit and Breman. This university, as with Montpellier in France, is highly influential in terms of the stature of its departments and the numerous graduates it produces who often go on to become, in turn, influential and well-connected alumni. In terms of soil and crop science, it rivals Montpellier; but it also has additional strengths that are particularly associated with understanding agro-ecosystems. It is this facet that began to become influential across the Sahel – but particularly in Mali – from the 1970s onwards, following the severe droughts, with Dutch support for training and research in IER playing a major catalytic role.

The systems ecology approach gained attention through two large and internationally high-profile research projects conducted in Mali, but with implications for the wider Sahel. The Primary Production in the Sahel (PPS) and the Production Soudano-Sahélienne (PSS) took agricultural research beyond a 'narrow' crop focus and introduced systems thinking to a generation of researchers.[12] According to one researcher, the PPS was:

> . . . *amazingly influential. It defined a whole scientific approach and what science was to Maliens. N'golo Traore, for example, ex-director of IER, was involved with PPS and later became Minister for Rural Development.*

The PPS, in particular, had a remarkable impact because, from years of research, a simple, clear and challenging message could be distilled. This sound bite was essentially that much that had gone before – predicated on the assumption that in the drought-prone Sahel rainfall should be the variable informing researchers – was misguided. Rather, the issue that was missed – albeit understandably – during decades of research was soil fertility. The implications of this were potentially huge, and it was controversial. Gaining acceptance of the message would depend upon maintaining the clarity, and on constructing networks of support. Neither of these should be taken for granted; rather, it needs to be emphasized that successfully asserting a certain position, as Latour (1987) argues, can be likened to a war, with key scientists strategizing, attempting to take over strongholds, enlisting new supporters in their ranks, and using whatever technologies will best ensure the end result. Of course, this might be overstated; but it is a way of thinking about the advance of scientific knowledge in a different way from the bland assumption that facts are usually incontrovertible and arrive out of nowhere to speak 'truth to power' (see Chapter 2).

A key actor in constructing a network around more systemic ways of thinking than had been experienced before, and in communicating the message about soil fertility through the PPS and the PSS, was Henk Breman, an internationally respected ecologist and – according to informants – 'a charismatic communicator', as well as 'a sharp strategiser'. Breman produced the one-line message that captured the imagination – 'fertilizer is irrigation' – and turned soils from a rather dry subject into a potent symbol of development. Breman was influential through these two projects and continues to exert influence today as director of the International Fertilizer Development

Center (IFDC) in Africa, where he plays a key role pushing soil fertility as a rural development policy issue across West Africa, and as a board member of the IER. The role of Breman in constructing a network of individuals and orientations within organizations believing that soil fertility is an essential policy issue is hard to deny (see, also, Chapter 3).

Soil fertility as an issue did not, however, sweep all before it after the publication of the PPS reports during the early 1980s. It has taken other studies involving other individuals and slightly different approaches to push a soil fertility agenda on further. Key to this has been the translation of soil science into some of the idioms of development planning and economics. The nutrient budgeting studies of Stoorvogel and Smaling (1990) are important here (see, also, Chapter 3). These soil scientists, also from Wageningen, put 'hard' figures on the shortfall between import and export of nutrients at different scales. While the extrapolations upon which plot-level research is transformed to macro statement have been criticized, the impact of being able to hold up statistics that support a general impression, and to say that this is why yields are declining (you are using X kilogrammes per hectare of nitrogen (N), and Y kilogrammes of phosphorus (P) less than you are putting in, for example) has been extremely powerful. The work of van der Pol (1992) took this further by calculating for Mali-Sud the percentage loss of agricultural income derived from exploitation, captured in his graphic term 'mining' of soil capital. His figure of 40 per cent of farm income deriving from depletion of soil nutrient capital (1992: 23) and the implications that the reserves might collapse or the 'elastic snap' are widely cited. For example, Bingen (1998: 275) footnotes van der Pol, and comments:

> *The environmental degradation associated with cotton production is well known. The cultivation techniques 'mine the soil', and the very 'success' of the crop puts severe pressure on limited and ecologically marginal land as smallholders save their capital in the form of cattle.*

The use of economic arguments to support the 'soil mining' claim has been an important route to communication with policy-makers. One senior Malian official commented: 'We don't have time to look at all the scientific data. We need simple results. I am interested in the costs, benefits and social impact.' But, of course, it is not only the data and its presentation that are important. A scientist who adopted a somewhat different position from the mainstream view of the productionist narrative commented:

> *The senior officials must always listen to what the donors are saying. They have no facts, no data to justify their position. Sure, I can extrapolate the figures to get a big number. But will they listen to me? No!*

CONSTRUCTING THE NARRATIVE

Scientific facts are built, not received; they rely on techniques and conventions around which consensus is constructed. Facts get taken up through the construction of actor networks, something key individuals in the Malian context have been effective at doing (although others in the process are necessarily excluded). The extension of actor networks is thus embedded in processes of mutual construction between policy-makers (and donors) and scientists (both local and expatriate) (see Chapter 2).

But how has the productionist soil-fertility narrative fitted into, and been shaped by, the cotton production context discussed above? There has been statistical evidence of declining yields in recent years in the core older cotton zones (CMDT, 1999: 3). This is the kind of information that can be used to fit with several different stories. One interpretation of declining yields is that it provides evidence of a soil fertility crisis. This was put to us by a number of informants. However, moving from a sense of acknowledgement that this is an issue to one of urgency, and to devising plans of action and allocating budgets, depended on seizing the moment and having in place a compelling story line that provided both a diagnosis of the situation and offered a solution. The soil fertility narrative, as it relates to the cotton sector, entailed demonstrating that, firstly, there is evidence of a fall-off in yields, which is explained as a consequence of not paying enough attention to soil fertility. Traditional methods of regenerating soils, such as fallowing, have – it is argued – become less feasible, and compensating for this by replenishing soil capital in other ways has become impractical. Soils can be mined for a certain period, the argument goes; but, in the end, your capital (the stock of nutrients in the soil) will run out. Some commentators we spoke to used the image of elastic – it will stretch and stretch so far, but at some point it breaks. So, too, for soils: the decline may plateau for a while; but, eventually, there is a real danger of a much more substantial and serious collapse. This scenario has received considerable attention, given the importance of cotton to the economy and to numerous livelihoods, and the political significance and weight of the CMDT.

The narrative goes on to articulate what must be done to right the ship. The first possible option is to make better use of organic sources of nutrients. Given the concentration of livestock in Mali-Sud, this is plausible. However, it is ultimately only envisaged as a complementary option. There is, the argument goes, simply not enough grazing land to produce sufficient manure to provide the amounts of nutrients required. What, then, is needed is concentration on mineral fertilizers: better usage, more tailored applications, wider availability, and increased use per unit of land. A senior soil scientist made the case to us vociferously: 'I've shown it to them quite clearly – add more bags of fertilizer and you'll get higher yields. We can triple yields.' Alongside the clear present-ation that more bags of fertilizer added to soils correlates with more bags of cotton, there is a second theme, which is about rebuilding soil capital. Here, the argument is that for phosphorus it is possible and desirable to invest in large-scale applications, and that these will have long-term pay-backs. A senior agronomist, adopting the language of economics, observed: 'Investment in soil fertility is the same as building a dam or bridge – it's a capital investment with long-term returns.' Similarly, 'getting the prices right' was a familiar refrain among many commentators. For example:

> Now millet and sorghum are fetching a price, some farmers are moving to fertilizer for sorghum and millet and maize, slowly; if the prices are right, farmers are using fertilizer. Some are doing this now. But you can't reach high yields with organic manure, you need chemical fertilizer.

A niche had been found, then, for presenting the case for soil fertility management in a crop production-focused sense. That the recent expansion into new cotton zones, and further extensification in the future, will help to maintain aggregate yield increases is not denied; but there is recognition that old areas continue to be important, and that in the new areas intensification has to be considered from the outset.

The argument, made in this way, had become compelling, with policy-makers gradually convinced of the need to allocate resources to implement suitable programmes for the long-term public good. As a local World Bank official argued:

> Soil fertility management is a long-term issue. If you talk to farmers, they don't see soil fertility as a problem. They are looking for the day-to-day problem – food. They see yields going down; they don't see how to stop this. They don't see concrete results. To invest in this you need a long-term perspective. It is hard to undertake this work. There will have to be a long-term programme, and slowly soil fertility will increase, yields will increase and farmers will see the results. This will require external help.

A LAND MANAGEMENT NARRATIVE

The previous section documented the development of a productionist soil fertility narrative in Mali. This, we argued, has had particular purchase because of the political importance of maintaining and increasing cotton output. As evidence of declining yields has received greater attention within the CMDT, key actors, at various points, have been able to make the case that soil fertility is the critical variable that needs addressing if a fully fledged crisis in the cotton filière is to be avoided. Actors have mattered, we have suggested, but so have contexts – particularly the close links between agronomists and soil scientists – and so, at times, has systems ecology, and the production-oriented parts of the bureaucracy. Understanding these settings and patterns of interaction has been key to understanding why soil fertility has a high profile and is framed this way, and why the policy process has a certain shape.

However, a second framing of the soil fertility issue is also identifiable in Mali. Again, this has been promoted by particular actors and also emerges from deeply embedded discursive contexts: the concerns of specific scientific disciplines, bureaucratic histories and the particularities of patterns of state formation and development. This framing we cast as a 'land management' narrative.

What are its core elements? Examination of donor and government policy documents, and interviews with a range of stakeholders, suggest a deeply held belief that population growth, combined with poor practices and a lack of technical innovation, are contributing to a crisis of land-based natural resources. The introduction to the National Environmental Action Plan (Plan National d'Action Environnemental – PNAE), for example, asserts:

The perceptible increase in the population, the persistence of unfavourable climatic conditions, and of extensive and inappropriate farming systems, have contributed to the degradation of natural resources and the environment, thereby accelerating desertification (Ministère de l'Environnement, 1998: 4).

Similarly, documentation for the Lutte Anti-erosive claims:

Woodlands and pastures are rapidly decreasing (50,000 to 75,000 hectares/year for south Mali). . . Extrapolation is dangerous, but it can be suggested that the recent acceleration of erosion has already led to the loss of 10,000 hectares of old cotton growing land. . . environmental degradation can be seen as due to a maladaptation of present farming systems to the vulnerable environment of southern Mali, given the current population pressure (van Campen, 1991: 135).

The Green-Com page of the US Agency for International Development (USAID) website comments of Mali:

The Saharan desert is steadily encroaching on what was once arable land in Mali. Since most Malians depend on subsistence farming to ensure their livelihood, desertification translates into an immediate threat to survival and an urgent need for environmental education.[13]

Links are also made between the land degradation and management debate and concerns with production. A senior official in the PNAE commented:

The CMDT is the same as the ON [Office du Niger]. They emphasize production. Now we are second in Africa, but we could be last because we are not paying attention to land degradation. Intensive production will destroy the Sahelian soils. So, sustainable approaches are needed – integrated, holistic approaches.

The land management narrative posits problems of desertification, defor-estation, soil erosion, overgrazing, water resource depletion and soil fertility decline as fundamentally interrelated. They are all issues of land manage-ment, and are integral parts of pastoral and farming systems, agro-pastoralist interactions and patterns of natural resource utilization by communities. As the problems are perceived as being interconnected, they require integrated solutions, rather than approaches that isolate one specific issue. Therefore, in relation to soil fertility, a senior official working on the PNAE and the Con-vention to Combat Desertification (CCD) commented: 'Fertility is essential to the CCD. If you protect soils, you have fertility, and if you protect other resources, then you have soil fertility.'

In identifying different framings, it is degrees of emphasis that are signif-icant. Those who advocate integrated land management approaches would not necessarily disagree with the assertions about soil fertility emerging from a productionist angle, and vice versa. But the relative stress placed on either approach, and the importance attached to one framing over another, will be critical in terms of overall decisions about resource allocation and systems of management and regulation. At the extremes of either framing, of course, there will be fundamental disagreements over fertilizer use, or the degree to which short-term production increases should be achieved at any cost, or whether land should be taken out of agricultural use for the regeneration of natural resources.

This section seeks to explain the emergence of this 'land management' framing and to identify how it fits into current policy processes. As with the production narrative, concerns about land management and degradation in Mali are historically deeply rooted. Where certain types of science have been closely linked to policy and bureaucracy, and where certain styles of argument, metaphors and pieces of information have wide currency, there is a strong tendency for policy to follow a particular track.

Colonial science and bureaucracy

The land management narrative dates at least to colonial times. There is now a substantial literature that documents the vital role of natural resource specialists in colonial bureaucracies in establishing a widespread intellectual and practical commitment to certain perceptions of African environments (Anderson and Grove, 1987; Fairhead and Leach, 1996; Swift, 1996). Concepts such as deforestation and desertification, which have resonated persistently as powerful symbols of crisis in the minds of policy-makers and publics for decades, find their origins substantially in the work of botanists, geographers and foresters in colonial service. In French West Africa, two key figures were the botanists Chevalier and Aubréville. Both worked for extended periods in the Francophone colonies, and both rose to senior positions in the admin-istration: Chevalier as botanical consultant to the Afrique Oriental Française (AOF), and Aubréville as General des Eaux et Forêts des Colonies (within the AOF) (Aubréville, 1956: 7; Catinot, 1982: 3).

As with many of the colonial scientists currently of interest to environmental historians, both Chevalier and Aubréville were highly committed
visionaries, equivalent to those who might be identified today as policy
entrepreneurs. Chevalier, for example, serving as head of a permanent mission
for colonial agriculture in Indochina in 1911, is described as a 'scientific czar'
by Pyenson (1993) in his history of the exact sciences and French colonialism
and is labelled as one of the key 'warrior scientists' of French colonialism.[14]
Both wrote extensively on land degradation, with Aubréville's 1949 book
Climats, Forêts et Desertification securing wider currency and authority for ideas
of natural resource degradation. What is particularly significant is that, as
Fairhead and Leach note, 'the renowned French botanists who had created the
degrading vision had, by the end of the colonial period, become the most
senior figures in the French colonial environmental administration' (1996: 113).

These natural scientists did not simply advise policy-makers or offer
suggestions as to how bureaucracies should be structured in order to tackle
technically defined problems; they were critically placed to take far-reaching
decisions themselves. This meant not only that future patterns of problem-
setting, training and disciplinary focus would be shaped substantially by their
legacies, but that, as administrators, they were particularly well placed to
implement programmes and formulate legislation that accorded with their
scientific findings. The consequences of this, in terms of prohibitions and
restrictions on communities, and the role and rights of the state in relation to
natural resources, are hard to overstate. In West Africa, this meant that all land
– cultivated or otherwise – not formally titled became state land under the
Code Dominale. At the same time, forests were reserved and policed by a new
department, Eaux et Forêts (Hilhorst and Coulibaly, 1999).

Environmental rehabilitation projects also followed from this concern with
desertification. In 1934, Stebbing, an official with the Indian Forestry Service,
in an Anglo–French mission, toured through British and French West Africa
and wrote extensively of poor agricultural practices, bush fires, the cutting of
trees and overgrazing. Quoting a French colonial officer, he argued that the
desert had advanced at a rate of 1km a year over the past three centuries. He
then became a key figure in initiating rehabilitation schemes comprising land-
use planning restrictions on grazing and cultivation, forest reservation and the
initiation of a vast shelter belt scheme to prevent the further march of the
desert. These schemes, as Swift (1996) notes, were the precursors to post-
colonial government and donor efforts to tackle desertification that followed
the 1977 UN Conference on Desertification in Nairobi.

Local land management: *gestion de terroir* approaches

One particular way that donors and government have tried to address land
management, and therefore soil fertility, has been through *gestion de terroir*
schemes. Painter et al (1994) argue that, after the critical Sahel drought of the
early 1970s, there followed a series of integrated rural development (IRD)
projects that concentrated on agricultural development:

> *These large IRD projects [however] generally took little account of the*
> *socio-economic and agro-ecological diversity that characterized the project*
> *areas. . . they apparently did not appreciate that smallholders were*
> *involved in a variety of income-generating activities, other than*
> *agriculture, which were essential to ensure their livelihoods (Painter et al,*
> *1994: 448).*

Poor performance of these projects led to scepticism about the agricultural development focus, and at the Comité Inter-Etat de Lutte Contre la Secheresse au Sahel (CILSS) convened seminar in Nouakchott in 1985 there was a strong reassertion of the 'need to link improved agricultural techniques with anti-desertification measures' (1994: 449). The consensus was that 'homogenous development zones be organized through close collaboration with rural communities' (Rochette, 1985, in Painter et al, 1994: 449).

Gestion de terroir from the mid-1980s became a key way of linking soil fertility and land management. While there were small-scale NGO projects, *gestion de terroir* in Mali is strongly associated with the substantial government and donor programmes, the Programme Gestion des Ressources Naturelles (PGRN) and Gestion des Resources Naturelles (GERENAT), funded by the World Bank and the Deutsche Gesellschaft für Technische Zusammenarbeit (GTZ) respectively. These projects were clearly seen as tackling a deeply rooted environmental crisis (World Bank, 1996a).

Gestion de terroir projects operated through the development of natural resource management plans for tightly defined geographical areas. Within these areas land use would carefully be planned, with different areas given over to pasture, woodland or agriculture. In this community-based rural development, the village development committees of targeted communities draw up plans, or *schémas d'aménagement*, which might entail rehabilitation projects, such as windbreaks, stone lines, check dams for gullies, reforestation, closing-off of particular areas, or dune stabilization.

Gestion de terroir projects have been critiqued in various ways. One criticism is that they rely very strongly on particular conceptions of space and territory. This knowledge about the salient ways in which the world is organized, is in fact, quite normative and has a political function. The core of this is the notion of the *terroir*, which as a concept is rooted, Painter et al (1994) show, in the work of French geographers such as Pellisier and Sautter who worked in the 1950s for ORSTOM (now the Institut de Recherche pour le Développement), producing the series *Atlas des Terroirs Africains*. The *terroir* idea assumes that people belong in communities that are clearly locatable within fixed and bounded geographical spaces – 'a territorial vision of society', as Dimier (undated) argues in a paper on the policies of the French colonial governor Delavignette.

These fixed geographical spaces can be understood as linked to a particular type of colonial bureaucracy seeking to order people and space, and then, subsequently, to post-colonial development structures that value administrative order over complex local realities. As Degnbol (1996: 2) comments:

These projects still tend to focus on technical and administrative solutions to what are fundamentally issues of power relations. Instead of approaching the problem of how to transfer authority from government authorities to local government staff, and from government structures to local populations, large donor-funded projects concentrate on how to ensure an efficient implementation of preconceived plans through the strengthening of existing structures. Thus, in an extreme version, such projects may adopt a purely technical approach in which terroir *activities take the form of a traditional extension package.*

Degnbol goes on to argue that programmes 'did not escape the classical structure of having a programme management unit in the Ministry of Environment with a heavy hand in all decision-making acitvities in the field' (Degnbol, 1996: 11). Equally, these programmes were not very participatory, often imposing a particular view of environmental change. Officials in the PGRN explained that the aim of their work was: 'to make them [local populations] sensitive to the natural resource problem. . . to make them realize it is necessary to fight against degradation with many technologies'. To achieve this: 'All participate to understand environmental problems in the village.'

The post-Rio policy process: action plans, conventions and ministries

The narrative reflected in the *gestion de terroir* projects took a slightly new turn in the post-Rio period, with the development of sustainable development planning strategies – notably, the Convention to Combat Desertification (CCD) and the National Environmental Action Plans (NEAPs). Thus, parallel to the narrative about production and output, narratives focusing on combating environmental degradation are prominent in national policy debates. Such a focus has been widely promoted by donors in the wake of the Sahel droughts of the 1970s and, subsequently, the 1992 United Nations Conference on Environment and Development (UNCED) in Rio. This narrative identifies poverty and food insecurity with broad processes of environmental degradation, including desertification, deforestation, soil erosion and overgrazing. Soil fertility decline is linked to these concerns as a central issue that needs to be addressed in order to halt land degradation.

The PNAE project document puts a slightly different spin on the problems of cotton-farming areas in Mali-Sud, in contrast to the productionist focus discussed earlier:

One may observe that the CMDT is faced with such problems as uncontrolled and ever expanding clearings, excessive exploitation of forests, overgrazing, abandonment of spaces that have become non-productive and soil erosion. One may note that cotton agriculture uses large amounts of fertilizers and pesticides. This use of chemicals must be

rational and controlled, as it may have harmful consequences on humans,
animals and water resources (Ministère de l'Environnement, 1999: 31).

Donors, as we have said, play a key role and many of their resources are channelled through the Ministry of Environment, which has responsibility for the Rio conventions, such as the CCD, and the preparation of NEAPs, as well as supporting some *gestion de terroir* projects. Throughout the 1990s, this resulted in a plethora of conferences, discussion forums, consultation exercises, action plans and pilot projects, supported by external funds. These all had the imprint of the international environment and development debate on them, with participation and sustainable management being the key buzzwords. However, some questions can be raised as to how embedded such processes have become. An official from the PNAE office commented on the process of 'participation' used in the national action plan development:

> *We informed the people of the environmental problems of Mali, then left them to discuss their regional issues. The challenge, however, is education and training. It will take time, but things are beginning to change. People talk of the environment now. We need to send more missions to con-scientize people. We need to take national debates to the local level in a language they can comprehend. That's important in a democratic country.*

One donor official, though, was somewhat more cynical about the process: 'Yes, we are involved because the other donors are too. But I am not convinced. There are too many conferences and workshops. What are they actually doing to improve things?'

As with the productionist narrative, discussed earlier, action plans are developed in a particular national bureaucratic context, through which donors pushing a land management approach must work if they want such ideas to stick and result in projects and programmes on the ground. A Ministry of Environment (MoE) was formed in Mali in 1993 in the wake of the UNCED process, as in many African countries. However, it merged again with the rural development ministry, the Ministère pour le Développement Rural et de l'Eau (MDRE), shortly afterwards. A Ministry of Environment was created again, however, in 1997, arguably to create a position in government for key political interests. The PNAE notes:

> *The MoE is responsible for the development and implementation of the national environmental policy. As such, it is in charge of: ensuring the coordination and implementation of actions for combating desertification and the advance of the desert; arousing the commitment of the populations around fighting ecosystem degradation and preserving the quality of the living environment (Ministère de l'Environnement, 1999: 5).*

In the late 1990s, the minister was perceived as one of the key players in domestic politics and, in this respect, the ministry was well connected. Yet, in other respects it remained weak in that it lacked a field presence comparable to the MDRE or the CMDT. This caused various tensions. At one level, it became clear from our interviews that there was friction between the MoE and the MDRE. Some argue that the MoE should deal only with urban environmental issues, while others argue that the MoE should deal with rural development, as well as pushing the environment as a cross-sectoral theme in all policy areas. Here, some of the tension arises in that the mandates are not always clearly defined, resulting in competition for projects and funds between the two ministries. The political power of the ministry, some would argue, was demonstrated when the Eaux et Forêts department was recreated in the MoE as an enforcing and implementing arm (the National Direction for the Conservation of Nature), rather than moving it in toned-down form to the MDRE.[15] Many people view this as near disastrous, given that the draconian Eaux et Forêts was one of the first government departments to be reformed after democratization. Conversely, the much-publicized reform of the MDRE is viewed as being in something of a mess, with its division into three new functional sections yet to convince many commentators.

This also means that, while the donors have a strong and clear narrative in relation to land management and some successful projects, and strong coordination through the GTZ of the CCD process, there is also understandable interest and pressure to try and translate the donor concern with environmental management into funding mechanisms for a planning and implementing bureaucracy. Hence, in May 1999, there was a large round table that looked at funding the NEAP through the MDRE, and this attracted widespread donor interest, with soil fertility a key theme. But concerns were still expressed about how to proceed in a fashion that is non-bureaucratic and addresses the concerns of meaningful participation.[16]

To sum up, alongside the soil-fertility productionist narrative, a land management has emerged that raises a different set of concerns as priorities for action. When these two narratives are contrasted historically and institutionally, they can be seen to be associated with very different networks of actors, with different styles of science, and with different forms of bureaucratic organization. These, we will see, have important implications.

This land management narrative has also, however, pitched itself as being concerned about soil fertility. In this, it competes for attention with the production-centred narrative. Of course, the two narratives do not always stand in opposition to each other. At times, there are explicit attempts to combine a focus on environment and production. The emphasis through the 1990s on sustainable development was one such attempt at bringing these two strands together. The next section looks at one attempt to build a major policy process for soil fertility, the Soil Fertility Initiative (SFI), a process that required the construction of networks between the two narratives.

COMPROMISE OR CONFLICT? THE CASE OF THE SOIL FERTILITY INITIATIVE IN MALI

This chapter has set out two distinct narratives about soil fertility. It has sought to show that they are associated with different types of knowledge production and science, with different actor networks, and emerge from different bureaucratic settings. These narratives, we suggest, do not contradict per se, but reflect differences of emphasis. These different emphases can, however, be important. During the 1990s, in order to build substantial activities around either theme, it became necessary to speak in the post-Rio language of sustainable development. This vocabulary emphasizes the environmentally friendly sides of production initiatives and the developmental benefits of protecting the environment. As a manager of the Malian National Environmental Action Plan (Plan National d'Action Environnemental – PNAE) framed his work: 'The language of sustainability is what we talk, not just the language of production.' This section looks at one attempt to bring the two soil fertility narrative strands together through the development of an SFI for Mali. The SFI, as a case study, shows a very concrete policy process around soil fertility, and highlights some of the difficulties in translating a compelling narrative into policy, particularly where there are different framings of the issue combined somewhat uneasily.

The Malian SFI is embedded in an international politics of soil fertility. Knowledge and power in relation to policy for soil fertility are not limited to national boundaries; rather, they are importantly tied up with global discourses about an African soil fertility crisis (as discussed in Chapter 3). In understanding this process, then, it is important to be aware of differences in perception and interests between national policy actors, and also the linkages that are formed with international actors. Mali was one of the core countries targeted by the SFI. The international prioritization of soil fertility provided an opportunity for those looking for action on soil fertility at a national level. As a senior Malian working in the MDRE put it: 'In the past, there have been lots of small initiatives which have been very fragmented, with limited impact. We want something rapid, over a large area that will have a big impact. We need a national plan.' Another official in the IER reiterated the soil mining narrative and the need for a major initiative:

> *The average Malian can't see the problem of soil mining. Now we have a national plan. It must be based on the decentralization policy – a regional-based approach. I am pushing for the plan. The minister says, if you think it is a problem then go ahead and work on it. Profit maximization is not what we have in mind. In some areas they need 10kg of inputs per hectare; where can farmers find that in manure?*

A window had now opened, as donors became concerned with tackling soil fertility in Africa. Politically, too, there was plenty of commitment. As a World

Bank official commented: 'The French and the CMDT want a long-lasting source of cotton – so they are into sustainability these days.'

A space emerged. However, making effective use of the opportunity entailed building a network that articulated something more than a straight-forward production-focused line. The initiative would need to be framed as addressing land management more broadly, and in a multi-faceted manner. A review document produced for the Malian SFI articulated the need to:

> [p]ut in place a multidisciplinary unit, playing a role as advisor to the minister on matters of soil fertility management policy and coordinating the activities of different programmes working on natural resource management (translated from Gakou et al, 1996: viii).

The World Bank task manager covering West Africa and the SFI suggested that the initiative should be seen as linked to a wider land management agenda: 'The aim is to harmonize the SFI and the Convention to Combat Desertification.' Accordingly, approaches were made to the major land-management rural development operation in Mali, the Programme Gestion des Ressources Naturelles (PGRN), for funding of the action plan. The in-country World Bank manager working on soil fertility noted: 'There will be links to key projects such as PGRN and PNVA [Projet National de Vulgarisation Agricole, the national extension programme]'. Equally, there would need to be an emphasis on both organic and inorganic solutions to soil fertility. A broad-based coalition of support for an initiative could not be built if only inorganic fertilizer-based strategies were promoted. This being the case, an integrated nutrient management was advocated (Gakou et al, 1996).

As well as addressing production and wider environmental concerns, the Malian SFI also needed to be effectively framed as participatory in conception and elaboration. During the mid-1990s, when the context was one of decentralization and donor emphases on participatory development, it was important for policy processes in relation to any large-scale initiative to attempt not to be top-down in style and to be open to the expression of different interests. Accordingly, the terms of reference for the regional working groups developing the National Action Plan on Soil Fertility placed considerable emphasis on adopting a participatory way of working. It is noted, for example, that preparation of the plan should entail 'a participatory and decentralized approach'. The note goes on:

> This team will approach the task in a participatory manner, working closely with technicians working in rural areas (extension, research, farmers' organizations, NGOs, projects working on natural resource management). . . Discussions will be open and may use different techniques such as PRA and knowledge, attitudes and practice studies (translated from Ministère de la Développement Rurale et de l'Eaux, 1998).

In different ways, then, a broad network of support would need to be con-structed to facilitate elaboration and implementation of the SFI, cutting across ministries, donors, NGOs and others. With the emphasis on participation and land management, a network of actors would have to be put together that facilitated compromises between different framings of the problem at hand and different, sometimes competing, interests. The degree to which these attempts at constructing this inclusive network around the initiative were successful is discussed below.

The first plank of the SFI in Mali was the production of a report on soil fertility as part of a four-country pilot study conducted by a key task manager working on soil fertility at the World Bank (Gakou et al, 1996). The report looked in depth at the fertilizer *filière*, and at explorations of the possible use of rock phosphate as a soil fertility amendment. It also laid some emphasis on broader forms of land management, referring to the Lutte Anti-erosive in the CMDT, for example. This document was presented at the key SFI meeting in Lomé in November 1997. The initiative had already been launched inter-nationally with much fanfare at the World Food Summit in late 1996, and a coalition of international bodies had been mobilized in support (see Chapter 3). The Lomé meeting brought together donors and national representatives to look at how to plan programmes of action in different national settings. The Malian representatives at the Lomé meeting returned enthused. Commenting in late 1997, one observed:

> We have seen other countries like Burkina Faso getting support for soil fertility issues. Now with the SFI, the World Bank is behind it. It's an international issue. The donors are interested because it relates to food security. When we came back [from Lomé] we pushed the minister to go for it [the SFI]. He is keen. He sees it as a priority.

A few months after the Lomé meeting, in February 1998, the World Bank task manager for West Africa visited Mali to launch the SFI nationally. His visit was followed shortly afterwards, in March 1998, by a technical consultancy coordinated by the United Nations Food and Agriculture Organization (FAO). This group provided technical support for the development of the initiative, and included a cotton agronomist with long experience of Mali working within the CMDT, an FAO official and the World Bank task manager for Mali. Following this, three working groups were created who were charged with determining the parameters of a future initiative. One team defined the nature and degree of soil fertility degradation with a view to targeting interventions; the second had to come up with a review of available technologies to tackle soil fertility decline; and the third was to look at policies across the fertilizer supply chain. This third group would also examine the potential of developing the Tilemsi rock phosphate deposit, with a factory at Markala, near Segou, as an alternative to relying on other sources of phosphate. Regional working groups were to consult with a variety of relevant stakeholders on the causes of, and possible solutions to, the problems of soil degradation, culminating in regional workshops, where, according to the Malian technical advisor to the SFI: 'The national study would be presented so that people understand the problems of SFI and agricultural production.' This, in turn, would lead to the development of regional action plans, presumably with the recommendations of the national study well represented (World Bank, 1998b).

The Malian SFI was, then, underway. There was a national background study, working groups and a steering committee set up in the MDRE, bringing together figures from IER and the key MDRE planning section, the Cellule de Planification et Statistiques (CPS), NGO representatives, and representatives of other government bodies such as the PNAE. With such an infrastructure in place, long-standing national interest in soil fertility and a substantial international focus, the Malian SFI was well placed to become a major planning and policy activity for soil fertlility management. It was, after all, well linked to the key networks of the international SFI, which included the International Fertilizer Development Center (IFDC), whose director in West Africa, Henk Breman, had been so influential in raising the soil fertility issue in Mali since the 1970s, as discussed earlier.

However, despite the flurry of early activity, the Malian SFI gradually ground to halt. Towards the end of 1998, the World Bank task manager for West Africa visited Mali on a mission. Negotiations were held with different government departments over funding and procedures for the next stages of the process. Nevertheless, shortly after this visit it became clear that no more funds would be forthcoming, and the initiative was effectively on hold. The working groups were not able to go on further with their activities, and plans for the development of a National Action Plan, as well as chances of a programme of investment, seemed remote.

For many involved in the process, this was intensely frustrating. There had been effort and commitment, and there was a strong sense that soil fertility was such an important issue to Malian development that it required large-scale action, with some urgency. A Malian soil scientist commented exasperatedly at the slow pace: 'We are locked into the starting blocks.' Why should the Malian SFI have run into problems when, as we have seen, it was attempting to tap into two powerful policy narratives that have historically been very influential in Mali? What exactly complicated this policy process, which, apparently, effectively linked a range of international and national actors? The rest of this section attempts to unravel this in order to suggest where the complexities in the policy process lay, what the difficulties were in implementing plans and making them concrete, and why, ultimately, it is difficult to wrap competing framings up in one package.

At one level, it might be argued that the fact that donors and a national government fail to agree on a plan of action or programme of investment is far from surprising. In a range of settings, it is possible to find examples of different visions emanating from national and external agencies, and of it being difficult to negotiate appropriate compromises. Equally, personality differences or intractable contests over details can, though seemingly small, become the grit that slows up the cogs of a policy process. In the Malian case, it is possible to find voices offering these explanations: clashes between individuals, difficulties over proposed budgets and even per diem rates. As the senior soil scientist commented: 'Because of difficulties between the World Bank, the FAO and the Malian government, funds have not been made available – there are money problems! Who knows why – I've heard several reasons!' However, it is important to look beyond 'money problems' to broader contextual influences on the policy process. The soil scientist commentator continued: 'Policy-makers are not rational; there are too many interest groups, too many compromises. They want to please John, Peter and Paul.' Understanding the difficulties around building a successful coalition is important in order to learn lessons of wider relevance.

One of the main problems of the Malian SFI is that, despite attempts to pitch itself as addressing the concerns of both production and land management narratives, in substance it took a strongly production-oriented approach. Many of the key figures involved took positions where soil fertility was framed primarily as an agricultural production issue, rather than one in which wider land management issues were central. The production focus and the links to cotton production, in particular, are clear. Many of the key consultants involved in the project were cotton agronomists. One member of the original FAO consultancy mission was, as mentioned, an agronomist in the CMDT; two of the authors of the key background report presented at Lomé were IER cotton agronomists, with one of them head of the cotton programme in the IER. The third author was an agro-economist, and head of the farming systems team in Sikasso, a key CMDT region. Similarly, the chair of the steering committee was also a senior IER cotton agronomist.

The fact that key inputs were made by this type of personnel, and that the large part of their careers have been spent on working to improve cotton production – important as that undoubtedly is – makes it unsurprising that activities associated with the Malian SFI had a strong cotton-production orientation. This is borne out by looking at the way in which the working groups framed the soil fertility problem, emphasizing management of the fertilizer *filière* and exploring the possibility of wider use of rock phosphate, linked to the construction of a fertilizer factory, in order to improve production.

So, ultimately, the Malian SFI can be seen as framing soil fertility in a particular way, despite the added gloss of sustainable development rhetoric. At its core – despite the attempted inclusion of a diverse range of partners on committees and in advisory meetings and (admittedly, rather half-hearted) efforts at 'participatory' consultation – was an attempt to construct a network linking cotton production, the development of rock phosphate as a fertility source (CMDT, 1996), and the construction of a factory as an improved source of that phosphate (see the following section). This network linked up the economics of a fertilizer factory, knowledge claims about the appropriateness of rock phosphate and maintenance of the outputs of the cotton *filière*. This is a very particular network, associated with particular forms of expertise and political and economic interests; as we shall see, it was not sufficiently strong or embracing for the SFI to move beyond the early stages. Certainly, it was not the network that we suggested was necessary if the two competing narratives were to be reconciled in one activity. Three particular problems with the network can be identified. Firstly, the emphasis on rock phosphate as the soil fertility solution relies on a network of support forming around this; key policy players and investors must then be convinced of the necessity of a factory. Secondly, the strong production focus can be seen as a reflection of weak links to other stakeholders who need to be incorporated in the network in order for it to gain credibility. Finally, the emphasis on cotton carries with it significant political and economic connotations which reach far beyond the narrow confines of the debate about soil fertility.

Rock phosphate and a fertilizer factory

For many looking at the Malian SFI, the key interest of most individuals involved was perceived as being the creation of a fertilizer factory. An official in the CMDT commented: 'The SFI in Mali is about the fertilizer factory. There are high-reactivity sources in Mali, which, if problems of application are overcome, can be very important.' Another commentator put it to us bluntly that: 'Malians want the fertilizer factory. So, if you say there isn't a soil fertility problem, then you won't be popular.'

There are two issues here. The first is around the analysis that phosphorus is a key limiting factor for Malian soils, and that the use of rock phosphate is the most appropriate way to tackle it. The argument in favour of using local sources of rock phosphate is that it is an alternative to depending upon expensive and sometimes erratic imports of phosphorus fertilizers. However, it also has links to an important international debate about the possibility of recapitalizing soils through one-off applications of volumes that are far higher than would be applied for a single cropping season (see Chapter 3). The model in West Africa has so far been Burkina Faso, where there has been a Soil Fertility Management Unit in government, and plans to develop local sources of phosphate, again with a factory. As Sanchez et al (1997: 35) comment in a key text on African soil fertility: 'The basic strategy is to use Kodjari PR [rock phosphate] to correct P [phosphorus] deficiency as a one-time capital investment paid for by the government via donors.' Hence, it is argued: 'The high residual effect of PRs has an important bearing on agronomic and economic evaluation of PR use in West Africa. This is an area that has often been neglected, since calculations are made on the basis of one season's production.'

However, the merits of the one-off investment are strongly contested by scientists, with some arguing that the uncertainties around such a strategy are huge. Nevertheless, it is still argued that smaller applications of rock phosphate make agronomic and economic sense (Buresh et al, 1997). While these assertions sound confident, further knowledge uncertainties complicate the picture. Particularly problematic is that, even with smaller doses, farmers have not been keen to use rock phosphate. There are a variety of reasons for this including the fact that, as a powder, it blows away in the wind. More broadly, many doubt that it is as effective as other nutrient sources. Hence, as Gakou et al (1996: 67) concede:

> *Despite the numerous results from agronomic research, the performance of demonstration trials and the extension efforts of development organizations, the farmers have largely not adopted rock phosphate, as yet.*

Or, as a donor representative put it: 'Rock phosphate – farmers won't buy it. It takes five years to show any benefits, and they only notice returns on a yearly basis'.[17] Another senior official in the IER commented:

> *There are serious problems because farmers will not pay for this even if it is subsidized. Fertilizer blows away with the wind. Farmers are not following extension advice. So, we are thinking about mixing it – urea and PNT [phosphate naturel de Tilemsi]; but we can't think about subsidizing it because the country has no money. We can think about ways to make them use it. If we don't use it, society will pay because we are mining the soil.*

Disputes around the efficacy of rock phosphate as a fertility amendment become more complicated where wider economic and political questions are brought into the frame, alongside the knowledge and practices of farmers. For many, the core problem with rock phosphate, in fact, lies with the factory and whether, despite the apparent desirability of having a national production source, it would be cost effective. It is here that the role of the World Bank in the soil fertility network becomes important. For some, demands for donor or government funding of a fertilizer factory amount to industrial or agricultural production subsidies – exactly what the policy reforms associated with structural adjustment had condemned. For the World Bank, a fertilizer factory, if it really made economic sense, would have to be a private-sector invest-ment.[18] As a member of one of the SFI working groups commented to us: 'The WB [World Bank] is floating around; you can't subsidize anything. Rock phosphate – you must be joking! It'll never happen; the World Bank is an important decision-maker in Mali.'

Ministerial mandates

The productionist emphasis is also reflected in the weak links between the MDRE and the MoE, an issue already hinted at earlier. Despite the attempts at inclusion and coordination, different mandates and conflicting bureaucratic politics prevented the formation of a strong network around the SFI. Despite the attempts by the World Bank to encourage some level of harmonization between the SFI and the CCD (in the Malian context, the PNAE), there appeared to be little in the way of substantive linkage. A senior figure from the PNAE commented: 'We went to a workshop [on the SFI], but we don't know much about it, and so can't criticize it.' Another senior official working in the MoE commented that he had never been told anything officially about the SFI at all: 'We know they are doing something. We are not told formally, only informally, by accident.'

This official went on to expand on the generic problem of initiatives being perceived as belonging to one ministry or sector, and therefore of no interest, or possibly a threat, to other ministries. He reflected on the difficulties in his work with the PNAE of making links to other ministries, where each ministry was interested in its own projects and securing more projects and funding, but was little interested in forming significant partnerships with other ministries:

> We asked for meetings with other ministries. . . agriculture, transport; but it didn't work. There was no understanding that the PNAE has implications for different ministries. It's a political problem. The MDRE is not involved in the PNAE. It is interested in production not protection, crudely. They are just into the filières.

But if those in the MoE view the MDRE as interested in 'production not protection', there are equally strong views on the other side of the fence. These centre on the perception that 'MDRE is the manager of cultivated land, but monitoring should be done by the MoE'. However, the MoE, as we have seen, had already by May 1999 raised considerable donor funds for field-level project activities, including projects on soil fertility in the CMDT area. This was all outside of the SFI's remit. In one sense, the MoE – and associated PNAE, CCD and *gestion de terroir* groupings – did not need the SFI, as they already had a significant slice of the donor cake and projects were in the pipeline.

This tendency to 'projectize' activities in relation to donor-funding requirements has a set of particular consequences in Mali. Projects become something like departments, associated with particular bureaucratic fiefdoms and tightly guarded budgetary resources, rather than activities that weave their way between departments. Therefore, people talk about Programme Gestion des Ressources Naturelles (PGRN), or Projet National de Vulgarisation Agricole (PNVA), or the Plan National d'Action Environnemental (PNAE) in the sense of it being a government division rather than a government activity. This can be understood as a key bureaucratic context that has fundamental implications for the policy process, where projects offer power, prestige, control over resources and patronage, and rent accumulation opportunities. Such bureaucratic demarcation is also seen, to some extent, in the way that different agro-ecological zones are almost divided into 'states within states', particularly for the CMDT and previously for the Office du Niger (ON). It is also the legacy of the Operations Développement Rurales (ODRs), more broadly, despite many having changed substantially or disappeared in the wake of structural adjustment. This tendency to create well-defined empires, rather than transversal operations, or even activities that are a subset of a larger entity, produces a particular type of bureaucratic politics that impinges on the policy process quite negatively where – as with the discourse of sustainable development – cross-sectoral interaction is required.

Given the importance that the World Bank attached to building a network between ministries, and of linking the SFI to the PNAE and the CCD, it is clear that these problems of enrolment in a network were central to the fate of the SFI. The World Bank official said: 'We are bringing ministries together to look for synergies, and both are in the steering committee.' But he acknowledged problems: 'The Bank intervenes at a higher level and says: "Look, if you want resources, then get your act together."' The sense that people were not getting their 'act[s] together' was strong.

The World Bank, economic reform and the politics of cotton

The fact that there were problems between donors and national ministries is hard to dispute: this can be illustrated by contrasting the comments of an official in the Cellule de Planification et Statistiques (CPS) and those of a World Bank official. The member of staff at the World Bank commented: 'In Mali, the work is dragging a bit – there is not enough commitment from local teams; they are still building local ownership.' Whereas the official in the CPS commented: 'There are some problems with the World Bank. We have a feeling they come with general ideas and don't try to understand specific reality.' Clearly, this is a fundamental problem – if people do not agree with what you want, you can say they are not 'on board', and there is no local ownership. However, it is equally the case that asserting local ownership may mean fundamentally reframing the policies and programmes that emanate from donors. What this meant, in practice, according to the World Bank official, was that: 'In terms of the Mali team, we are decentralizing away from the CPS because they are too slow; we will go to the ON or the CMDT.'

This comment is significant for the fate of the SFI because the relationship between the World Bank and the CMDT is, as we have seen, in many ways one of the most important political relationships in Mali. The World Bank has pushed unsuccessfully in the past for privatization of the CMDT (Tambora, 1999). Recently, this has been on the agenda again, with the CMDT weakened, to some degree, by low world cotton prices and bad publicity following resignations of senior staff for financial irregularities.[19] On this occasion, however, the World Bank has had more leverage, perhaps, than in the past to push for change. The reason for this is that it is playing a key role in organizing debt relief for African countries under the International Monetary Fund's (IMF's) Highly Indebted Poor Countries Initiative (HIPC). Though the details are unclear, it seems that implementation of the recent HIPC debt relief agreement will rest on introducing greater competitiveness into the cotton sector. The press release announcing the agreement documents the condition as follows: 'satisfactory implementation of a set of agreed structural reforms, including continued implementation of reforms under the cotton sector restructuring plan'.[20]

What is the relevance of these wider processes for the SFI? Given the importance of cotton to the SFI, and the key role of the World Bank in determining the degree to which local ownership has been created – some interpret this as acceptance of external conditions – it is easy to imagine that the SFI network has, to some extent, been undermined by the weakness of the wider networks within which it is embedded, particularly those linking the CMDT and the World Bank. The soil fertility narrative gets disrupted when the role of the cotton *filière* is brought firmly into the story. It is here, as we have seen, that substantially different diagnoses and proposed solutions, and, indeed, political and bureaucratic interests, coexist.

Actor networks, Latour argues (1987), are powerful and effective when all the engaged actors can 'agree' on their roles (and when non-human agents – in this case, soils and the cotton *filière* – fit into the roles prescribed) (see Chapter 2). The *filière*, for example, is critical to the fate of the soil fertility narrative. If the reform of the *filière* under a liberalization programme can be set aside as another story and another dispute, somehow irrelevant to the case for doing something about soil fertility, then the network may cement around a productionist story line. However, if the *filière* continues to be perceived as a key part of the story, then a wider range of disputes is introduced, and an effective actor network may, as we have seen, not emerge.

The unravelling of an initiative

For a variety of reasons, then, we have seen that the SFI has not been a success so far in Mali, despite the existence of two powerful narratives about soil fertility. Part of the reason, we suggested, was that it was not possible to effectively build networks bridging these two narratives. Some of the local network linkages were weak – particularly between the two ministries – and the knowledge network around the phosphate issue was in disarray. In addition, the links between the global and the local were not as firm as would have been necessary in order to have Mali as a key part of the international SFI. This was because the cotton/soil-fertility nexus identified by the SFI exposed tensions between the World Bank and the CMDT's and Malian government's own strategies for liberalization and economic reform. There has also been a sense that there is indecision within the World Bank itself on how to proceed with regard to the SFI, and the perception on the Malian side of receiving mixed messages from Washington has not facilitated progress with the initiative.

What we have seen, then, is that – because of particular bureaucratic and political contexts and despite the inclusive rhetoric of sustainable development – the difficulties with building broad-based policy on soil fertility were substantial. The SFI failed to combine the productionist and land management narratives, despite this being a condition of success. It also set out to be participatory and, therefore, implicitly to be open to many voices and interests. However, participation in this case could only be participation within highly constrained and predefined limits. In many ways, this was because the policy process for soil fertility was strongly linked to a particular context – that of cotton, fertilizers and the CMDT zone. However, the policy process might take a new shape if contexts were to alter. There are possibilities that this may, indeed, be happening, and this forms the theme of our concluding section.

NEW SPACES, NEW DIRECTIONS?

This chapter, so far, has outlined two dominant ways of framing soil-fertility policy options. We have suggested that these approaches are shaped strongly by bureaucratic and political context. The influence of particular narratives is very much dependent on these settings, and on the networks built by actors who push a particular view. This final section again emphasizes the importance of contexts, and looks at how the changing economic and political background identified at the beginning of the chapter is potentially creating new spaces for new approaches to rural development. These new approaches, we argue, have implications for the (re)framing of soil fertility questions, and may, over time, lead to very different types of policy initiative (see Benjaminsen, 1997).

Currently, dominant approaches to soil fertility management originate from periods when the state – both the colonial state and the newly independent post-colonial state – exercised relatively firm economic and political control. Before 1991 in Mali, the political system was tightly controlled, with the world of policy managed by a largely unchallenged bureaucracy, albeit with donor influence. Economic activity was again controlled firmly by the bureaucracy – the line ministries and the parastatal Operations Développement Rurales (ODRs). These patterns of state activity, perhaps exemplified most strongly by the *filière*-based organization of the CMDT, but also by styles of interaction between science and policy, reflect the legacy of the colonial state. Histories of state formation leave powerful legacies for current policy activity and political behaviour in ways that are shaping but not determining. In recent decades, donors also have played a key role, given Malian dependence on aid flows.

These contexts, however, changed substantially from the 1990s. Today, the state is still important and donors wield considerable influence; but new actors are emerging as potentially highly important participants in policy processes. In addition to broad, but not complete, economic liberalization, Mali now operates with a far more democratic political system than in the past. As one commentator observed: 'In 1992, the system changed completely. There has been a massive growth of civil society and a suspicion of government. But there has also been a lot of confusion.'

Civil society organizations have grown rapidly and now increasingly occupy the political sphere, alongside different components of the state (Monga, 1995).[21] In addition, trends towards decentralization have increased the possibilities for – and expectations that there will be – civic participation in governance.

In these new contexts, new activities are taking place that may suggest new directions for rural development. Much of this activity is localized in the sense that it emerges from village settings; but, increasingly, small programmes are spread across *cercles* and even become some of the key rural development activity in entire regions. In the Fifth Region, for example, there is a range of increasingly networked NGO activity, which combines village resource management activities with new initiatives where communities are involved in drawing up local conventions to regulate resource access and management (Hilhorst and Coulibaly, 1999; Winter, 1998; Chevenix-Trench et al, 1997).[22] What is interesting about a lot of this type of micro activity is that productionist and land management issues are often practically integrated around live-lihood concerns in ways that are often not apparent in the policy narratives and activities proposed at the national level.

New avenues in research are also opening up. Research – particularly farming systems research – has begun to experiment with new participatory methods and techniques (Defoer and Budelman, 2000; Defoer et al, 1996; Defoer et al, 1999a, 1999b; Dembelé et al, 2001). As a result, people are beginning to think about new ways of linking research and extension to allow better expression of farmers' needs and interests (Budelman, 1996). As farmers are now seen by many as legitimately having a voice in research, the develop-ment of forms of 'citizen science', as a counterpart to mainstream agricultural science, may be emerging.

Alongside these new forms of practice associated largely with NGOs, there have also been other expressions of local concern. For example, the burning of factories and threats to withdraw from cotton production in CMDT areas, as well as disputes over irrigation fees in the ON, may be more than sporadic outbursts. During the 2000-2001 cropping season, farmers in Mali-Sud refused to plant cotton, complaining about low producer prices despite the efforts of the CMDT (and even the Malian Union of Cotton and Food Crop Producers – SYCOV – when it had come to agreement with the CMDT) to persuade them otherwise (Haramata, 2000). These conflicts can be seen as challenges to the way in which production is framed in dominant policy narratives, centred on a questioning of the dominant mode of organizing production and, therefore, on livelihoods in the cash-cropping zones.

Together, all this activity potentially challenges dominant approaches to soil fertility policy. In the emergent livelihood-focused approaches, soil fertility is not isolated as a technical input, as it is in the productionist approach, or identified as something that requires crisis environmental management, as in the land management framing. Instead, soil fertility management is seen as one of a set of broader livelihood concerns, wrapped up in questions of access to resources for livelihoods, institutional issues of tenure security, and socio-economic dimensions of, for example, market access.

An example of how this can mean a fundamental reframing of policy problems was put to us by one researcher. He challenged the basic premise of a soil fertility crisis, and argued that when problems were looked at through a lens that is sensitive to the diversity of farming livelihood practices, very different conclusions might be reached. He argued:

> *There is no fertility problem, per se. Stagnant yields in some areas may be explained by the diversion of cotton fertilizer to maize and other cereals after devaluation. In some areas (for example, around Sikasso), yields are increasing. The real problem may actually be pest build-up.*

Likewise, a donor official noted: 'Desertification is not a problem. One year the desert comes forward, the next it comes back.'

So, a new series of challenges may be emerging. The first of these relates to the dominant way in which knowledge influences policy – which, as we have seen in Mali, is a particular type of scientific knowledge refracted through a particular bureaucratic and political context. New political and policy spaces associated with, and fostering, civil society activity may push new, alternative types of knowledge – often local technical knowledge, or knowledge informed by the realities of local livelihood issues – into the policy process. Secondly, there are challenges to production-oriented approaches, particularly where they are associated with certain tightly controlled styles of bureaucratic and political management – as with cotton. Thirdly, there are challenges to the type of management associated with land degradation approaches, especially where these rely on particular styles of bureaucratic management or instrumental project participation.

In relation to the SFI case study, these new directions may have important implications. Firstly, the dynamism and expressions of agency at the local level challenge the implicit assumptions of the SFI that farmers are passive actors who will fit smoothly into centrally planned schemes to increase agricultural output. There may be pressures for production and marketing of agricultural commodities to be more locally defined, and more responsive and adaptive to changing market realities and livelihood opportunities. This, in turn, may have significant implications for the continuation of the *filière* as a system of economic and political organization. Secondly, as we have seen, some of the political and bureaucratic contradictions within the somewhat fragile coalition may become more marked if grassroots pressures – protests against the CMDT, for example – and awareness of alternative livelihood and land management approaches increase. This may require a substantial rethinking of the SFI as it now stands, and even the development of new actor networks that frame the issue in very different ways, suggesting different types and styles of intervention.

The charge, of course, remains that these new emerging discourses and practices are too scattered and dependent upon external support to really have an impact on the policy process. There are clearly numerous areas – particularly non-ON or CMDT areas – where there is no NGO activity, and debates about, or activities in relation to, policy are virtually non-existent. A recent and extensive study of livelihood activities in Dalonguebougou in the Segou Region revealed that this area existed with absolutely no regular state or NGO activity (Brock and Coulibaly, 1999). And discussions with others suggest that this is often the pattern for large parts of many *cercles* in the dryland zones. In these areas, it may be very difficult to engage the state effectively.

It might also be argued that in order for these new activities to have a wider impact, it will be necessary for democratic decentralization to work effectively. But questions remain as to whether decentralization will facilitate the challenging of dominant policy narratives (Ribot, 1999). With much initial activity surrounding decentralization centred on local political manoeuvring, the securing of symbolic projects and general administrative confusion, the opportunities for 'local voice' to enter broader policy discussions is limited at this point. Of course, at this early stage it is difficult to tell what will result in the long term. Some argue that one danger with decentralization is that there is a lot of talk; but in the end, the centre and, crucially, the line ministries refuse to relinquish management, legislative functions and budgets effectively to local levels. Others argue that even when they do, it takes a long time to create effective democratic local politics, and that the tendency is more likely to be towards the 'politics of the belly' (Bayart, 1993), where sub-localities compete and politicians attempt to deliver visible symbols of development, such as community centres, rather than negotiate solutions to complicated local problems.

But, equally, decentralization may create space. While there will be local stories that detractors will point to as failures, the key point about decentralization may be that it potentially provides the space to create a legitimating discourse that enables previously excluded groups and perspectives to challenge conventional wisdoms and policy agendas. Here, new actor networks could be constructed, which could become new axes for the practice of policy, bringing local issues and innovative experiences and micro-experiments into national level debates, or linking up, for instance, protests about the CMDT with critiques of the *filière*, as well as examples of local livelihood initiatives that augment production and embrace issues of natural resource management. Under this yet-to-be-realized scenario, soil fertility might come to be talked about in very different ways.

6

Environmental Policy-making in Zimbabwe: Challenging the Technocracy?

INTRODUCTION[1]

From colonial times to the present, a range of scientific research has documented apparently alarming trends in soil erosion, soil fertility decline, deforestation and rangeland degradation in Zimbabwe, as elsewhere in Africa. This technical knowledge has, in turn, helped to shape a process of policy-making – both for colonial administrative programmes and, also, post-independence government policy and development aid (Beinart, 1989; Drinkwater, 1991; Chibudu et al, 2001). The aim of this chapter is not to weigh up the arguments for and against an environmental crisis. Instead, our point of departure is that there is a significant enough consensus that land degradation orthodoxies are problematic to ask how it is that these views are maintained in policy, and, subsequently, whether spaces exist for the expression of alternative perspectives.

The chapter is organized as follows. The next section sets out how the environmental debate is framed in Zimbabwe. This leads into a brief discussion of the role of the state and different actors in the policy process. The following section looks at the styles of scientific knowledge and the interactions between science and policy that inform discourses on the environment and, in particular, soils management. We then examine a range of changing contexts that are influencing policy processes in Zimbabwe before examining whether these have resulted in a challenge to the 'technocracy' through an examination of a series of case studies of attempts at new styles of research, planning, regulation and extension.[2] A final section looks at the extent to which the contours of a new type of policy space are now emerging in Zimbabwe.

FRAMING POLICY

Since the early colonial era, concrete programmes for natural resource management in Zimbabwe have consistently reflected particular discursive framings of environmental problems.[3] These framings have often been expressed in a distinctly narrative style. A range of commentators has illustrated how colonial land use and natural resource policies were based on assumptions that traditional farming practices degraded the land.[4] This certainty about wide-spread environmental degradation in the communal areas has continued to the present day.[5] Indeed, Malthusian assumptions about population increase progressively leading to a degradation of natural resources were repeatedly articulated in our interviews, and are also in evidence in both grey and academic literature.[6]

Such views of a growing crisis that requires urgent action were made to us by a range of different informants with different technical backgrounds, and with different positions in various organizations. They were articulated by senior and influential figures, as well as by junior staff, scientists and non-scientists, and those outside of state institutions, as well as by those within them. An international non-governmental organization (NGO) director working on natural resource management made the point in stark and alarmist terms: 'People live off raping the soil and raping the forest.' A worker with a smaller local NGO set out the challenge as: 'Natural resources are getting scarcer and scarcer in the communal areas – it's a tragedy of the commons.' A senior official in the Department of Natural Resources commented:

> *Look at the deforestation we have now. Rural reforestation programmes are not that successful; they are cutting more than they are planting. Erosion on grazing lands is greater than arable lands, but arable lands are also eroded, particularly hillsides, streambanks and streambeds, despite the legislation.*

A more junior official working on conservation in Agritex (the national extension agency – now AREX, the Department for Agricultural Research and Extension) made it clear that pressure on marginal lands was the major issue he faced in his work: 'Increases in population are leading to cultivation of waterways and steep slopes.' In relation to soil fertility, a senior soil scientist commented: 'There is serious soil fertility depletion in the smallholder sector. . . Soil fertility is associated with a lack of food security. . . if you come to Zimbabwe in 20 years, we'll be just like Ethiopia.' On soil conservation, Henry Elwell, a key figure in the Zimbabwean soils debate, is quoted as predicting that: 'If soil erosion rates are allowed to continue at existing levels within our lifetime, crop failures will be the norm, water will become scarce, and most of our resources will go towards feeding a vast, starving rural population.'[7]

These, we would argue, are not an unrepresentative selection of quotes; rather, they represent widely held and historically deeply rooted views of highly precarious people–resource dynamics in rural areas. These narratives, as we will show below, are shaped by the policy process and influence the way in which those involved in the policy process act.

CONTINUITIES IN POLICY-MAKING

Such narratives about land degradation frame particular practices of research, planning, regulation and extension. This section looks at bureaucratic and political contexts more closely in an attempt to see how, historically, they have contributed to creating and maintaining a certain view of interactions between people and natural resources, resulting in a particular – and remarkably static – set of policy prescriptions over time.

The view that people in rural areas need to be told how to manage natural resources and, essentially, to be instructed how to farm can, as we have noted, be traced back to colonial times. An array of legislation, decrees and regulations defined how soils, trees or wetlands were to be used, reflecting the relationship between the colonial state and local populations. The strategies used and the relative emphases between different approaches, of course, varied over time, often with substantial conflicts over these issues emerging within the scientific community and government bureaucracy (Alexander, 1993). However, the broad pattern is clear and hard to contest.

Exactly why this happens can be debated. On the one hand, it can be argued that colonial authorities claimed that Africans were inadequate farmers or managers of natural resources because they needed moral or political justifications for the seizure of fertile land by white settlers and the relocation of blacks to the reserves. As Munro (1998) argues, there needed to be a Land Husbandry Act to justify the Land Apportionment Act (1930). Likewise, Drinkwater notes: 'Land apportionment not only had to be maintained, it had to be justified' (1989: 288). A rationale for state activity in the reserves had to be provided because of the 'uncertain status of public authority in the reserves'(Munro, 1998: 84). Others have argued that the predilection for straight lines in grazing schemes, settlement areas and land-use plans found favour and were promoted with such vigour because they facilitated control and surveillance of rural populations (Robins, 1994, 1998).

An alternative view would be that technicians simply believed profoundly in the superiority of 'modern' European farming practices. While there was an early recognition that land degradation was an issue in the white commercial farming areas, this was seen to be more significant in the 'native reserves' because of the 'backward' nature of traditional farming practices. In the commercial farming areas, this was responded to through voluntary agreements and generous incentive packages promoted through the Intensive Conservation Area approach. By contrast, it was assumed that – because of the lack of responsiveness of native populations to technical recommendations – a more top-down, command-and-control response was required in the African farming areas. In turn, in order to safeguard the food-producing commercial sector, a rationale for land alienation could be made on technical grounds.

In the post-colonial period, an essential continuity is evident. The same assumptions about the backwardness of rural natural resource management strategies and agricultural practices has continued in the activities of the agricultural extension agency, the Department for Natural Resources, and in land-use planning activities (see, for example, Drinkwater, 1989). Despite some attempts at overhauling environmental legislation, many of the colonial rules and regulations have persisted.[8] The Master Farmer scheme continues, restrictions on streambank use persist and standardized recommendations for soil conservation measures remain in place. Again, there are different explanations. As Hill (1994: 227), in an article on the politics of wildlife in Zimbabwe, puts it:

> *The state uses conservation policies in much the same way it uses taxation, investment, interest rates or land resettlement policies: to establish and extend its own interests, which in a new and independent polity centre on authority maintenance and creation.*

An approach to state intervention has emerged where positivist scientific and technical knowledge is wedded to a Weberian mode of administration: a form of 'technocracy' (Habermas, 1973; Fischer, 1993b; see, also, Chapter 2).[9] Drinkwater (1991), for example, identifies in state activity the progressive spread of technocratic rationality over alternative types of knowledge. The state, it is argued, is absolutely central because 'modern', 'rational' and 'technical' approaches are so embedded in its mechanisms, composite parts and institutional practices. This meant that, even with the transition to a new government of entirely different hue after independence, state officials have continued to operate with the same technicist, modernizing mindset. This continuity between the pre- and post-independence settings (at least until recently) highlights how, despite obvious shifts in political regime, the embedded nature of bureaucratic attitudes and practices, shaped by science, provides the reason for the persistence of a particular style of state response to environmental and land management issues.

SCIENCE AND THE POLICY PROCESS

In the Zimbabwean context, science has often provided the basis for such planning and regulatory practices, as well as a culture of fixed recommendations in extension. Examining these models and recommendations, we argue that the underpinning data for these approaches reflects, to an important extent, social and political commitments, relying on particular audiences and practices to support claims to validity. We suggest, too, that this type of science achieves influence through the construction of actor networks, incorporating bureaucrats and politicians and international and civil society organizations. These networks engage in processes of co-construction, recursively shaping the way in which science is studied and policy is made (see Chapter 2).

Science, since colonial times in Zimbabwe, has existed in a close relationship with the state and its policies. In the colonial era, scientists largely concentrated on agricultural production in the commercial sector. The work that was carried out specifically on communal area questions was limited.

Thus, the framing of questions and the policy advice that emerged was very much located in the white-settler agricultural context. Wider environmental concerns also emerged through the colonial administration and through contact with consultants from outside. Thus, for example, concerns about drought and erosion were spurred by the South African Drought Commission of 1922 and the experience of the 'dust bowl' in the US (Beinart, 1989). Similarly, ideas about pasture degradation and livestock management regimes were, in a major way, influenced by Pole-Evans, an eminent pasture scientist who provided evidence to the native enquiry on natural resources in 1939 (Scoones, 1996). Within the then Native Department, agricultural officials focused on 'reserve' agriculture; but their numbers were small and their practice so bound up with day-to-day administration that the opportunities for innovation remained limited. A few key individuals, such as Emory Alvord, however, pushed particular innovations for small-scale agriculture – in his case, a model of 'mixed farming' based on crop rotation and manuring (Alvord, 1930; Scoones and Wolmer, 2002). This was a key part of the centraliz-ation policy from the late 1920s and was the technical centrepiece of the Native Land Husbandry Act of 1951, perhaps the most ambitious of all state attempts at technical intervention during the colonial era (Garbett, 1963). While, of course, there was debate and dissent within both the technical and admin-istrative arms of the Rhodesian state (Alexander, 2000), this does not detract from the significance of the dominant discourse.

In the post-colonial period, many of the earlier core assumptions and approaches have continued to shape the practices of science. An NGO director summed up this style: 'Particularly for soils, the cry of Alvord is what we are hearing today – we still think the solutions are the same.'[10] The solutions, in this view, are through policy change, informed by scientific expertise and implemented by technical extension, leading to the promulgation of legal directives setting out how rural populations may utilize natural resources. He continued:

> We don't know better because the way we do science has not changed. Going out and measuring slope changes, soil-loss estimation methods – all these come from the turn of the century; there is no fresh way of doing science.

The influence of science on natural resource policy can be traced through a variety of models and approaches that have guided policy development. These include the 'mixed farming' model, promoted since the 1920s as a way of organizing agricultural production; mapping and planning frameworks that have guided land-use and settlement designs; key pieces of data about natural resource trends that have informed policy direction, such as the figures for annual soil losses of 50 tonnes per hectare; and specific directives and fixed recommendations, such as the 30-metre rule for streambank cultivation, as well as the huge variety of cropping, soil conservation and fertilizer recommendations and regulations. It is these models, maps, plans, data sets, directives and recommendations that have formed the basis of state-led intervention strategies since the colonial era. Within agricultural extension, the Master Farmer programme epitomizes this approach. This is an archetypically technocratic approach to working with smallholders, involving the filling-in of record books detailing planting, fertilizer applications and conservation measure construction, all executed to the letter as advised by extensionists. These practices, backed up by science, help to frame and order policy problems and, in turn, provide the legitimacy and authority for particular state interventions.

The social construction of scientific facts

One of the characteristics of scientific practice is to claim objectivity and neutrality: scientists uncover and document facts, and the facts speak for themselves. In this view, the link between science and policy is taken as unproblematic. Of course, many scientists do not necessarily adopt a positivist view of scientific activity. As we shall see, many are quite candid about the contingencies surrounding scientific knowledge claims. However, awareness of uncertainty has a habit of disappearing when science interacts with policy. When policy-making is presented as being based upon objective and neutral facts, it can also be framed as a purely technical activity. Scientific knowledge can – unwittingly or not – provide the justification for the interventions of both a technocratic state and, increasingly, other policy actors.

In many cases, when apparently 'hard' scientific data is interrogated and facts are retraced to their origins, it emerges that particular bits of knowledge may be far from certain and, indeed, may possibly rest on quite dubious assumptions. Similarly, mapping the paths along which facts move to positions of influence may reveal the importance of particular events, specific practices and, often, the central significance of the strategies of scientists, particularly in their interactions with policy-makers. The case of the much-quoted Zimbabwean soil-loss data is a useful example. Plot-based soil-loss figures have been immensely influential both within Zimbabwe and further afield. One politician, we were informed, picked up on the data and made a speech claiming that Zimbabwe was losing enough soil each year to fill two goods trains stretching between the earth and the moon. However, discussions involved with those producing the data suggest reasons to view the figures with care, implying the need to be careful about what conclusions are drawn. A scientist involved in this research commented to us:

> *The numbers came out of a hat. . . the figure of 50 tonnes per hectare came from the same source as US soil-loss tolerance. It was just a wild guess from a conversation we had one evening on how to extrapolate nutrient losses. We wanted a figure for arable lands, a wild figure. . . Our footnotes say that. Retrospectively, it was good that we made it a round number.*

The figures may be treated with great caution by those who produced them; but after appearing in scientific papers and reports, they get taken up by others and develop a life of their own, and, in the process, they achieve power and influence. A comment made by an NGO worker reflects the way in which particular individuals, and the science with which they are associated, have gained positions of influence and status in Zimbabwean natural resources debates:

> *When we think about soils we think about soil erosion. And the key studies for this are by Whitlow, Elwell and so on: their erosivity formulas that have helped us with classifications.*

How did this influence come about? Part of the explanation is that figures are useful when you are trying to make a particular case. A senior Zimbabwe Farmers' Union official commented that having data at his fingertips in meetings was often crucial to the outcomes of discussions:

> *The more alarmist the information, the more you are probably going to win it. People want quantified information about the state of affairs. But no one has time to compete with figures. If I say X per cent rate, no matter what the figures are, I get better results.*

The soil loss figures achieved influence because politicians, government officials and donor agencies latched onto them. Indeed, in this instance, the very existence of particular – and, arguably, problematic – scientific data was a result of pressure applied by one policy actor. A senior soil scientist commented: 'FAO pushed us desperately to extrapolate for macro-figures. . . However many health warnings we put, they just went ahead blithely. Popular publications then picked this up.'

This work on soil erosion is used as a key piece of evidence for a land degradation crisis in the document *Conservation and Rehabilitation of African Lands* (FAO, 1990). A box entitled 'Zimbabwe: the hidden cost of soil erosion' refers to the 1986 reanalysis of the data from the Henderson experiments of the 1950s. It argues:

> *The financial cost of erosion per hectare per year varied from US$20 to $50 on arable land and from US$10 to $80 on grazing lands. The implication of these figures is that erosion is a massive 'hidden' cost on the economy of Zimbabwe – as, indeed, it must be in nearly every other African country (FAO, 1990: 10).*

The scientific experiments thus give authority to the United Nations Food and Agriculture Organization (FAO) case. They are neatly summarized, caveats are dropped and the information is translated into economic terms in order to give more impact.

The power of scientific knowledge comes not from its incontrovertible status as a depiction of reality, but from the construction of actor networks supporting specific knowledge claims (see Chapter 2). This may involve processes of strategizing on behalf of scientists and it may also involve other actors joining up together with their own agendas. The power of the knowledge and the influence of the science come from the degree to which the enlisted actors are themselves powerful, and the degree of solidity and stability of the network (see Latour, 1987). The construction of scientific facts involves processes of 'black-boxing', where disputes are closed, and fundamental uncertainties or questionable premises are concealed from further investigation, or are just simply ignored. So, for example, uncertainties around experiments from the 1950s are black-boxed in the production of evidence of a crisis several decades later. Scientists whom we spoke to currently at work in Zimbabwe were quite clear that, if their work was to engage people who mattered, it involved black-boxing uncertainties and making trade-offs between rigour and impact. One scientist commented:

> One of the key things researchers can do is to present the situation as really bad. . . If policy is going to be influenced by researchers, then there has to be an alarmist message. . . We need broad-level scenarios rather than ecosystem complexity. Many conclusions are derived from plot level. You increase the scale and, of course, extrapolation is difficult and there may be errors. Scientists rely on facts at a smaller scale – but the question is what message you want to present. To drive the message home, it is worth including a large element of error. . . Don't be afraid even if there are inherent inaccuracies.

Another researcher put it this way:

> If you want to push something through, you must bring it down and simplify it. Make it something they can understand. From complicated scientific data, you pull out the simple elements. . . In the real world you have to take risks. . . How long do you have to have an experiment running before you make a decision?

Science, it is often assumed, neutrally and dispassionately observes biophysical realities, and documents what is happening to the environment. Scientific findings are presented as rational inputs to be translated through government and administration into policies and programmes. But science, as we have seen, is not as value free as this idealized image would have it. The complexities of scientific findings are often lost in the process of producing clear, intelligible messages for busy audiences with wavering attention spans.

There are several explanations for this. In some cases, scientists are clearly aware of the need to make trade-offs and to produce arresting messages that have real purchase. It is enough, they argue, that the disputes over the assumptions upon which assertions are constructed can be dealt with elsewhere in more 'technical' arenas. Successful engagement with those who establish policy priorities, who guide funding and who can influence career paths and reputations may be important motivations. Others – the majority, perhaps – are more reluctantly pragmatic. Premature closure may be necessary in order to appear relevant, and may be no bad thing if it engages people in debate while further refinements to propositions and processes of experiment continue. Others may, while being aware of the limitations of their work, still be convinced that the broad point they are making is correct, or self-evident, so that limited evidence is not perceived as a problem. Here, received wisdoms, we argue, transmitted through society and bureaucratic and scientific practice, have powerful structuring roles in ongoing processes of knowledge production and policy.

The mutual construction of science and policy

While scientists may actively try to shape policy agendas, the process is, as we have suggested, two-way. Politicians and bureaucratic staff also have their own agendas, and pick up on and ignore different types of science and scientific information. Scientists strategize to promote their findings. While this is, of course, not altogether surprising, there are cases where, in the desire for impact, any attempt at circumspection is lost.[11] One scientist commented that in the 'campaign' against soil erosion, certain 'technical fixes are more acts of faith than acts of science'. Thus, science shapes the agenda for policy interventions; but, at the same time, what scientists work on is shaped by research policy, the difficulties of getting decision-makers interested, and, often, the need to find backers in government and other agencies. For example, a group of researchers we spoke to were far less upbeat about influencing policy on soil fertility compared to soil erosion:

> You can see gullies on TV. People can feel them creeping. So, publicity is easy for gullies. But you can't see chemical imbalances. You talk to reporters about soils and they strike out the nutrient aspect and concentrate on soil loss. It's hard to communicate to politicians that poor soil fertility leads to increased soil erosion.

As they noted, soil erosion – particularly, gullies – has received most of the attention in the Zimbabwe land-degradation policy debate. Work on soil erosion in Zimbabwe has a long pedigree. Some of the earliest articles in the *Rhodesia Agricultural Journal* commented on the potentials for severe soil erosion. The Henderson experiments, referred to above, for instance, were one of the first long-term attempts on the continent to establish soil erosion rates under different conditions (Hudson, 1961). The work of the soil conservation section of the Institute of Agricultural Engineering, particularly under the guidance of Henry Elwell, has, as already noted, been enormously influential in raising the issue of soil erosion and testing and extending mechanical soil conservation technologies. In addition, numerous surveys have attempted to document soil erosion levels and potential hazards across the country through a variety of assessment techniques (see, for example, Stocking, 1986; Elwell, 1974, 1983, 1987; Elwell and Stocking, 1988; Whitlow, 1988). Together, this network of scientists and technicians has offered a consistent set of messages: soil erosion is bad and it is getting worse, and here is a range of tested technologies that will stop it. While the way some of the data is used to make this case can certainly be questioned, key advocates of urgent action have not been afraid of sounding the alarm bells. For example, Elwell (1987: 8) commented:

> *Soils, particularly in the communal areas, are rapidly degrading. Vast amounts of nutrients are being lost annually. . . on current evidence it seems probable that, within our own lifetimes, the subsistence sector will no longer be able to feed itself.*

One of the key institutional aspects of this network has been that, unlike other research groupings based in the University of Zimbabwe or the Department of Research and Specialist Services (DRSS) in the Ministry of Agriculture, the Institute of Agricultural Engineering had a direct route to the extension arm of the ministry, being formally under Agritex. In many ways, this blurring of the research and extension distinction, which, until recently, was institutionally defined, has proved important in getting the message out and incorporating new technologies and management practices within extension recommendations.

While undoubtedly resulting in high-quality scientific results and an important expansion of understanding (for example, Hikwa and Mukurumbira, 1995; Kumwenda et al, 1995), work on soil fertility has not gained the profile that soil erosion research has. In part, this may be because of the apparently less inviting or easily communicable nature of the subject – soil nutrients, microbes and so on do not make good TV and newspaper material. But, also, it is due to the lack of cohesiveness of the scientific networks, spread as they have been over several institutions and multiple departments. With some exceptions, much of this work has remained effectively isolated from policy and extension concerns located at the more 'pure' end of soil science. Thus the actor networks that have formed have remained fragmented and lack the necessary diversity across science-extension policy areas. And without the 'policy entrepreneurs' in the mould of Henry Elwell, the soil fertility debate has remained less prominent, although in significant ways it is still influential.[12]

In various ways, then, these actor networks are involved in an ongoing process of producing facts that lend support to particular narratives of environmental degradation. Through the engagements between scientists, policy-makers, international donors, the media and others, this process contributes to the mutual construction of science and policy, and the creation of a particular style of Zimbabwean technocracy that has proved remarkably resilient. The widely held perceptions, entrenched institutional practices and the persistence of legislation, regulations and recommendations all bear witness to the apparent efficacy of the core actor networks involved in soils management and land degradation issues in Zimbabwe.

However, do changing contexts result in new activities, new styles of research and new technical and institutional practices? Whether these emerging approaches provide a fundamental challenge to the 'technocracy' – and, hence, the practices of research, planning, regulation and extension – is explored in the case studies below. Before moving to the case studies, however, it is worth outlining briefly some of the changing contexts found in Zimbabwe.

CHANGING CONTEXTS

By the late 1990s, policy processes operated in very different contexts from those during independence in 1980 when the new Zimbabwe African National Union–Patriotic Front (ZANU–PF) government took power with strong backing from the rural population (Bratton, 1987b). Party structures were then key in asserting state control, and an ambitious programme of reform was announced through a series of five-year plans. The creation of a decentralized system of local representation through village development committees and ward councils was announced in 1984 with the stated aim of encouraging a decentralized process of rural development (De Valk and Wekwete, 1990; Helmsing et al, 1991). However, by the 1990s, the grand aims announced since 1980 had not been realized. Many of the early gains in improved service provision had slowed, land reform on any significant scale had not materialized, poverty levels had increased and the new local governance arrangements were increasingly critiqued (Makumbe, 1998). The structural adjustment programmes initiated from 1991 had also weakened the state through restructuring and retrenchment.

By the late 1990s, the political legitimacy of the ruling party, ZANU–PF, was increasingly being questioned, culminating in both significant electoral challenges and civil unrest from 2000 (Raftopoulos, 2001). The revival of the land reform programme under the fast-track model seemed to push aside of many of the standard planning frameworks in favour of a popular mobilization of 'land invaders' (Alexander and McGregor 2001; Moyo, 2000). The combination of state-led (or at least sanctioned) political violence and the reconfiguration of political authority – particularly at provincial and district levels – has, for some, signalled a rejection of the modernist, technicist, developmental objectives of the 1980s and 1990s, replacing these with a populist, nationalist perspective with new norms, institutions and politics (Worby, 2001; McGregor, 2002), although in some settings the technocratic impulse remained, despite the apparent chaos and confusion (Chaumba et al, 2002a).

Over the last decade or so, international actors (for example, international financial institutions, NGOs and bilateral donors), the private sector (such as business lobbies and fertilizer and seed companies) and 'civil society' players (for example, farmers' organizations, churches and local NGOs) have come to have a greater influence on the state in policy discussions (see Skalnes, 1989) – although in recent years influences have changed. The following sections look at these other connections, focusing on the context up to 2000–2001.

Global connections

Zimbabwean officials are increasingly exposed to what has been labelled a 'global environmental discourse' (Yearley, 1996). National NGOs and line ministries do not only exist within networks that are coextensive with national borders. The United Nations Conference on Environment and Development (UNCED) in Rio in 1992 and its follow-up in Johannesburg in 2002 are the most obvious examples of international fora bringing together national actors and attempting to shape national projects around a common international agenda. The conventions associated with the Earth Summit in Rio were regularly mentioned by informants during interviews as important in shaping percept-ions of environmental issues in Zimbabwe. What appears to have emerged is an internationalized 'epistemic community' (see Haas, 1992; see, also, Chapter 2) around the environment–development debate, with key actors in Zimbabwe in government, NGOs and the research community linked to wider inter-national networks. In this international context, epistemic communities are effective because they are able to target individuals in national ministries and to promote an approach to environmental problems that goes beyond narrow national interest concerns. Many of our informants made this point to us. A senior figure in the Ministry of Agriculture put it that: 'Environment has become a big issue because of the international environmental bandwagon.' A Zimbabwean working in one of the multilateral agencies commented that: 'There is lots of awareness about the conventions. . . so many people talk about desertification and biodiversity depletion.'

Zimbabwean state actors, at least at senior levels, have a fair amount of interaction with others in the international environmental community. How this translates precisely into modifications of views and changing perceptions of interests is hard to gauge. But it is clear that the involvement is substantial. Someone with close familiarity with the Ministry of Environment commented that: 'half the ministry is gone for half the year dealing with environmental protocols and treaties. . . per diem hunting'.

Not only are national actors increasingly exposed to the environmental community outside of Zimbabwe; at least until recently, international actors also had space and opportunities in Zimbabwe. One example where a bilateral donor has been important in the environmental policy process was in pushing for, and providing technical assistance to, the drafting of the Environmental Management Bill (from 2002 passed as an Act). The drafting and presentation of this bill was fairly high profile, linked to a process of consultative meetings and hearings and extensive newspaper coverage. Reactions to the bill were mixed. One perception that was often repeated to us was of the bill as a donor-dominated activity. A senior researcher commented: 'CIDA's [Canadian

International Development Agency] role is key. At a guess, the act is 80 per cent Canadian and 20 per cent the Zimbabwean lawyer in the ministry.'

The 'per-diem hunting' or 'squabbling over shopping trips', which another donor official identified, have perhaps meant that ministry officials have not been as proactive as they might have been and that, correspondingly, donors and expatriate advisors have had more influence on the process of policy formulation. There is a serious concern about this lack of focus and capacity within the environment ministry. One person commented: 'The MMET [then Ministry of Mines, Environment and Tourism] is a disaster area. To get them to do anything is well nigh impossible.'

The picture that emerges of this period, then, is that the state has continued to shape policy processes, albeit through processes of interaction with donor agencies and some limited forms of public consultation. Policy processes, then, often seem to be encouraged by donor activity, with state officials often appearing not to have particularly coherent projects, and leaving international discourses about environmental management and frameworks for sustainable development – mediated through expatriate consultants – to exert considerable influence. As one senior donor official commented:

> *Ministries of environment in Africa are often offices to bring in donor money. It's because we love action plans and the rest of it. There is lots of political pressure to respond to the environmental agenda at the HQ. They breathe down our neck and send lots of consultants with their own agendas.*

Yet, apparently, none of these factors have substantially altered the fundamental direction of Zimbabwean environmental policy. While the preparation of the Environmental Management Bill was associated with various forms of consultation, one commentator reflected on how this had become increasingly limited as criticisms were raised (IUCN, 2000). According to the director of an NGO, the new bill is 'a command-and-control approach. . . full of dos and don'ts, standards and compliance'. The technical approach supported by scientific knowledge, and implemented through, essentially, top-down bureaucratic and administrative procedures, apparently remains intact. Thus, even though international debates and actors may have become more important in the policy process, they have not fundamentally challenged the basis of practice – in this area, at least. In fact, in many respects, such connections have acted to reinforce and sometimes extend existing technocratic perspectives. Next, we want to ask whether the same can be said of national NGOs and other actors in civil society.

NGOs and 'civil society'

Today, there are numerous registered NGOs in Zimbabwe (Muir, 1992; Vivian, 1994), alongside a host of other more informal community organizations (Bratton, 1987a; Thomas-Slayter, 1994). Many NGOs are involved in some way or other in environmental and land management issues as most of their work is focused on communal areas (Ndiweni et al, 1991; Vivian and Maseko, 1994). They range in size from outfits of a handful of people – sometimes based in the communal areas with very limited budgets and operating capacities – to large, well-funded organizations with national coverage. Most NGOs, whether classed as 'Northern' or 'local', rely on external donor funds. These funds flooded in during the post-independence period, resulting in a boom period for the NGO sector during the 1980s. For those involved in environment and development activities, this boom was sustained into the 1990s through engagement with the international convention processes leading up to, and following, the 1992 Rio conference. This helped to raise profiles and broaden credibility. For example, reports by the Zimbabwe Environmental Research Organization (ZERO), Environment and Development Activities, Zimbabwe (ENDA) and other environmental NGOs at the Earth Summit have been widely quoted and have increased the standing of those organizations and, at least until recently when many donors have withdrawn, their ability to attract funds (see ENDA/ZERO, 1992).

The relations between NGOs and the state are not necessarily confrontational (Mungate and Mvududu, 1991).[13] The ZERO/ENDA piece, for example, was part of the Zimbabwean government's own submission. Many NGOs also work closely with the state in service delivery, and make up for some of the lack of government capacity in rural areas – one of the major consequences of structural adjustment during the 1990s. As one commentator put it: 'In the 1980s, NGOs and government were at loggerheads. Now [1999] the government is more cooperative because they are filling a gap, because they don't have officers at grassroots or district levels.'

The growth of networks and coalitions, embracing both government and non-governmental officials, has been important in recasting the way in which some areas of policy are thought about. There is much blurring of boundaries. At one time, the same individual may be a government official, help run an NGO, be a respected academic commentator, and be a player in the business community. Indeed, when one talks to NGO officials, they are clear that it is their strong personal connections with key figures in government (often old colleagues or classmates) that facilitates their work.[14] For example, one provincial NGO official told us: 'With the permanent secretary, I can go and see him straight away as we were at college together. With the minister, it's more of a problem; but then the permanent secretary may arrange it.' At the provincial level, such interactions are even easier. One NGO worker commented: 'Masvingo is a small place. We all know each other. If we get on, we can do business.' Particularly significant is the flow of personnel between donors, government and NGOs. One NGO official commented: 'One of our senior officers was a senior secretary in the Ministry of Environment. This is now a help in building networks and passing on ideas.'

While such networks may help encourage new ideas to blossom, on other occasions there is sometimes a tendency for NGOs to simply implement government policy in their own programmes. Thus, many NGO resource-management projects – whether woodlots, soil conservation or wildlife management – are indistinguishable from their government equivalents. Indeed, in many instances, government officials are employed by the NGOs to oversee the project on the ground. Other NGOs, in contrast, have made use of close links with government and have taken advantage of new opportunities to experiment with innovative approaches to natural resource management. As we shall see below, some of these new initiatives have been important in challenging the current state-led approaches to environment and natural resources. An NGO director put it like this: 'These days, NGOs can get in and define the parameters of state involvement.' Others are more sceptical. For example, another NGO official spoke rather resignedly of her organization's involvement with the drafting of the Environmental Management Bill:

> *Our NGO was set up to influence policy. We do research and then provide solutions and recommendations. All this is successful to a limited extent. For example, the core ideas for the Environment Bill came from the ministry. We proposed changes but things remained the same.*

NGOs are, of course, not the only civil society players in the policy process. The farming unions, the private sector and more diffuse rural movements all play a part. The Zimbabwe Farmers' Union (ZFU), for example, seeks to represent communal area and small-scale farmers. It is a membership organization that extracts levies to cover its operational costs. While membership is not high in relation to the overall farming population, it does have a large potential constituency. Although, in the past, it has been criticized for simply representing the interests of the farming elite, it has made recent attempts to address wider concerns. Through its policy and research sections, it attempts to raise issues with government, both through formal and informal channels. An official in the ZFU reflected that: 'Five or ten years ago, it was a controlled environment – now it is a liberalized environment with many more actors. This requires new lobbying techniques – more lunches and more dinners!'

In addition to these rather more formal elements of civil society, a range of informal movements and followings can be identified in the communal areas, which, in various ways, influence the policy process. For example, during and after the devastating drought of the early 1990s, a large following emerged across the south of the country behind a young female spirit messenger, Ambuya Juliana. She proclaimed that the drought was the result of a combination of lack of respect for the ancestors, linked to the adoption of inappropriate technical policies and interventions. She urged her followers to reject extension advice regarding 'modern' seeds and inputs, to abandon development projects that used cement and wire fencing, and to return to 'traditional' ways (Scoones et al, 1996). It is, of course, difficult to assess the impact of such movements; but over quite some period during the mid-1990s and across a wide area, extensionists and development project workers had to adapt their approaches and take account of shifting local opinions as influenced by Ambuya Juliana and her followers. Other self-proclaimed prophets, leaders of the proliferating new Christian churches and traditional spirit mediums and messengers also offer advice and recommendations – perhaps not framed as 'policy' as such, but nevertheless introducing greater complexities within the processes of implementation on the ground (Maxwell, 1999). In recent years new political actors, notably war veterans and associated youth militias have entered the fray, often setting up parallel processes of governance and administration in rural areas, particularly in the new resettlement schemes (see Chaumba et al, 2002b).

The private sector

Since the liberalization of the economy during the 1990s, and before the economic implosion of the period 2000–2001, the private sector had become increasingly important. In the past, the largely white commercial interests in agriculture and industry were represented through highly influential lobby groups, such as the Commercial Farmers' Union (CFU) (Herbst, 1990). These groupings remained important through the 1990s, although with deregulation and liberalization the opportunities for direct influence from the farming union on government policy has diminished. With the major land redistribution initiatives from 2000 onwards, the commercial farming sector, and its political and economic influence, has been significantly weakened.

Through the 1990s, the growth of the private sector – for instance, in the agricultural supply and marketing sector – resulted in major changes in systems of seed provision and fertilizer supply, as well as in the growth of contract-farming arrangements. Privatization of formerly state-owned operations and the entry of South African and multinational companies transformed the agricultural sector and, hence, the policy networks associated with it. One manager of a local fertilizer company commented on this change:

> Today it's the multinationals who want to control the industry. By contrast, we local industries need to be liked. We can't keep saying commercial, commercial, commercial, when there's such a gap with the small scale. Government no longer controls us, but applies pressure. Government is well connected in industry.

Thus, the links between the state and the private sector are well entrenched – through boardroom appointments, advisors, consultants and other forms of patronage. These offer ways and means of applying subtle (and sometimes less so) pressure from both sides. Beyond the conventional agricultural sector, a range of other private-sector interests is increasingly important in the environmental policy debate, particularly those associated with the tourism, hunting and safari industry. These groups, while not having the organizational infrastructure of the long-established CFU, do exert considerable influence in the day-to-day implementation of policy initiatives – such as the Communal Areas Management Programme for Indigenous Resources (CAMPFIRE), a community-based wildlife programme – through the structuring of markets, the enrolment of key figures and behind-the-scenes political lobbying.

New players, new processes?

So, during the 1990s, did increasingly articulate and high-profile NGOs, private-sector players and other civil society actors effectively challenge the political effects of an apparently technical state-driven policy process? One academic with much experience in the NGO sector took a decidedly pessimistic view. He argued, somewhat prophetically, that NGOs tend to get involved in fairly limited technical debates rather unreflectingly and miss the broader political issues such as land reform: 'They are raising the flag on issues with narrow constituencies and not thinking squarely what the issues of the country are.' This lack of coherence and strategizing, he argued, meant that 'environment' – which might have been a suitable entry point for tackling larger issues of resource access – has in some sense lost some of its potency due to the lack of astuteness, vision and tactical skill of those in the NGO movement: 'Business is buying into the environment debate. CAMPFIRE has been coopted. The thunder has been taken out of environment.'

According to this view, civil society has not effectively dealt with the burning political issues that underlie technical deliberations about natural resources. In the Zimbabwe setting, of course, this centres on the 'land question'. In a sense, this mirrors what has happened with international actors – these actors have been new and important players in national policy processes, and, to some extent, agendas look broader for their involvement. But these changes, it can be argued, have not fundamentally altered the framing of policies or the way in which solutions are thought about as, in their enthusiasm for 'environmental' projects, the donors have also skirted around the more fundamental policy issues. A senior advisor in a bilateral aid agency argued:

> There has never been a policy for small farmers here. When government applies for money from us, they ask for irrigation, boreholes and so on. There is still the assumption that small-scale farmers are just small big farmers.

Scepticism is also voiced about the role of NGOs. A senior government official we spoke to observed: 'NGOs are often founded to raise money and create jobs. Their motives are essentially private ones and not focused on environmental issues.' Others argued that the 'big issues' were not being broached as they were too sensitive. One commentator observed: 'There is a conservatism among the bureaucrats – and this despite a wide knowledge of alternatives. They don't want to tamper with food production. It's too politically risky.'

There are, however, reasons to think that such views are overly pessimistic and that important changes are unfolding. These have been initially at the micro level – essentially around experiments in participatory agricultural and natural resource management – which, over time, have been linked to new forms of science that challenge strongly positivist and exclusionary approaches to knowledge. Taking advantage of complex bureaucratic settings, 'room for manoeuvre' (see Clay and Schaffer, 1984) was created in some quarters. The degree to which such initiatives took hold and began to transform the policy process (up to 2000 at least) is explored in the following section.

PARTICIPATION: EXTENDING OR CHALLENGING THE DOMINANT DISCOURSE?

Given the changing contexts of the 1990s, to what degree has the technocratic paradigm, so evident from the colonial to the post-independence era, come under challenge? Did the technocracy come under threat from new, emerging discourses and practices centred on more 'participatory' approaches to development? Or did such practices simply reinforce a technocratic, instrumental pattern, with the basic narratives underlying previous practice going unchallenged? We explore these questions through a series of case studies that look at key features of technocratic practice in agriculture and natural resource management; they look in detail at research, planning, regulation and extension.

The key question we ask is, given the changing architecture of state and civil society interests, what room exists for new perspectives to enter the policy debate and challenge some of the core assumptions and premises of the conventional policy framework? Are there new 'policy spaces' (see Grindle and Thomas, 1991) opening up, with new policy entrepreneurs associated with new actor networks, offering radically new perspectives on policy issues? Are there, as a result of such shifts, any emerging opportunities for new ways of co-producing science and policy arising from interactions between different kinds of science and policy actor? Are there, then, possibilities for new, more diverse, inclusionary and participatory forms of policy process? Or, by contrast, are these apparently new ways of talking about and doing things simply extensions of existing webs of authority and control, where fundamentals are not challenged? Is it the case that, although networks may be extended and new actors enrolled, an essentially similar set of policy perspectives emerges that is simply dressed up with the gloss of participatory rhetoric? In these cases, we explore the degree to which 'participation' – which comes in many shapes and forms – has the potential to fundamentally shift the nature of the policy process, challenging the conventional discourse on environment and development, or whether such initiatives prove a convenient diversionary tactic, effectively extending mainstream discourses through a new form of 'political technology', this time dressed up in the paraphernalia of 'participatory development' (see Chapter 7 for further discussion).

Certainly, contemporary Zimbabwe offers an interesting setting for exploring these questions. The new buzzwords of development – participation, empowerment, decentralization, indigenous knowledge and so on – are widely used across the spectrum of policy actors (Makumbe, 1996). No conference, workshop or seminar is complete without some commentary on the potential benefits of participatory approaches, whether in the minister's opening speech, or in the submissions of NGOs or farmers' groups. Through the 1990s, participatory rural appraisal (PRA), and similar local-level analysis and planning approaches, became the *sine qua non* of development activity in government, NGOs, and even the private sector, provoking a growth in entrepreneurial consultancy activity in the area, as well as a plethora of networks, newsletters and exchange programmes focused on participatory themes.[15] As one local-level researcher in Masvingo exclaimed: 'Participation is coming like a bomb!'

In the following sections we look at four case studies where apparent attempts at encouraging a more participatory approach to policy and implementation have been tried in recent years. The first two cases focus on local-level negotiations over knowledge and how these are reflected through the practices of research and planning. The first dwells on an exploration of how new interactions between scientists and farmers emerged through farmer participatory research initiatives in the field of soils management. The second looks at district environmental-action planning initiatives, where cross-sectoral participatory planning for environment and development issues has been encouraged as part of a national response to Agenda 21. The second two cases look more at the institutional and organizational settings for new initiatives in participation within the two key government agencies dealing with regulation and extension, the first within the Department of Natural Resources and the second within the pre-2001 separate extension agency Agritex.

Research: new spaces for alternative forms of knowledge?

The growth of farmer involvement in the research process has been an important shift in recent years within large parts of the conventional research establishment. Everyone now encourages farmer involvement in field experimentation based on 'participatory research'. But what are the implications of this change for the policy process, and the interactions between farmers, scientists and policy-makers?

What is common to all such initiatives is the emphasis on showing people things: erosion, yield increases, new technologies, indigenous conservation practices. Through the more radical styles of farmer participation, alternative knowledges are increasingly influential. Through such experiments, demonstrations and pilot activities, some of the technocratic science portrayed earlier has been contested in a number of ways – firstly, in terms of its internal assumptions, as issues of complexity and uncertainty receive more attention; and, secondly, in terms of its biases towards exclusivity, as alternative forms of knowledge and popular science are better articulated and promoted through the creation of alternative actor networks.

The debate over wetland use, for example, has fuelled a great deal of controversy in Zimbabwe over many years (Scoones and Cousins, 1994). While the actual legislation associated with wetland use for agriculture has not changed, the attitudes of officials have shifted significantly during the last decade. This has been the result of consistent lobbying by a loose network of researchers, government officials, NGO workers and farmers. Through a series of research projects, pilot and demonstration activities, media coverage, and workshops where a range of wetland-use advocates and policy actors were brought together both within Zimbabwe and at a regional level, a perceptible shift in approach has resulted.[16]

The head of the former Agritex Soil and Water Conservation Branch reflected on the various actors who had influenced his thinking. In particular, he acknowledged the role of Zephaniah Phiri, a farmer from Zvishavane district who was once arrested for cultivating a wetland, but since has developed his farm as a demonstration site with regular visitors from across Zimbabwe and overseas. He also acknowledged the Contill research project within Agritex as another key influence:[17]

> *Farmers are often very vocal. Mr Phiri, for example, was extremely vocal in a workshop. He said Agritex and DNR [Department of Natural Resources] have hindered me, but only now you appreciate me. . . Researchers are also influential. The work on conservation tillage was important, and the work on participatory technology development and experimentation. I saw this initially as pressure from outside. To begin with, it was very rough. Then I realized it was worthwhile to look at a new system.*

Constructing actor networks is simultaneously a process of building and extending knowledge, with experiments, pilot projects or demonstration farms – in part – acting as opportunities for 'witnessing'. Experiments are set up, key people witness what is claimed and, if they support it, facts are extended (see Chapter 2). While the conventional tools of science – graphs, statistics and so on – matter (as we have seen with the soil loss data), researchers argue that they generate real support when they can show things. As the soil fertility researchers quoted earlier noted, it was the visual impact of dramatic gullies, not scientific data per se, which had the impact on policy profile. In discussing experiments on conservation tillage, a researcher commented: 'People prefer yields to conservation effectiveness, but if tied ridging can show yield gaps, then we can discuss conservation. Seeing the size of cobs matters!'

The contexts for new styles of participatory research and action are enormously varied. Much interest exists in pockets within the mainstream agricultural research establishments (in particular, the former Department of Research and Specialist Services of the Ministry of Agriculture – now part of AREX – and the University of Zimbabwe); but NGOs, the farmers' union, extension agents and others are also engaged in various types of farmer participatory research. Researchers engaging with farmers effectively by-pass the hierarchical structures of the transfer-of-technology paradigm, where research, guided by policy priorities, is supposed to lead to extension and the transfer of information and technology to farmers. By enrolling actors across these divides – farmers, extensionists, researchers, policy-makers – researchers working in a more participatory mode can establish new ways of doing things more quickly than is the case when they rely on formal procedures and bureau-cratic structures. For example, a researcher involved with the conservation tillage project Contill explained how they got around the official position that prevents the dissemination of formally unproven technology by labelling their activities as 'testing':

> Testing is a way of getting around not being able to implement. We call it research, not extension. For those involved, it's an excuse to do things their bosses wouldn't approve of. To get around the rules, you have to have a research project nearby. There is a very fine line between demonstration and research, and you can't demonstrate unproven technology.

This has provided scope for extension officials, researchers and farmers to try out new soil management and conservation options that had not been formally approved, and thus effectively creating new policy through a process of research and implementation on the ground.

Other forms of policy influence emanate from the documentation of particular projects and activities of farmers in the communal areas. For example, the extensive work carried out on 'indigenous' soil and water conservation and land-use management practices by researchers, NGOs and others has provided a legitimacy to types of practice that, in the relatively recent past, were at best frowned upon and sometimes banned outright.[18] While often notionally illegal and contravening policy guidelines, such practices are frequently accepted as appropriate activities by extension workers, and, indeed, are used as demonstration visit sites for other farmers. For instance, the soil and water conservation specialist in Masvingo commented on one farmer whom he had recently visited in Zaka:

> It is quite beautiful if you saw what that farmer did. Then you wouldn't worry about erosion. This was well conserved – he was a model farmer. DNR won't give him any problems. He didn't need a permit; he had a permit in his head.

Farmer participatory research takes a variety of forms, ranging from the nominal involvement of farmers in implementing experiments already designed by research scientists, to a fuller engagement, involving the design, implementation and analysis of research in collaboration with researchers. In the former case, participation is limited, and the opportunities for new forms of knowledge and action to emerge are constrained, with – more often than not – the standard technicist solutions that issue from conventional science simply being extended to a wider group. However, other forms of participatory research do potentially allow new voices to be heard, and a different type of science to emerge, based more upon local understandings of key issues and problems. The effective linking of actors across the conventional divides offers the potential for new forms of knowledge and practice to enter the policy process. Very often, this occurs through the extension of new forms of practice through informal networks, and the acceptance of this by an expanding group of actors. This may not result in a formal change in policy – as with the wetland case, or much of the soil conservation measures – but this may not matter if accepted practice shifts in response.

Planning: experiences with district environmental action planning

Another example of the new participation emphasis was the attempt to bring different line ministries together with local communities to develop District Environmental Action Plans (DEAPs). The DEAP process is seen as an attempt to implement the National Conservation Strategy developed during the mid-1980s and to provide a district-level focus for post-Rio Agenda 21 activities (Mukahanana et al, 1998). The approach fits within a wider trend of the last decade towards greater decentralization of governance and public service provision to the district level.

The DEAP process was established during the early 1990s with support from the United Nations Development Programme (UNDP), with an office initially placed in the Department of Natural Resources. A consultant with experience in participatory planning approaches was hired through the World Conservation Union (IUCN) to initiate the process in a number of districts and to develop a methodology and training package. By 1999, DEAP activities had occurred in a number of districts in the country, each involving a range of line ministry, district and NGO officials. DEAPs are seen as an attempt to develop the capacity of district-level administration and to create mechanisms for community-based management of natural resources.

An official in the UNDP spoke to us highly enthusiastically of his experiences: 'We have started a revolution which could influence future policy formulation: once people articulate their needs, no government can resist.' The DEAP process draws its inspiration, in particular, from the CAMPFIRE community-based wildlife programme, now a world-renowned attempt at widespread participatory resource management centred on local and district administrative structures. One commentator involved in the CAMPFIRE programme for some time observed:

> CAMPFIRE *was the first non-command-and-control approach, a new vista for management of animals, trees and soils. Once people know their rights, you can't go back. The district administrator was a feared man; now people want to do it for themselves. They demand their rights.*

In a similar vein, a DNR official argued: 'There are lots of fights over wildlife revenues. CAMPFIRE has opened up a window for accountability which DEAPs are trying to work with.' Within the DNR, DEAPs are seen as a radically new approach to natural resource management, an approach that will allow the department to break away from its past associations of draconian, top-down policing style. The former deputy director commented:

> We believe that people with resources should manage. So there have been greater attempts to involve people in policy formulation. CAMPFIRE exemplifies this, and DEAPs, too, empower communities.

This optimistic angle on the DEAP process – that it really is the beginning of a new type of inclusionary planning and policy-making – was not shared by everyone we spoke to. A general criticism is that the DEAPs that have emerged are simply long lists of demands for basic infrastructure and services, with different line ministries putting in bids for roads, clinics or schools, rather than imaginative plans emanating from the community for natural resource management. A provincial official in Masvingo commented: 'People expect dams, irrigation schemes, roads and boreholes.' While the emphasis on the standard products of rural development is important, there is also a sense among some that the whole process was too donor reliant, and, in fact, is poorly linked to higher levels of line ministry planning and budget allocation. It also presents a major capacity problem at the district level. As one advocate observed: 'For DEAPs, you need three to four people for seven days per village for the assessment and action planning. It ties the whole district staff up.' Commenting on the donor dominance of DEAP activities, a senior environmental researcher put it that:

> DEAPs' negative side is that they are just donor driven – they die when donors leave. It's all at too high a bureaucratic level. All this natural resource reform needs to be right down at the ground.

It is possible to see the DEAP process as more technocratic planning rather than genuine participation and empowerment. While there may be public involvement, it does not appear to be sufficiently linked to broader questions of resource access and other more political issues to constitute a real shift. DEAP as a policy approach constructs its subjects as participants in a planning frame, but not one that they actually control, because they have to continue to fit within the broader resource allocation and political commitments of government. As one senior figure in the DNR commented: 'The aim is to have DEAP as part of the core Rural Development Council planning process.'

   The question, then, is to what degree can participatory initiatives at the local level – whether based on farmer participatory research or district-level environmental planning – have an effect within the existing structures of government and bureaucracy? To what degree can participatory approaches to policy-making, planning and implementation become institutionalized within settings that, as we have seen, have long histories? It is these questions that we pursue in the following two sections, which look at changes in the two key government departments dealing with environmental regulation and agricultural extension – the Department of Natural Resources (DNR) and the former Agritex.

Regulation: refashioning the Department of Natural Resources

In recent years, there has been a gradual shift in the way the DNR operates. This department has, historically, been the body that polices rural communities and ensures that natural resource legislation is being respected. It has the power to fine farmers who cultivate wetlands, for example, and the power to grant discretionary licences to those who are following practices that are technically illegal.[19]

DNR has many fewer operational staff than Agritex, the agricultural extension agency. There is typically only one DNR official per district, whereas there will be over 30 agricultural extension agents. Restricted numbers and dwindling government budgets make it hard for DNR officials to go out and fulfil their policing role. One DNR officer commented in 1999, even before the major economic collapse which followed, on their day-to-day operational challenges: 'Fuel has gone up 60–70 per cent. The cost of spares has gone up, so it is difficult to go out and look and see what is happening.' A senior official put it that DNR has had to move to a more community-based advisory role because it has simply been impossible to enforce regulations: 'Unless you send in the army, gold panning and deforestation will go on.' Another official commented: 'You can't have a police officer behind every tree.'

In some instances, there is evidence of a growing realization among DNR officials that the earlier picture of rural populations who need to be policed into good natural resource management is no longer always appropriate. And, furthermore, where rules are infringed, there may be a logic that reflects alternative knowledge about how to manage natural resources effectively and maintain livelihoods. Given the DNR's statutory obligations to enforce the environmental legislation, however, a new, more discretionary, stance presents many dilemmas. A DNR official discussed a case of an NGO illegally experimenting with wetland use. The DNR forced the community to apply for a licence: 'They applied and the community got approval. We may not be against these things, but we must respect the law of the land. It's my responsibility to see that government policy is implemented at this level.'

Taking advantage of policy spaces, researchers can effectively shift policy discussions incrementally through enrolling particular officials. One such DNR official recounted the story of how 'illegal' research was first ignored and then noticed by higher officials, provoking a shift in regulatory practice from the Natural Resources Board:

> They started trials and I went round. People were ignoring the policy. So it came up in Harare and people started asking, 'What is happening in Masvingo?' And so last week we sat down and they applied for approval from the Natural Resources Board.

Thus, in the context of the DNR, certain changes are afoot. In its desire to recast itself in a positive light, and to reject its past policing role as much as possible, the department has wholeheartedly embraced a range of community-based natural resource management initiatives. CAMPFIRE, DEAPs, community forestry and so on are all heralded as part of a new era. The attempts to revamp environmental legislation by the ministry have also been welcomed as part of the reinvention of the department. Despite its critics, the new Environmental Management Act is hailed internally as a radical new step that sweeps away past colonial legislation and emphasizes holistic environmental assessment.

This new view, emerging slowly from the late 1980s, has been accepted with greater flexibility and discretion by field officers in their day-to-day work. But such officers are put in a difficult position. On the one hand, they are encouraged to operate under a new regime that emphasizes community involvement and participatory management. Yet, they are also expected to implement and enforce the enormous array of complex, restrictive legislation. They must operate in the often fraught milieu of local politics. As one local extension worker from Chivi communal area pointed out:

> *There is a lot of politics involved. You have to ignore it, because of politics. I have never seen a DNR officer give a ticket because of this. When elections come, the politicians say, don't harass these people. You have to be quiet. If not, you will be quickly transferred.*

So, does such discretion and flexibility result in participation, or simply a less draconian form of state-led environmental managerialism? It seems that some basic features of the DNR's structural setting mean that the result, by and large, has been the latter. The dominant and, in many respects, incredibly powerful role of the Natural Resources Board puts limits on the flexibility of the organization to shift both its policies and practices, as does the nature of the legislation that it has been obliged to oversee. The limited resources of the department – both in terms of personnel and overall budget – also mean that the scope for innovation and change remains constrained. Thus, a rather instrumental form of participation is the result, limited by the broader setting. Without the obligation to enforce regulations, Agritex, the former agricultural extension agency, had perhaps more opportunities to adopt a more flexible, inclusive style. However, as with the DNR, it too carries with it a long history of very different ways of operating.

Extension: organizational change in the extension system

In the late 1990s Agritex underwent a process of organizational development labelled 'change management'. This process began formally in Masvingo province in 1994 under the auspices of the provincial head, and with support from organizational development and participatory extension consultants employed through the Deutsche Gesellschaft für Technische Zusammenarbeit

(GTZ). Since then, the provincial process won national support and began to be implemented nationally, following the promotion of the director to a senior national position (Hagmann et al, 1999).

Broadly, change management came about because of a growing realization among key figures that the command-and-control approach with which Agritex had historically been associated was not producing effective results. For example, a senior officer in Masvingo observed: 'Hundreds of land-use plans are produced every year, but only grazing is ever implemented; besides that, nothing else happens.' A key figure in the process commented that a change was needed from a 'technical quick-fix' approach to a more 'problem-oriented' approach:

> *We learned that extensionists should be partners not teachers; there should be open diagnosis and we should be less production oriented, looking, instead, at the full range of income-earning possibilities. We need client assessment, more stakeholder involvement, peer assessment – not the old attitude of 'I'm the expert for this ward'. . . 'the expert assistance model of development' is nonsense.*

A range of reasons was identified by people whom we interviewed as leading to this commitment to change. One theme was the realization that lower-level extensionists were interacting with farmers and other actors outside of the organization and were following practices that contravened official positions. These grassroots officers were then not feeding back, or were dissembling to superiors. A junior agricultural extension worker commented on this:

> *We try to avoid the Master Farmer regulations on cattle ownership. We cannot say that you don't qualify because your cattle died in the drought. We convince our superiors, who say no problem as long as training days are covered and oral tests are passed. For controversial things, we look at the situation. Such policies are never authorized; they are still being debated at head office. But we can get on with things on the ground.*

Awareness of the actual practice of extension implementation and its implications for policy filtered back up the system. But this was only gradual. As one district extension officer observed: 'Water does not flow upwards easily.' Another key factor that facilitated the shift in perspective was the effect of a constellation of well-linked NGO/research projects in Masvingo province. The 'three key stimuli', according to the then acting provincial head of Agritex, were the Chivi-based Intermediate Technology Group project, concentrating on farmer empowerment and demand-led research and extension; the Integrated Rural Development Programme (IRDEP)/GTZ participatory extension project; and the conservation tillage farmer participatory experiments.[20] During the first part of the 1990s, these combined to offer experiences – field days, seed fairs, workshops, exchange visits and study tours – which helped to change the perceptions of key personnel in the Agritex bureaucracy in Masvingo and, later, further afield. These projects suggested entirely new approaches to research and extension that engaged with farmer knowledge and practice, and built on new understandings of the logic – and sometimes superiority – of farmer approaches to utilizing natural resources.

The three Masvingo projects were not isolated activities. They can be taken as experiments with fundamentally different ways of initiating rural development. The findings and practices that emerged from them flatly contradict many long-established policy directions – for example, promotion of inter-cropping, new tillage techniques and forms of conservation. As the impact of these experiments was extended, policy – particularly policy in practice – began to change. This gradually permeated upwards through the Agritex hierarchy to the head office, where even the Master Farmer programme came under review.

Not surprisingly, the changes that unfolded did not occur without a certain amount of resistance. A researcher commented:

> *In 1991–1992, there was a really strong debate about Contill. Contill really goes against the Alvord recommendations – talking of inter-cropping and unclean weeding, and not straight lines. Monocropping is very entrenched in Agritex.*

However, at least in Masvingo province, in a few years, key elements of the participatory approach that was advocated took hold. An official with the Masvingo-based IRDEP programme commented on changes within Agritex: 'A few years ago they would have laughed at ITK [indigenous technical knowledge]. Now there has been an attitudinal change for extension agents. They are training them in participatory approaches.'

So, how did these experiments, projects and unconventional practices both within and outside of the organization lead to wider changes? One explanation is that key individuals, convinced of the validity of alternative approaches, were able to strategize and build alternative actor networks in a similar manner to those in which dominant scientific–bureaucratic actor networks had emerged in the past. Many of these networks started out quietly and in isolation, but gradually expanded to involve a wide range of farmers, extensionists, researchers and practitioners across a multitude of organizations. Over time, there were enough visible results to enrol higher-profile protagonists, such as the provincial Agritex head. A consultant observed, 'These micro-pilots are essential: they tune in the senior people.' When the provincial head got involved, he was able to use his authority and links to highlight the results of the projects, and to achieve official endorsement for a process of change within the bureaucracy. At a workshop in 1993, 'The national director sat there and saw the provincial director talk about organizational development. He said, "That's a risky area. We'll call it a pilot project for two years and if it is good we'll all share the glory; otherwise it's your problem."'

But such tactics and strategies of individuals as members of actor networks cannot be seen as separate from wider changes, which opened up an area of policy space for a discussion about participatory forms of extension that had not been present before. The early 1990s were characterized by severe financial cutbacks in the public sector due to structural adjustment and the withdrawal of loan funding to agricultural departments. As discussed earlier, this put a major strain on government departments, including Agritex, restricting their ability to fulfil their mandate. It also resulted in a drop in morale – no longer, it seemed, was Agritex the prestigious, premier technical extension agency in Africa that actually 'worked'. Thus, during the early 1990s, key people in Agritex were looking outwards for new ideas, new directions and, indeed, new sources of funding.

The donor support from the German government that allowed Agritex Masvingo the opportunity to experiment flexibly – without undue reliance on central funds and the ministry's bureaucratic procedures – was undoubtedly significant, as was the close interaction with the trio of projects working in the province at that time. By the mid-1990s, these projects had accumulated significant experience and were beginning to show some really positive results, if at a very small scale. This was sufficient to give confidence to key Agritex officials that real alternatives existed, which, on the one hand, were potentially more cost effective and, on the other, delivered real successes that farmers clearly appreciated.

The space offered by the national Agritex directorate for a Masvingo pilot was also important. By 1993, preparations for a new phase of World Bank lending were already in the offing, and the need to rethink extension strategy and organization was highlighted by a range of consultants' reports for the World Bank and other donors.[21] In addition, a political push was increasingly evident with the appointment of Dr Olivia Muchena as deputy minister for agriculture, who was well known from her days as a University of Zimbabwe lecturer in extension and a strong advocate of a participatory approach.

Thus, during the late 1990s, a range of factors combined – political pressures and budgetary constraints; delivery problems across the extension service; advocacy of new approaches through NGO and pilot projects; the creation of new actor networks across organizations; and the actions of a few key 'policy entrepreneurs'. Such factors created some 'room for manoeuvre' in one of the largest government departments in the country. This had not existed before, but did allow the space for introducing new, participatory ideas in ways that potentially offered real opportunities for change.

The emperor's new clothes?

Each of the case studies has highlighted some of the potentials of participation, but also the clear limits. In many cases, as we have seen, an instrumental form is evident, where prevailing discourses and practices go largely unchallenged. A 'participation gloss', in other words, does not alter the technocracy by shifting deeply embedded practices of conventional research, planning, regulation or extension. In other instances, more fundamental changes have been observed where policy spaces have been opened up by new configurations of actor networks, with new forms of bureaucratic practice emerging. This has often started at the local level through the discretionary actions of so-called 'street-level bureaucrats' (see Chapter 2), but sometimes has permeated upwards and outwards into structural organizational reform.

Yet, the examples we have identified have remained limited to re-negotiations over technical knowledge, with little evidence of more direct challenges to structural issues of politics and power. It could be argued that such shifts – while on the surface appearing to be progressive and amenable to change – operate on the margins and are not played out in more contentious and political arenas, such as around issues of land access. In such situations, participation is limited to consultation since the consequences of addressing explicitly political issues through participatory processes have not been countenanced. As one informant commented during a discussion of the 1994 Land Tenure Commission: 'There were lots of consultations. . . but it's not a technical issue; you're kidding yourself if you think it is. It's political.'[22] An awareness of the consequences of more politicized forms of participation was expressed by one senior government official who commented ominously: 'Empowerment can be politically dangerous, especially where you don't practice democracy. It's a time bomb.' The events of the last few years in Zimbabwe have perhaps proved him right, as clampdowns on independent political activity have taken place. Policy around key contentious issues such as land are today being played out in a highly politicized arena with, at times, violent consequences, rather than in marginal renegotiations of the technocracy under the banner of participation.

CONCLUSION

This chapter has looked at the policy processes that have produced a particular style of natural resources policy in Zimbabwe – a style that has been associated with the production and reproduction of a set of environmental crisis narratives, which became embedded in particular institutionalized practices around research, planning, regulation and extension. This approach emerges from the way in which science and bureaucracy mutually construct one another potentially depoliticizing awkward, more political questions by framing them as technical. Tracing the continuities of policy practice from the colonial to the post-colonial era, we have also elaborated on some of the state interests in maintaining such a technocratic approach.

However, as we have shown, for a variety of reasons, in the 1990s, policy processes have began to show some change, allowing room for international and civil society actors; and state agencies, as our analyses of Agritex and the DNR suggest. What this means for policy processes is as yet unclear. Our examination of the DEAP process, for example, suggests there are reasons to be concerned that the new emphasis among policy actors on participatory planning and consultative mechanisms is simply an extension of the earlier technologies of governance, albeit in slightly new forms, but nevertheless with the same political effects.

An alternative view claims that participation is not just being used instrumentally; rather, a range of actors had begun to build networks that run through state and civil society and potentially result in quite a different type of policy practice and process. In this view, lower-level policy actors, such as farmers, field researchers and development practitioners, may exercise agency and actually create policy and thereby broader social and political realities too. In many ways, this requires more testing and experimentation. What are the limits of citizen science and the creation of witnessing experiences? When are visits and workshops, the careful construction of projects or NGO steering committees, or the manipulation of personal connections likely to offer returns? What are the limits of lower-level policy actors' agency? Can the cumulative effect of such new practices result in more fundamental change, particularly in more contentious arenas such as land reform?

At this juncture, given the wider macro-political and economic changes ongoing in Zimbabwe, it is unclear what the 1990s experience of 'participation' ultimately means for the policy process. It may be that it simply becomes an extension of a well-established technocracy, continuing to reinforce narratives on environmental and agricultural policy that have long been at the centre of state-led initiatives, although now in a 'participatory' guise. Or it may be that there really are new opportunities for people to articulate their realities, and that participatory approaches may be a vehicle for challenging the political assumptions upon which much technical policy rests. For this to take place, new actor networks will need to be built, and new forms of knowledge and practice skilfully articulated. This, in turn, requires sensitivity to the new policy spaces created by the new contexts emerging with currently tumultuous broader social, economic and political change. With such contexts changing so rapidly, it is unclear what the future will hold. But what our case studies suggest is that the rigid frameworks of the past are being challenged in various ways with the potential, as yet far from realized, for new forms of policy process to emerge.

7

Spaces for Engagement: Science, Experts and Citizens

INTRODUCTION

This book has been about the interactions of science, expertise and policy-making across different contexts. In the preceding chapters, we have shown how technical and political issues are intertwined in the process of policy-making. In order to understand why particular policies persist, we have shown how it is important to understand not only the scientific framing of issues – the narratives that tell the policy stories – but also the way policy positions become embedded in networks of actors, funding, professional and other relationships, as well as in particular organizations and institutions. Such interactions cross boundaries between the local and the global, and therefore disturb categories – such as the state or civil society – which circumscribe much conventional political and policy analysis. With a focus on issues of knowledge and expertise, we must look beyond the conventional structural analyses of political science to the sometimes less obvious, but no less important, discursive politics of expertise. This means investigating the generally overlooked processes by which scientific and technical policy arguments become routinized and lodged within particular bureaucratic and administrative practices.

In this book we set out to explore how policy change occurs or, as in many cases, remains constant, taking the example of land management in Africa as our focus. As laid out in Chapter 2 and subsequently explored in Chapters 3–6, we have found a number of analytical lenses useful in this enquiry. With our focus on knowledge – and particularly the relations of expert scientific knowledge to the policy process – we 'followed the actors' and traced the networks of knowledge that they create. We have, in turn, examined more broadly the creation of a discursive politics, and the ways in which more complex discourse coalitions or epistemic communities are formed. Such an analysis, in turn, without rejecting conventional structuralist analyses of politics and interests, brought in a micro-focus on actors, their networks and the exercise of agency.

In the area of environmental policy-making, such a perspective high-lighting knowledge, practice and power, we argue, is important, since science and technical expertise has such a central role in framing, shaping and implementing environmental policies. Perhaps this is particularly so in the context of so-called 'global' environmental issues, where science and expertise have become bound up with the negotiation and implementation of international agreements and protocols. The scientific and policy communities that engage in such processes move easily between Washington and Addis Ababa, Rome and Bamako, and – while being part of a more global knowledge elite – remain, in certain key ways, connected with particular places and contexts.

Our focus on the interaction of science and policies points in many of our case examples to a particular style of policy practice that, in its technocratic incarnations, emphasizes science-led managerial, instrumental and interventionist approaches as the basic practice of development. With particular types of science creating a frame for policy intervention, the practice of development thus inevitably incorporates the categories and practices of such framings, reinforced, in turn, by the institutional settings within which such knowledge is created. This process therefore demarcates the boundaries of inclusion and exclusion – deeming certain people expert, others ignorant; and certain people able to speak, and others not. The form of governmentality emerging from such a style of technocracy thus results in an implicit vision of whose perspectives and interests matter in policy processes.

This clearly has implications for the potential for citizen participation. As we have seen in many instances, farmers' perspectives have been excluded from policy debates about land and soil management in Africa, despite their experience and knowledge. In this chapter we first offer a reminder of the contexts for policy-making discussed in the case study chapters, and examine the degree to which a technocratic approach to policy-making excludes alternative views in these different settings. Next, the chapter moves to a discussion of the possible spaces for the engagement of citizens in the policy process, examining, in turn, spaces created by international connections, national governments and parties, and citizen action of various sorts. Drawing on the case study material, we examine the relationships observed between knowledge, expertise and policy-making. The final section turns to an assessment of the prospects for citizen participation in policy processes, and highlights positive experiences to date.

CONTEXTS FOR POLICY PROCESSES IN AFRICA

Internationalized science policy

One of the recurrent features of policy processes surrounding land management in Africa comprises the connections between local, national and international processes. This theme has been emphasized particularly in Chapter 3 through our discussion of the Soil Fertility Initiative (SFI), but also in the context of the country case study chapters that followed. We have identified a characteristic style of international science, wedded to crisis narratives and often linked to major initiatives. Wrapped up as this is in the complex world of donor organizations, international research centres and global policy moves, it brings with it a certain form of politics and policy.

The practices of international science are linked, as we have seen, across space through funding connections, collaborative research networks and collegial interactions. Thus, in the debate about soil fertility, we saw the importance of the nutrient-balance modelling approach in framing the debate. Emanating from a consultancy funded by the United Nations Food and Agriculture Organization (FAO) and carried out by two Dutch researchers from Wageningen University in the Netherlands, the approach was widely taken up by others. The research of another Dutch researcher in Mali, for instance, was – as we saw in Chapter 5 – highly significant in the policy debate there. Nutrient balance studies were subsequently funded in many other sites through connections made between African researchers and Wageningen with European Union (EU) funding support. As the approach – its assumptions, methodology and black boxes – became part of normal practice and institutionalized within research institutions (via further projects, PhDs and so on), the process by which such science helps to mutually construct the policy problem is consolidated.

The coalitons that form around a particular scientific diagnosis – whether soil recapitalization through rock phosphate application or nutrient balance modelling – may have a major influence on the way in which issues are thought about in policy and funding circles. Often driven by effective narratives and good story-tellers, the effects can be widespread and dramatic, spreading across national boundaries and creating what, at first, appears to be an international consensus through a standardized approach.

But, as we have seen for the case of the SFI, such dominance is never complete. While international science and policy is, at first glance, homogenous and totalizing in its influence, when looked at in a more disaggregated manner, there is far more diversity in practice and perspective than would first appear. International science and policy-making is carried out in diverse locations, each of which – to varying degrees – take on a local character. Thus, when intersecting with other scientific cultures and policy styles, the apparently all-powerful international discourse coalitions must transmute and adapt in order to survive.

Science and technical policy is, thus far, from being universal, and it is these interactions across scales and between competing coalitions and networks of actors and ideas that characterizes the national policy processes of Ethiopia, Mali and Zimbabwe. However, in order to understand the nature of these interactions, a more comprehensive look at the characteristic styles of policy-making in each of the countries is needed. This requires us to examine the broader social relations of science, citizens and policy in the context of different 'regional modernities' (see Agarwal and Sivaramakrishnan, 2000); the history of relations between scientific and technical expertise and the state in the construction of development; and the bureaucratic, political and economic setting for policy-making in each national setting.

ETHIOPIA

As introduced in Chapter 1, and explored further in Chapter 4, from the imperial rulers to the modern presidents, Ethiopia has been characterized by strong, centralized state authority. Development has often been conceived as part of a larger technocratic vision that could be realized through the commitment and authority of the central ruler. Thus, when President Meles Zenawi became convinced that the Sasakawa Global 2000 (SG2000) package approach was a potential solution to long-term food insecurity and famine in the country, he wasted no time in making it his high-priority project. From a pilot project in a few sites, it moved to a national programme with targets of millions of farmers in under five years (see Chapter 4). This big, high-profile, technical project replicated in many senses – both practically and symbolically – the big prestige development projects of the past, whether the integrated rural development projects of the 1970s, the package programmes that followed, or the major soil and water conservation programmes of the 1980s. In each case, these were, in some senses, impressive achievements. Technical expertise was mobilized and applied, funds were raised and whole bureaucracies turned around to deliver. But, at least in the early phases, there was little consultation or opportunities for reflection. This was a politically and technically driven solution that required firm central direction. In Ethiopia, with its strong aid dependence, international ties are key. Yet in interactions with outsiders, there is always a strong assertion of Ethiopian independence, and a definitively Ethiopian mark is imposed. Thus, even though the Sasakawa Global 2000 (SG2000) initiative was externally driven – with advice from Nobel Laureate Norman Borlaug and ex-US President Jimmy Carter – it was quickly 'Ethiopianized' and claimed to be nationally owned and conceived (see Chapter 4).

Within the context of a highly centralized system, with a politicized and centrally controlled bureaucracy, a highly selective form of regional autonomy is permitted. This results in differences in relationships between state and citizens dependent upon historically informed ties with the centre. The contrast between Tigray in the north and the Southern Peoples' Region, for example, is stark, with Tigray reflecting a politics of liberation and close ties to the current national rulers and the Southern Peoples' Region reflecting a politics of conquest and control. There are, therefore, varying degrees of bureaucratic room for manoeuvre on the ground, resulting in different practices of government bureaucrats, as well as the functioning of non-governmental organizations (NGOs) and other civil society organizations.

A form of politically directed, channelled and managed participation is allowed, based on the Tigrayan model of political mobilization. This sets the boundaries for development-style consultations, where, under well-defined parameters, rural voices may be heard. Thus, orchestrated consultations were conducted, for instance, under the aegis of the National Conservation Strategy and numerous participatory rural appraisals (PRAs) are conducted for the planning of projects and interventions. The degree to which such consultation results in real debate and opportunities for dissent is limited. An independent press exists, but is closely monitored. Debates by academics and others are similarly observed. The contentious and fragile politics of the Ethiopian state creates an apparent need for central control for fear of national disintegration and regional and ethnic strife. A technocratic, expert-led regime, therefore, exists at the centre of the policy process; it is highly centralized, with only selective alliances created outside to generate ideas and, particularly, financial support.

MALI

By comparison, Mali has a relatively weak state, which, as discussed in Chapter 5, is highly dependent on external support, especially from France. Cotton is perhaps the key economic resource for the state, and thus the technical transformation of agriculture – bolstered by a strong productionist narrative for the cash-crop zones – is seen as critical. Policy-making is therefore very much about the core economic areas and the complex relationships between the state, political parties, the parastatal Compagnie Malienne pour le Développement des Fibres Textiles (CMDT) and cotton farmers.

While farmer organizations were originally simply an extension of this state technocratic system in the cotton areas, more recently – in the context of the relatively new democratic era since 1991 – they have taken on new roles. The last decades have also coincided with a period of structural adjustment and a decline in state patronage of cotton areas. Farmers' unions have, in the last few years, exerted more influence – strikes, burning of depots, and withdrawal of labour and support have all had major impacts. The result is that the long-term compact between the state and the cotton sector – based on complex, long-established patronage relationships – is potentially breaking down as farmers assert themselves more and carve out an identity that is different from that ascribed to them from the colonial era as simply cotton producers for the state. This may foreshadow a rather different set of power balances and the emergence of a new form of policy process in the cotton sector in the future.

Beyond the cash-crop zones, as described in Chapter 5, state influence is relatively limited, restricted to a range of *cercle* and commune officials and a very thinly spread service-support infrastructure. In these expansive dryland areas, day-to-day politics are governed by often very local considerations, mediated by traditional leaders and local 'big men'. It is an open question as to what policy and participation means in these areas – such settings are a far cry from the cotton zone, where a complex mix of international, state, commercial and local voices enter the fray. Participation in such settings may mean engagement with a local NGO project or an occasional involvement in a consultation initiated by a ministry in Bamako with support from one donor or another. For the most part, policy is something that happens elsewhere. But this situation may change with the emergence of a decentralized system of local governance with the potential, as yet unrealized, of more local decision-making and budget allocation. Here, the experiments in community organization and participation – led largely by NGOs – may provide an interesting basis for an extension beyond the project areas of their pilot activities into the mainstream of a changing local state.

ZIMBABWE

Through the colonial era, there emerged a strong technocratic state apparatus. While focused on the commercial areas in terms of support and incentives, the control of the African rural population was seen as critical. Thus, in contrast to Ethiopia and Mali, a plethora of laws, regulations and recommendations were formulated and enforced. Policies that restricted cattle numbers, banned wetland cultivation, prescribed how people should farm, defined the form of soil conservation that should exist, and so on emerged from a close relationship between a particular type of dominant colonial science and the emerging state apparatus. Bound up in bureaucratic practice and procedure, such policy approaches became deeply institutionally embedded. As described in Chapter 6, with independence, there was a remarkable continuity in policy style, despite a sea change in politics. This occurred despite the fact that many of the laws and regulations that continued to be enforced, often with renewed vigour post-1980, were the very ones that rural people were mobilized against during the liberation war by the guerilla fighters who became the post-independence leadership. This contradiction can only be understood through a fuller understanding of the embedded nature of the technocratic bureaucracy, and the resilience of particular ways of thinking and acting.

During the 1990s, however, this strong adherence to the letter of the colonial approach began to waver. A number of factors contributed to this, as discussed in Chapter 6. Firstly, the efficacy of the state in enforcing restrictive laws and regulations in remote rural areas lessened as a result of adjustment policies reducing state capacity. Secondly, bureaucrats – particularly those at the front line in the field – increasingly questioned this way of doing things. They realized that it was not effective and that they, as a result, were unpopular characters in places where they lived, and in relation to people with whom they had often close personal links. Thirdly, and building on and responding to the first two reasons, NGOs and other groups began to experiment more fully with alternatives through a whole range of pilot projects and experiments, picking up on international shifts in development thinking that emphasized more community-based, participatory approaches. This combination of factors meant that, by the end of the 1990s, some alternatives were being mapped out and, in some cases, were being implemented with the assistance of state agencies over wide scales.

But the late 1990s also coincided with the rise of political tensions in the country. For the first time, electoral politics became a contest between parties, rather than simply being run within the Zimbabwe African National Union–

Patriotic Front (ZANU–PF) political machine. The agitation of the union movement, the creation of the Movement for Democratic Change (MDC), and the constitutional referendum all contributed to the assertion of a political alternative to the ruling party. The re-emergence of the war veterans as a political force and the politically motivated farm invasions that followed from 2000 have fuelled a level of political tension, intimidation and uncertainty that has put on hold many of the emerging participatory alternatives that appeared to be blossoming earlier. Perhaps, Chapter 6 conjectured, such alternatives were simply mirages that were created in the unreal world, generated by donor funding; perhaps, also, without the resolution of the core political issues around land and democracy in the country, they were never going to last.

SPACES FOR ENGAGEMENT

We started this book with an observation and a challenge. The observation was that, despite contrary evidence and divergent practice, mainstream policy positions on environment and land management in Africa stick with remarkable tenacity. The challenge was to examine why this was so. The previous chapters have highlighted a range of factors that give rise to this situation, but also point to the ways in which policies do change, and how new perspectives emerge and become part of the mainstream. How this happens is, as we have seen in the previous section, very much dependent upon the context for policy – political, economic, social and environmental. This suggests equally that contexts for participation and citizen engagement with policy will also be highly contextualized. It is worth asking at this stage, then, given the nature and context of policy processes in each of the three countries, what spaces for engagement exist for alternative perspectives on environment and land management that go beyond the mainstream 'received wisdoms'? Are there possibilities for challenge, for reframing and for different forms of practice? Are there different approaches to conceiving of the relationship between science, expertise and citizens, in ways that challenge the technocratic visions emerging from the state and the alliances with international networks? Are there new discourse coalitions that suggest new possibilities for an alternative policy process, as well as new knowledges, institutions and practices?

These are, of course, big questions that we can only address in a very partial way. In the following sections we outline some of the experiences of 'participation' in policy that have emerged from our case study analyses. What are the limits and constraints, possibilities and opportunities, of a participatory policy process in these different settings? In asking these questions, we want to go beyond the somewhat glib rhetoric about participation that has dominated development discourse in recent years in order to situate an understanding of participatory engagement in policy in our located analyses. Clearly, we can only comment specifically on issues relating to environment and land management in Ethiopia, Mali and Zimbabwe. Different issues will arise in different fields and in different contexts; but our hope is that such an analysis will point to broader questions about the relationships between science, policy and citizens that will allow more general reflections on questions of democratizing expertise in environmental policy-making.

Across the case studies, there are a number of ways in which policy change occurs – ranging from forging connections at the international level, to linking up with research–action projects, to engaging with the local state or political parties, to encouraging citizen action of various sorts. The following sections draw on the case material presented in Chapters 3–6 in order to highlight some of various ways in which 'participation' is constructed, ranging from the instrumental to the more active, as well as the interactions with the policy process that occur as a result. From this assessment, we then move to examine how, across the case study contexts, the relationship between expertise and citizens is defined.

International connections

Relationships between locally developed knowledge and expertise and that developed in the context of international circuits and networks is a key feature of the policy stories analysed in each of the case study countries. As already noted, variable relationships have been developed that depend on the form and composition of the networks, their origins and organization. What comes through strongly, however, in the context of policy debates over land management in Africa, is that internationalized discourse coalitions are key. In Chapter 3, we explored the emergence and apparent stumbling of the SFI as an example. Similar sources of funding, similar members of networks, similar concern with particular policy narratives generate a striking commonality between a range of international environmental policy initiatives. Thus, for example, links between the Consultative Group on International Agricultural Research (CGIAR), national agricultural research institutes and the Rockefeller Foundation have been an important influence in Zimbabwe (Chapter 6). In Mali, donor-funded activities (particularly through the French and Dutch foreign aid) have created particular styles of science and policy practice (Chapter 5). Regional alliances – often created through donor funding – are also important links across countries. Thus, for example, the Southern African Development Community (SADC) in Southern Africa, the Francophone zone of West Africa and East Africa all have various soil-related initiatives and networks allied to them, supported by different donor organizations (see Chapters 3–6). Whether we can talk of an international expert epistemic community (following Haas, 1992) that relates to this field, or, instead, a set of overlapping but deeply intertwined communities and networks, is unclear. What is evident, though, is that most of the groupings whom we encountered (with certain rare cases excepted) replicated and reinforced, in national contexts, mainstream policy discourses that were based on a particular crisis narrative, which linked soil fertility decline or soil erosion to a downward spiral of food insecurity and poverty (Chapter 3).

How the internationalization of policy discourse and networks plays out in relation to particular settings is, as we have seen, a key question. Across the cases, different responses were observed. In some cases, an argument for the dominating power of international coalitions can be made, with the shaping of knowledge, practice and institutions heavily determined by international influences – often through the guiding power and conditionalities of donor funding. Very often – adopting wholesale the core narratives of the international debate – is a basic requirement for gaining access to such funds. Thus, the stylized desertification narratives are repeated back – sometimes with tongue in cheek, sometimes not – in order to unlock the funding opportunities. With the post-Rio Convention to Combat Desertification (CCD) offering the potential (very much unrealized) for major donor investment in land management issues in Africa to provide cash to starved ministries of the environment, the response cannot be doubted as anything but a sensible one. That there is, generally, complicity in this interaction between donors and national governments suits all of those involved.

Yet, as we have pointed out before, such international dominance is never complete. International networks are composed of actors with 'local' connections, and the contingencies and uncertainties of local contexts must always impinge upon processes of implementation in particular places. As we saw in Chapter 3, the unravelling – or at least adaptation – of the SFI was very much influenced by such local responses and conditions. Participation in internationalized networks, then, can bring with it authority and stature, funds from international aid donors and sometimes legitimacy for alternative views (as in the cases where, for example, an advocacy of local or indigenous knowledges has been forwarded). However, as we have also seen, engagement with international networks may result in a narrowing or constraining of perspective, with the imposition of particular views and a required compliance with a predefined international discourse.

NGOs, researchers and pilot projects

Development aid – particularly, projects – has provided some opportunities, although the engagement of farmers in research, policy and planning is restricted. In all three countries, we encountered examples of projects set up variously by NGOs, researchers or sometimes government departments, where new approaches were being piloted that, in some respects, set a challenge to mainstream policy thinking and practice. Such projects also offered the opportunity for developing new relationships and networks – such as between an NGO pilot project and a government department – and therefore opportunities for moving from isolated field experiments to more fundamental change within bureaucracies followed. For example, in Zimbabwe, we refer to the coalition forged between an NGO, a bilateral aid project and, initially, the provincial state department of extension (Agritex) (Chapter 6).

However, such experiences were highly variable, and questions regarding their influence and sustainability were inevitably raised. The degree to which they offered real challenges to policy processes and opened up spaces for wider engagement depended upon the nature of the knowledge networks underpinning them, conditioned, in turn, by political, personal and funding connections. Some NGO projects, far from offering an alternative, served only to buttress and reinforce existing discourses and practices through the deployment of funding, external expertise and international connections. Thus, for example, the NGO SG2000 in Ethiopia promoted a particular type of seed-fertilizer package as the solution to food security problems in the country, bolstering the long-established Green Revolution policy narrative, and associated scientific and administrative practices of the Ministry of Agriculture (Chapter 4).

Such initiatives, located in pilot-project experiences, have had variable degrees of impact on the policy process. The SG2000 pilot in Ethiopia was clearly spectacularly influential, with the model acting as the basis for up-scaling a national extension effort backed by the president. As Chapter 4 documents, the network established both within Ethiopia and outside was impressive, including a former US president, a Nobel laureate, the president of the country, the World Bank, key multinational commercial concerns, and a range of highly respected scientists and others. The directive-based technocratic approach that was advocated fitted neatly with long-established Ethiopian policy styles, and therefore was easily incorporated within the existing bureaucratic and administrative machinery. The Zimbabwe agricultural extension story also involved building a strong network, but was more tentative and incremental; nonetheless, it was, for a period, successful. The network was built over time, first in one district, then in a province, then nationally. Involvement of key government officials early on allowed for wider ownership of ideas and experiences. International legitimation through publications, exchange visits and so on brought prestige and so authority both to the projects and to those government staff associated with them. This gradually built confidence in the approach and trust in the network, resulting, ultimately, in policy shifts that created a funded institutionalized space within government for the extension and expansion of the pilot work. Other examples, however, although widely appreciated – and the site of numerous visits and the subject of endless seminar presentations – remain isolated islands of experimentation without generating such broader impacts.

Decentralization, the local state and planning

Many individuals have argued that opportunities for participation can, potentially, be created through ongoing processes of democratic decentralization. In different ways, as discussed elsewhere, such processes are happening in each of the three case study countries. But the consequences on the ground are very different, with different implications for citizen engagement in policy processes. In Ethiopia, as already discussed, the political system remains characterized by a high degree of centralization, despite granting variable regional autonomy. In Mali, decentralization processes are only just beginning following local elections. Here, there are clearly some prospects for both fiscal and political decentralization, although the mechanics of this remain unclear and will, no doubt, vary across the country. In Zimbabwe, decentralization has had limited effectiveness due to the lack of revenue of local government authorities. Now, the shift in the political centres of power has reduced the capacity and authority of local elected officials even further.

In all countries, central line ministries remain key, and donor funding can shift patterns of resource transfer significantly, often disrupting any potential for engagement at the local government level. Thus, across the three countries, the prospects for effective democratic decentralization – where local decisions are taken through local representative bodies – appear limited. Yet, despite these limitations, the creation of district and local councils, and the establishment of democratic representative processes at the local level, have created a new layer of representatives. This has had the effect of potentially building capacity for engagement in policy. However, from our analysis of experiences in Ethiopia, Mali and Zimbabwe, this potential was not yet realized. For example, councils in Zimbabwe are necessarily more concerned with beer-hall revenue collection than with substantial policy engagements. Widespread disillusionment with local elected authorities is also evident through the lack of participation in elections, with people surmising that spaces for change and opportunities for engagement at this level are very limited.

Despite the emergence of multiparty systems, policy distinctions between parties on issues such as agriculture and environment are often difficult to discern, and the political landscape is more influenced by ethnic allegiances, patronage relations and historical ties. Thus, for example, the Ethiopian People's Revolutionary Democratic Front (EPRDF) and its regional incarnations essentially exist to support the Tigrayan political power base in Addis Ababa. The ruling party in Zimbabwe, ZANU–PF, is predominantly a Shona party, albeit with complex subdivisions and internal contests. In Mali, Bambara politics are also important. The establishment of power has involved, in all cases, the striking of coalitions with potential dissenters (often across ethnic boundaries), resulting in often entrenched patrimonial political systems with little room for open debate and discussion. Where challenges have arisen, as in the case of Zimbabwe from the MDC, for example, these have been met with sometimes violent tactics of repression and silencing.

The case study chapters have all traced examples of government-led consultation exercises of various sorts. In Ethiopia, we looked at the National Conservation Strategy (NCS) led by the Environmental Protection Agency (EPA). In Mali, we examined the SFI and the National Environmental Action Planning (NEAP) process. And in Zimbabwe, we highlighted the processes surrounding the development of the Environmental Management Bill and District Environmental Action Planning (DEAP). All adopted the rhetoric of participation as the rationale for the approach, often promoting the idea that gaining access to local knowledge and farmers' views was central to more effective policy development. All, therefore, bought into the current vogue rhetoric, which puts listening to 'the voices of the poor' as a central task.

State-led activities of this sort are often heavily influenced by donor conditions and, as we saw in a number of instances, are very much part of negotiating project ideas. In each of the examples, the initiative, the design and, in some cases, implementation were driven by donors. In each case, our analysis of the practice revealed some basic limitations. In particular, across the examples, the consultations were essentially used as a mechanism for confirming a pre-set agenda, lending legitimacy to existing plans and policies. Where examples went beyond consultation to planning, as in the cases of District Environmental Action Plans (DEAPs) in Zimbabwe, bureaucratic limitations on the capacity for truly responding to local agendas and priorities constrained the opportunities for participation.

Citizen action, the media and environmental campaigning

Outside of the formal political/governmental system, other avenues may exist for exercising voice and influence. In Mali, for example, the protests against the cotton bureaucracy, in the wake of producer price reductions, could be read in relation to broad discontent, with the binding of farmers to a particular style of production and resource management (Chapter 5). Whether such protests result in reflections on broader policy approaches in the cotton zone in the longer term is, as yet, unknown; but the reconfiguration of power relations may yet have wider ramifications. In Zimbabwe, direct protest against govern-ment policies has been limited until recent times by the effective control of the state and the suppression of protest. Instead, a tradition of informal, often hidden, resistance has dominated. While certain agricultural practices, for example, are notionally banned or not recommended, in practice farmers may find ways of doing what they want to do – creating their own policy in practice. Government agents in the field may be complicit with such resistance, or at least exercise discretion and turn a blind eye.

Where wider forms of protest have emerged, they have often been artic-ulated through informally organized movements, such as the following of the prophet Ambuya Juliana, discussed in Chapter 6. In recent years, other protests have emerged in response to the economic crisis and the ongoing 'land issue'. Again, the degree to which these protests are coordinated, and can be fed into a recasting of the policy debate, is unclear, given the highly charged political environment of the moment. In Ethiopia, we did not identify much space for any organized or even spontaneous protest against state-directed policy. While the possibilities of passive, hidden resistance exist and are frequently exercised, the opportunities for more organized action are limited, given the centralized and often repressive form of state authority.

In all three countries, an independent media has expanded in recent years. However, certainly in the case of Ethiopia and Zimbabwe, this has been closely monitored by the state, and the licence for critical commentary is severely restricted. Cases of intimidation and even arrest of journalists have been reported in both countries. But environment and land management issues are seen as non-political, by and large, by the media, and column inches can be filled without any sense that boundaries are being challenged.[1] Very often, environmental coverage is derived from the international media, fed by news agencies and wire services, and therefore strongly reflects the international discourse on such issues. Thus, narratives of desertification, the backwardness of smallholder farming and the need for technical intervention are reinforced by much media commentary. The degree to which this coverage generates public debate is, however, very limited. The discussion that is seen in comment columns and letters pages tends to replicate the standard lines of environmental discourse more generally, without allowing for a more searching examination of issues, and a questioning of policies and their framings. In the media, standard forms of expertise – scientists, bureaucrats and, particularly, international experts – are given prevalence, and the coverage of local issues and perspectives tends to be parochial and often highly stereotyped.

In each of the countries there is a limited number of groups, usually formed as NGOs, who are active in campaigning on environmental issues through media work, public education, interaction in schools and so on. Very often, they replicate a Northern model of an environmental NGO, with a support base that is largely urban and often elite, and is connected to international (or at least European/North American) environmental groups. Zimbabwe has, perhaps, the most developed environmental NGO sector of this sort, with groups such as Environment 2000 emerging firmly as campaign groups around issues of wildlife management and parks development. They often are seen to replicate a classic environmentalist line, and – although they have strong links with the environment ministries – are dismissed by others as elitist and out of touch, particularly with black rural concerns. The presence of such environmental campaign groups is more limited in Ethiopia and Mali, reflecting their different histories and urban/elite composition. For those that do exist, the focus is more on urban environmental improvement, environmental education and micro-project work at the local level. In all three countries, other advocacy groups are also present – with varying degrees of freedom to operate, depending upon the political setting. These are often focused around rights issues, including land and women's rights, and have developed distinct networks, with few alliances with those working on rural development.

Where scientific institutions fail to address the concerns of citizens, this may mean lay people developing their own forms of scientific research and pushing these into the policy arena through a variety of means (see Irwin, 1995). The mobilization of such citizen science movements requires that such groups create a legitimate, authoritative collective identity around the framing of particular crises or the representations of facts and reality (Epstein, 1991). This may require alliances being forged with accredited experts who, for a range of reasons, may have 'dissident' views. It also may require that advocacy groups develop their own specialized forms of expertise and promote alternative scientific standpoints. In so doing, such groups must learn to speak in those terms defined by scientific and policy debates (Fischer, 2000), while – at the same time – speaking for a defined group (of farmers, poor people, women, etc). Across our case studies, however, there was little evidence of such a mass-based movement around environmental issues. Where more classic environmentalist NGOs existed, they very much replicated their equivalents in Europe and North America and were seen by many to be dislocated from local contexts. Where coordinated action across sites – including across countries – has occurred around alternative conceptions of knowledge about soils management, this has arisen from networked project-based links. The Indigenous Soil and Water Conservation project (ISWC), coordinated by the Free University of Amsterdam and linking practitioners and researchers across eight African countries, could be argued to be an example of a research-based advocacy approach, where case study documentation of indigenous practices has combined with a range of training, media work and national and inter-national policy-lobbying (Reij and Waters-Bayer, 2001). But given its origins in a donor-funded project, the ascription of it as being a movement is perhaps inappropriate.

Across these examples –from international connections, to pilot projects, to governmental and political processes, to citizen action – there are a number of possibilities, though constrained in various ways, for policy influence through various forms of citizen engagement with the policy process, both formally and informally, from above and below. In the final sections of this chapter, we turn to a consideration of such possibilities by looking at the relationships between knowledge and expertise more specifically and the opportunities for participation that potentially arise.

KNOWLEDGE, EXPERTISE AND POLICY-MAKING

Prospects for citizen engagement in policy-making are often looked at in relation to, on the one hand, the degree of state responsiveness 'from above' and the opportunities for citizen voice 'from below', on the other. State responsiveness is seen to be linked to such factors as supportive political contexts; the absence of patronage-based 'clientalistic' relations; statutory arrangements conferring rights to citizens; progressive organizational cultures in the public sector; public administration procedures; incentives and sanc-tions; and consultation and monitoring mechanisms and procedures, among others. Citizen voice, in turn, results from the capacity of citizen groups to raise awareness and to mobilize; broad-based membership of groups who demon-strate the social and political legitimacy of claims; interactions with the media that allow positions to be put forward; the existence of forms of accountability based on citizen monitoring and auditing; and the ability to form alliances with key politicians and decision-makers in state bureaucracies (Goetz and Gaventa, 2001).

As the previous sections have shown, such factors are all critical to our understanding of how policies change. In this section we concentrate more specifically on how knowledges are negotiated among actors, and particularly between 'experts' and citizens in the policy process. Analyses that stop at assessing the more organizational, administrative and structural features of state responsiveness and citizen voice, we argue, fail to address the relations of knowledge and expertise, which, as we have seen, underpin much environmental policy-making. With this focus on knowledge, then, we ask how more participatory forms of policy process can challenge the technocratic forms of rationality of mainstream science-driven policy-making, both as discourse and practice.

Across the varied settings discussed in this book, different relations of knowledge and expertise can be discerned. In some instances, despite apparent opportunities for citizen participation, this is circumscribed by pre-set agendas. Experts with credentials – often reflecting international connections and donor funding – define the contours of engagement. Thus, while farmers may engage in participatory exercises in order to prioritize land management options – and a suite of apparently responsive mechanisms exist for planning, implementation, and monitoring and evaluation – the technical solutions are already pre-set as part of technology 'packages', tested and approved by specialized science. A wider debate on their design, or even the need for them in the first place, is not part of the process. In this technocratic mode, despite apparent concessions towards consultation, farmers are constructed as subjects of development planning, and participation is, as we have seen, routinized and instrumental. This, in turn, creates a particular set of knowledge relations, allowing only selective inclusion in the process of policy-making.

The embedded nature of elite expertise, despite the rhetoric of participation, is, as the case study chapters show, widespread. This is apparent in both NGO-inspired programmes and in the programmes of state and international organizations. For example, in Zimbabwe, the DEAPs capture elements of an idealized decentralized planning process. Yet, partly through the methodology of the process and partly due to bureaucratic location and funding mechanisms, they allow only certain delimited forms of participation. Similarly, in Ethiopia, despite including participation in the label of the nation-wide Participatory Agricultural Demonstration and Extension Training System (PADETES), farmer engagement is highly circumscribed. Farmers participate in a predefined package programme, where their ability to question technical options is highly constrained, at least in the formal design of the programme. As already discussed, the degree to which decentralized local government or party politics allows for anything other than a deference to mainstream forms of expertise is also open to question. In many respects, as discussed above, much of the media commentary on environmental issues simply replicates dominant knowledge framings, allowing little or no space for alternative views to be articulated and debated.

Such 'top-down', 'expert-driven' development practice is opposed – particularly by certain NGOs – through populist arguments for 'bottom-up', 'indigenous' solutions. By putting forward an alternative form of expertise, based on what is claimed to be genuine and rooted, as well as local forms of knowledge and practice, such approaches challenge the mainstream scientific view. Whether the articulation of such perspectives has an effect on the mainstream practice of environmental management depends, of course, on the connections made, and the opportunities and spaces that exist for change in mainstream technical institutions. Shifts at the margins, at least, are observable in all three countries, largely through the mobilization of research–action projects with donor funding and pilot projects. Thus, in Mali, Dutch-funded work in Sikasso and Niono has developed participatory approaches to integrated soil fertility management (Chapter 5). In Ethiopia, the Farmers' Research Project in Wolayta has promoted farmer-based trials and surveys of indigenous knowledge (Chapter 4); while in Zimbabwe, links between projects have encouraged farmer-based participatory extension and research in Masvingo province (Chapter 6). These have had varying success in opening up conventional technical institutions to new ways of operating. They have achieved this by providing new sets of incentives to government officers, often very constrained by resources, and new reward systems and forms of credibility and authority that are frequently enhanced by the links NGO projects have with international organizations.

Yet, such a stance, which counter-poses an idealized and often romanticized indigenous knowledge with scientific knowledge, is open to question on a number of counts. By focusing the debate at the level of discussions about what is technically correct, such approaches often ignore rather more fundamental questions of how knowledge is created and controlled. Just as technocratic science creates the categories of 'backward', 'unscientific', 'ignorant' farmers and farming practices in order to justify the intervention of formal scientific expertise, advocates of so-called indigenous knowledge-based approaches, at their most extreme, will reify and glorify the categories of 'rural', 'local' and 'indigenous'. The result is that such approaches deny the possibilities of negotiation and deliberation of knowledge, and set up an advocacy position that relies on a new, but equally problematic, form of elite expertise.

A potentially more radical – although, on the face of it, more mundane – route has been to present a more basic methodological and epistemological challenge to conventional scientific diagnoses. By opening up the black box of scientific approaches to wider deliberation, this sort of enquiry is, in some respects, more challenging, as assumptions are exposed, uncertainties and indeterminacies are highlighted, and – in so doing – controversies are opened up. When this interacts with the policy process, this can be an explosive and unsettling mix. The deliberative approach emerges from a position that recognizes the contingency of different knowledge claims, and the uncertainties and indeterminacies inherent in much science-based knowledge for policy. It therefore places more emphasis on developing methods and institutions that promote communication and address policy issues through inclusive processes of argumentation.[2] These attempt to go beyond the contests of knowledge positions based on entrenched interest-group stances to effective deliberation and participation.

Fora for deliberation may be required within the scientific community, and in contexts where scientists interact with users. Some scientists, for example, are brave enough to go beyond the conventional frame and question the guiding assumptions of mainstream work. But such challenges may be frowned upon. For example, technical debates questioning phosphorous dynamics and recapitalization strategies (Chapter 3) have resulted in accusations of scientific dishonesty, selective publishing and censorship. But if a more reflective form of deliberation was permitted, alternative perspectives might be found.

Other debates, which are equally challenging, but on different themes, may emerge from interesting alliances between scientists and farmers in joint work in field settings. Farmer participatory research has become a catchall term for a multitude of practices, ranging from the allocation of a portion of a field, to agronomists' experiments, to fuller forms of collaboration. When more established collegial relations are struck up between farmers and scientists, new forms of experimentation may emerge and new methods of assessment may arise. With such different methodologies, the view of technology options and environmental risks may alter dramatically. For example, in Zimbabwe, farmers working with the government national research system's farming systems team have derived a programme of experimentation on soils management, and a range of assessment techniques based on adapted participatory appraisal approaches. By inviting other scientists, extensionists and farmers to their research field days, opportunities arise for sharing their experiments, derived both from their own understandings and insights and from those of scientists (Chapter 6).

In other instances, alliances between farmers and scientists may be required to gain legitimacy and authority for practices that previously were deemed unacceptable or even illegal. For example, again in Zimbabwe, university hydrologists and soil conservation engineers have worked closely with Zephaniah Phiri, a farmer from Zvishavane district in the dry south of the country, to provide scientific documentation of the efficacy of his notionally illegal wetland farming practices (Chapter 6).

PROSPECTS FOR PARTICIPATION

By asking different questions, initiating the search for solutions, exposing previously black-boxed uncertainties, and challenging received wisdoms, the technical basis of policy prescriptions can thus be opened to wider scrutiny and debate. The potential for such experiments in alternatives to flourish, and to take hold in policy discussions, depends, of course, on the highly contextualized politics of knowledge. As we have discussed at many points during this book, 'fact-building' for policy is less the result of a pure, rational quest for what is technically correct – this is, in any case, always partial and provisional – but more about the establishment of facts within networks. It is, therefore, the reach and influence of such networks and their stability in mainstream institutions, both nationally and internationally, that is key. Thus, the degree to which such alternative perspectives destabilize mainstream views depends, crucially, on relations of power and the degree to which alternatives can establish credibility and authority in the policy-making process.

Throughout this book, we have made the case that policy-making is complex, political and power-laden. We have argued that the science–policy relationship needs to be treated as a social and mutually shaping process. We have also argued that environmental policy-making needs to be seen as a discursive phenomenon, constructing reality and individuals as the subjects of policy in a variety of ways. In relation to particular policy processes, we have shown how policy approaches are influenced by dominant policy discourses and narratives, by powerful combinations of political interests, and by effective actor networks, which traverse national boundaries and link across conventional categories.

It is these dynamics, we argue, that – to answer the original question posed in Chapter 1– keep received wisdoms entrenched in policy. But we have also suggested that this should not lead to the pessimistic conclusion that policy processes inevitably end in an impasse; that nothing can change; and that alternative views are never heard and never have an influence. Each discourse, actor network or policy coalition involves institutional practices and inter-actions that are made up of the activities of individuals who are connected across a range of networks. It is at these multiple interfaces that there may be 'policy spaces' (Grindle and Thomas, 1991) or 'room for manoeuvre' (Clay and Schaffer, 1984) to promote alternative approaches to policy, galvanized by new forms of deliberative and participatory approach.[3] While, as we have discussed earlier in this chapter, these opportunities may be limited, they do exist and change does occur. A challenge for development, then, is to move from a nuanced, informed diagnosis of policy change processes, to encour-aging methods and mechanisms that foster more inclusion of previously marginalized voices.

Notes

CHAPTER 1

1   This is more the concern of a recent book looking at case studies in the same
    three countries (Scoones, ed, 2001; see, also, Scoones and Wolmer, 2002).

CHAPTER 2

1   For a selection of definitions of the term 'policy', see Walt (1994: 40–41);
    Parsons (1995: 13–16); Hill (1997: 6–7). For some useful reviews of policy
    process issues, see Lasswell (1956); Jenkins (1978); Lindblom (1980, 1990);
    Jordan (1981); Hogwood and Gunn (1984); Hill (1993, 1997); Parsons
    (1995); Hempel (1996); Healey (1997); John (1998).
2   See, for example, Apthorpe (1996); Apthorpe and Gasper (1996); Shore and
    Wright (1997) for literature in this vein.
3   See, for example, Lukes (1974); Bourdieu (1977); Foucault (1980), Latour
    (1986); Gledhill (1994) for different perspectives on the question of power.
4   For an introduction to policy analysis and policy research, see Weiss (1977,
    1992); Torgerson (1986).
5   J F Kennedy, for example, asserted: 'Most of us are conditioned to have a
    political viewpoint. Republican or Democratic – liberal, conservative,
    moderate. The fact. . . is that most of the problems. . . we now face are
    technical problems, are administrative problems' (Kennedy, 1963, quoted
    in Fischer, 1993b).
6   Fischer (1993a) documents the sponsorship of right-wing think tanks
    during the late 1970s and early 1980s and argues that they contributed
    substantially to the Reagan 'revolution', giving credibility to the interests
    of particular elite groups. It is possible, then, to see the growth of pro-
    fessional policy expertise as reflecting the growth of a market for ideas, a
    claim that undermines the professed objectivity of policy analysis (see,
    also, Smith, 1991).
7   See the debate between advocates of representative democracy and part-
    icipatory democracy (Pateman, 1970; Dahl, 1971, 1989; Barber, 1984;
    Morrissey, 1996).
8   For an early statement of the social constructivist position, see Berger and
    Luckmann (1972).

9   For an introduction to the science studies literature, see Knorr-Cetina (1981); Callon et al (1986); Woolgar (1988); Pickering (1992); Jasanoff et al (1995); Irwin, (1995); Gieryn (1995); Barnes et al, (1996); Jasanoff and Wynne (1997).

10   Actor-network theory, initially propounded by Callon and Latour (1981), argues that knowledge involves the enrolment of human (actors) and non-humans (actants) into networks contingent for their stability upon each actor and actant adhering to its role in the network. Such a 'symmetrical view' breaks down the Kantian 'great divide' between nature and society, and sees practice as the occurrence of nature and society being continuously made and remade (Callon and Latour, 1992). The 'extended symmetry' of the actor-network theory approach, however, has been criticized as leading to unnecessarily prosaic accounts that lack the political effect of more conventional sociology of scientific knowledge approaches (Collins and Yearley, 1992). See, also, Callon (1986b); Law (1986); Latour (1986, 1987, 1988, 1993); Murdoch and Clark (1994); Murdoch (1997).

11   For an account of the origins of the concept of experiment and the importance of 'witnessing', see Shapin and Schaffer (1985). On extending experiments, see Latour's account of the 'pasteurization of France' (1988).

12   Marxists, too, have made the case for policy being related to diverging interests in society – in this case, the struggle between different economic classes (see McLennan, 1989). Most commentators view Marxism as essentially a society-centred approach to policy change. The state is seen as reflecting the interests of the dominant class, or as another arena for class struggle. Later Marxist accounts (see the Miliband, 1969, and Poulantzas, 1973, debate) looked again at the role of the state and argued that the state may, on occasions, behave independently of specific class interests.

13   Groups are perhaps less clearly institutionalized in new social movements, making this phenomenon rather different from pluralism, but the point that the motor of change lies in society is similar.

14   Skocpol (1985: 13) also argues on the basis of her work on US New Deal agricultural policies that certain ministries may be powerful even when the state in aggregate is 'weak'.

15   Dryzek (1990) presents the Weberian model as the dominant approach to the social organization of policy and labels it instrumentally rationalist.

16   See Long (1992: 33–34) for an actor-oriented critique of linear models of policy: 'There is no straight line from policy to outcomes.' Long also notes that it is not only governments and development agencies who have policies, but also local groups who have 'programmes of development'.

17   See, also, writings within the 'new institutionalism' school in political science that emphasize the importance of institutional political contexts for policy outcomes (March and Olsen, 1984; for reviews, see Jordan, 1990a; John, 1998).

18 The management and organizations' literature also reflects on such issues. See, for example, Cohen et al (1980); Handy (1976); Crosby (1996), among many others.

19 See, for example, the following authors on advocacy coalitions: Sabatier (1988, 1998); Sabatier and Jenkins-Smith (1993); on policy networks and policy communities: Jordan and Richardson (1987); Jordan (1990b); Knoke (1990); Kenis and Schneider (1991); Marin and Mayntz (1991); Atkinson and Coleman (1992); Marsh and Rhodes (1992); Rhodes and Marsh (1992); Smith (1993); Dowding (1995); Rhodes (1997); on discourse coalitions: Hajer (1995).

20 This is, perhaps, particularly the case in settings where the legacies of colonial rule on policy, politics and the operation of the state are evident.

21 For further discussion, see Goldstein and Keohane (1993); Haas et al (1993); Vogler (1996).

22 Skocpol (1985) also makes the point in relation to state autonomy that it can be international actor-network linkages which enable states to receive information and to support and enable them to make policy independent of societal interests.

23 The following is an example of this. Stanley Prusiner, the Nobel Prize winning 'discoverer' of the prion protein responsible for BSE, was denied funding to study similar processes in sheep. Until the network of funding, and the peer and political support it entails has been established, there can be no research and, more importantly, no facts, no new knowledge and no incremental shift in social order (*The Guardian*, 11 June 1998).

24 An alternative definition is: 'A discourse is a shared way of apprehending the world. Embedded in language, it enables those who subscribe to it to interpret bits of information and put them together into coherent stories or accounts. Each discourse rests on assumptions, judgements and contentions that provide the basic terms for analysis, debates, agreements and disagreements' (Dryzek, 1997: 8).

25 See Roe (1995) and Leach and Mearns (eds) (1996) for case studies.

CHAPTER 3

1 By January 2003, 185 countries had ratified or were in the process of ratifying the convention. The governing body for the convention is the Conference of the Parties, where all governments who have ratified the convention are represented. Under the terms of the convention, each country is committed to designing and implementing a national action programme. While the convention is a global process and instrument, it has concentrated on Africa and is widely seen to have come into existence out of a concern for Africa, and also as a complement to the other conventions that were perceived by some as 'Northern' concerns. For more details, see www.unccd.int/main.

2 While it is true that the SFI is only an African initiative, it can still be thought of as a global problem because it was created by players within the global arena, and because it has a global 'spin': African soils are a global problem. It is also very similar to other land degradation activities, such as the Convention to Combat Desertification, which are concerned with several continents.

3 IFPRI does not in itself have 'a line' as a senior researcher in the institute commented to us. However, the key publications associated with the institute, such as the *2020 Vision Initiative* and the *World Food Prospects Report*, have provided intellectual support for a food gap perspective.

4 For other perspectives on the food gap, see Lipton (1999); Wiggins (1995); Dyson (1996).

5 Bilateral donors, the World Bank and the United Nations have agreed international development targets through the Development Assistance Committee of the Organization for Economic Cooperation and Development (OECD). These include the aim of reducing the number of people in extreme poverty by half by 2015, and, for the environment, ensuring the implementation of a national strategy for sustainable development by 2005, as well as a reduction in rates of loss of environmental resources by 2015. For more information, see www.oecd.org/dac/Indicators/htm.

6 Sasakawa Global 2000 currently operates in 11 African countries and seeks an African Green Revolution based on demonstration and transfer of packages of improved varieties and fertilizer. For more information, see www.energyhouse.com/sasakawa.htm and *Feeding the Future*, the magazine of the Sasakawa Africa Association.

7 See www.worldwatch.org.

8 Other important statements in a similar vein from this period include 'Blueprint for Survival' (*The Ecologist*, 1972) and *Population Bomb* (Ehrlich, 1968).

9 Scherr and Yadav argue: 'If accelerated erosion continues unabated, yield reductions by the year 2020 may be 16.5 per cent for the Continent and 14.5 per cent for sub-Saharan Africa' (Scherr and Yadav, 1997). For a statement of the seriousness of global environmental problems, see the *Global Environmental Outlook* produced by UNEP (UNEP, 2000).

10 Cleaver's 'nexus' ideas were particularly influential around the period when the SFI was getting off the ground. They are cited, for example, in the first paragraph of the important article by Sanchez et al (1997: 2) and in the key initial soil-fertility concept note produced by the World Bank (1996: 3).

11 The article is 'Soil Fertility Initiative: the *sine qua non* for boosting productivity', located at www.icrisat.org/text/news/soil_fertility_initiative (visited January 2001).

12 The argument is also made by Sanchez: 'per capita food production will continue to decrease unless soil fertility is effectively addressed' (Sanchez et al, 1997: 3). See, also, Pinstrup-Andersen et al (1999: 25); Oram (1995); Donovan and Casey (1998).

13 Comment recorded at the SFI Recapitalization Workshop in Lomé, 1997; www.ifdc.org/SoilFert.htm, visited June, 2000.
14 www.ifdc.org.
15 See, for example, World Bank (1996: 3); IFA (1998); Borlaug and Dowswell (1995). See, also, Bumb and Baanante (1996a, 1996b).
16 For statements of this position, see Borlaug and Dowswell (1995); IFA (1998); Quiñones et al (1997).
17 Different organizations tend to emphasize the importance of external inputs to differing degrees. Some, such as the IFDC and Sasakawa Global 2000, are strong advocates of inorganic fertilizers, while others, such as the Association for Better Land Husbandry, emphasize an organic approach. These days, most situate themselves within an 'integrated nutrient management' approach. This apparent consensus, though, hides some varied interpretations. That there are distinctly different interpretations of what the SFI entails was made clear by a manager in the FAO: 'Many interpret the SFI as fertilizer alone. . . but blanket application of fertilizer is not recapitalization.'
18 Sanchez et al (1997: 4) go on to argue that 'Africa is now losing 4.4 million [tonnes of nitrogen], 0.5 million [tonnes of phosphorus] and 3 million [tonnes of potassium] every year from its cultivated land. These rates are several times higher than Africa's annual fertilizer consumption, excluding South Africa – 0.8 million [tonnes of nitrogen], 0.26 million [tonnes of phosphorus] and 0.2 million [tonnes of potassium] [FAO, 1995]'.
19 See, also, UNEP's *Global Environmental Outlook*. 'An estimated 500 million hectares of agricultural land [in Africa] have been affected by soil degradation since about 1950, including as much as 65 per cent of agricultural land' (UNEP, 2000): www.unep.org/geo2000/english/0053.htm (visited February 2001).
20 Smaling himself claims: 'The average NPK balances for Africa were -22, -2.5 and -15 kg ha per year respectively. . . the implication of the figure is that, on average, Africa must supply 22 kg ha per year to balance the ledger, leading to a decline of the N stocks' (Smaling et al, 1997: 50). A more recent nutrient balance study has been carried out by Henao and Baanante for IFDC (1999). The figures they produce are found in the widely circulated IFPRI *World Food Prospects* report: 'About 86 per cent of the countries in Africa show negative balances of nutrients greater than 30 kilogrammes of NPK per hectare per year' (Pinstrup-Andersen et al, 1999: 25).
21 See, for example, the key technical paper for the SFI produced by De Alwis (1996: 3, 5).
22 A nutrient budget is a balance of five nutrient input and five nutrient output functions. The input functions are mineral fertilizers, organic inputs, atmospheric deposition, biological nitrogen fixation and sedimentation. The output functions are harvested products, crop residue removal, solute leaching, gaseous losses and run-off and erosion.

23   The degree of uncertainty and necessary 'black-boxing' to create the nutrient balance data is discussed explicitly by Smaling et al (1997: 49): 'The amount of data available to calculate the five inputs and the five outputs varied largely between and within countries. As a consequence, much available detail had to be dropped and discrete ratings developed for variables that normally represent a continuum. Quantitative inform-ation on atmospheric deposition, leaching and gaseous losses was very scarce. Instead of going by educated guesses, transfer functions were built. . . in which nutrient flow is explained by parameters that are easy to measure.'

24   Various other studies or projects exist offering aggregated information on land status for large areas. The Land Quality Indicators project, for example, funded by UNEP and the World Bank (Pieri et al, 1995), presents data on the pressures and the state of land at sub-continental scales – for example, semi-humid or dry areas of Africa.

25   For further discussion of the limitations of nutrient budget studies, see also Budelman and Defoer (2000), Scoones and Toulmin (1999) and Scoones (2001).

26   Take, for example, the nutrient budget figures quoted above. They appear again in the concept note for the SFI. They have changed slightly and this time they are unacknowledged. The impression might be given to an observer that these are World Bank figures: '700kg of nitrogen, 100kg of phosphorus and 450kg of potassium per ha are claimed to have been exported from over 100 million ha of cultivated land in sub-Saharan Africa over 30 years, resulting in "soil mining" over wide areas, with large negative nutrient balances the consequence' (World Bank, 1996: 3).

27   See Scoones and Toulmin (1999) and Scoones (2001) for further discussion of these.

28   Sanchez et al (1997: 11) continue: 'The above-defined nutrient capital stocks as discrete pools fit well with economic concepts. Nutrient fluxes during the growing period are synonymous [with] service flows in economics. Such fluxes subtract from the nutrient capital and are thus analogous to the concept of depreciation.'

29   The scientific advisory committee model is a key example, where experts are called in to offer advice on specific issues, or to 'do the science' and offer accredited knowledge about any given subject.

30   For example, the *Bulletin of the Soil Science Society of America* publication by Sanchez et al (1997), following a key meeting in Indianapolis in 1996. Another example is the 16th World Congress in Montpellier, where the idea for a soils convention emerged.

31   For example, SoilFertNet is coordinated by the International Maize and Wheat Improvement Center (CIMMYT) in Harare and involves research scientists from Zimbabwe and Malawi, with, until recently, support from a senior soil scientist seconded from a UK university.

32   See Penning de Vries and Djitèye (1982) for the scientific overview of the project, and Breman and Uithol (1984) for a summary with publicity materials.

33 Robert Blake's 'open letter' of 8 May 1995 is reproduced, in part, in *Fertilizers and Agriculture*, November 1995 (IFA, 1995).

34 Wolfensohn's reply (13 October 1995) is reproduced in full in *Fertilizers and Agriculture*, March 1996 (IFA, 1996).

35 Interestingly, slightly different emphases are placed by different actors on different networks and, correspondingly, on who did the key bits of enrolling. This can be seen to some extent – as we will discuss in the next section – as different organizations claiming ownership.

36 The contingency of these boundaries, and the social nature of the way boundaries are constructed between science and society, are discussed in Gieryn (1995). See, also, Shackley and Wynne (1996); van der Sluijs et al (1998); and Jasanoff (1996).

37 This is not to deny that there are not individuals with a high degree of conviction and commitment in any of these organizations.

38 IFDC (1996); www.ifdc.org.

39 The IFA is one of the seven founding organizations represented in the glossy publicity material for the Soil Fertility Initiative. The IFA magazine *Fertilizers and Agriculture* also publicized the important correspondence between Robert Blake and James Wolfensohn (November 1995 and March 1996 issues); see notes 33 and 34.

40 See www.icraf.org; presentation of ICRAF's work on soil fertility can be found at www.cgiar.org/icraf/inform/CorpReport.htm (visited February 2001).

41 See www.fao.org; for an organizational analysis of FAO in relation to forestry, see Brechin (1997).

42 The fertilizer section became the Plant Nutrition Service, and this service has recently been merged with the Land Management Service.

43 The integrated plant nutrition line coming from the IFA may, of course, be judged by some to be just so much 'greenwash' – attempting to appear balanced, moderate and environmentally friendly to diffuse potential criticisms of the fertilizer lobby.

44 The Dutch fertilizer industry, for example, funded the publication of a key collection of articles on soil fertility in Africa: van Reuler and Prins (eds, 1993) *The Role of Plant Nutrients for Sustainable Food Crop Production in Sub-Saharan Africa*. The volume contains articles by key Dutch soil scientists – Smaling, van der Pol and Janssen. An Ethiopian diplomat writes in the forward: 'therefore, I welcome the initiative taken by the Dutch fertilizer industry to invite independent research institutes to examine the relationship between plant nutrients, food production and the environment and to determine the place of fertilizer in sustainable agriculture in Africa'.

45 The UK Department for International Development (DFID) and the Swedish International Development Cooperation Agency (SIDA), for example, have sustainable agriculture strategies, both of which have been informed by consultancies by the International Institute for Environment and Development (IIED), based in London. Dutch research institutes,

such as ILEIA (the Information Centre for Low External Input Agriculture) and ETC, have also played key roles in advocating sustainable agriculture and participatory technology development to donors.

46   An example is Daniel Benor, founder of the highly controversial World Bank training and visit (T&V) agricultural extension approach. As one official commented: 'An anti-Benor faction in the Bank want to link SFI and farmer field schools. . . but everyone in the Bank is still looking over their shoulders at Benor, and new, adapted forms of T&V.'

47   There are 'anchors' at the cross-over points in the matrix; but, again, these lack mechanisms for the horizontal to routinely imprint on the vertical.

48   Brechin (1997) explains that for any bank, volume of lending and turnover, alongside loan performance, are key yardsticks for evaluation. This is important, of course, because the World Bank has to maintain the confidence of the international financial community.

49   The World Bank has, however, begun to recruit more sociologists and anthropologists in recent years – though the numbers are still small relative to economists, and they tend not to be task managers. However, according to Chambers, economists outnumber other social scientists by maybe 50 to 1 (Chambers 1997: 49–50). A basic organizational chart of the World Bank is available at www.worldbank.org/about/organization/orgcharts (visited February, 2001).

50   A report by one task manager notes that in-country staff have not always been enthusiastic about the SFI: 'The field staff shows little, if any, interest in helping with the initiative because it has no related staff week allocations, and also because the [World] Bank's management has not sufficiently stressed the importance of the initiative to field staff.'

51   A researcher outside the World Bank echoed the argument that the loans structure of the Bank biases it towards 'straightforward' investments: 'The SFI pointed towards the setting up of soil management units within national governments – an institutional measure which requires different processes, but not the type of thing that country economists are particularly interested in.'

52   A World Bank task manager notes in his report: 'In countries such as Burkina Faso and Senegal, governments already have a strategy for dealing with the soil fertility issue and are not inclined to make any change. Funding sources for implementing the strategy already exist. . . FAO assistance for drafting action plans, although politely accepted, is not being effectively used' (Prudencio, 1998: 5).

53   We have suggested a number of reasons for the unravelling of the Soil Fertility Initiative. To these might be added another – namely, that if there is a development industry, this industry needs new products, as everything has a shelf life. When we began this research, soil fertility stood at the apex of both the food and environment debate, and as such looked to become a major policy issue. Now, this appears less the case than before, and there are new priorities. At the time of writing, biotechnology and water are the key themes. Interestingly, both the environmental

188 UNDERSTANDING ENVIRONMENTAL POLICY PROCESSES

degradation and food gap narratives we noted earlier are articulated as powerfully as ever in the attention-grabbing parts of policy documents; but now they are lined up to generate enthusiasm for new causes. Of course, this can all be analysed as an in-built need to go on generating new ideas to keep everyone busy: researchers, project managers and consultants. But it also reminds us that there are always universes of actor networks beyond the one with which we are immediately concerned. So, there are water or biotechnology policy entrepreneurs and actor networks in the same way that there are webs of key protagonists in the soil fertility field.

54   New experiments in this area are emerging, known as deliberative inclusionary processes, or DIPs. These make use of new institutional mechanisms, such as citizens' juries, consensus conferences and electronic polling. For a review of the literature on DIPs, see Bloomfield et al (1998), Holmes and Scoones (2000) and Munton (2003).

CHAPTER 4

1   See, for instance, Clapham (1988); Andargarchew Tiruneh (1993); Ottaway (1990); and Young (1997).
2   See Donham and James (1986). Bahru Zewde defines 'southern Ethiopia' as 'a convenient category embracing those states and peoples which did not directly engage in, or were peripheral to, the imperial politics of Gondar' (1991: 16). Menelik's feat, he asserts, was to unify these areas and the northern highlands. Others, however, would frame the period of expansion between the 1880s and 1900 as the incorporation of these areas into the Ethiopian empire (Donham 1986: 3).
3   For example, the Peasant Agricultural Development Exchange Programme (PADEP), funded by donors such as the World Bank and the European Union (EU) since 1988, divided the country into eight agro-ecological zones and aimed to devise appropriate research and extension packages for each. In the end, however, resources were heavily concentrated on high-potential areas (Belshaw, 1990; World Bank, 1990: 76; see, also, Worku, 2000).
4   The Food Security Strategy was published in 1996. For a critique of the national strategy, see Masefield (1997). The strategy's approach is: 'To increase food production as quickly as possible, the strategy focuses on the diffusion of simple technology packages, off the shelf, within smallholder areas of reliable rainfall' (FDRE, 1996: 16).
5   The National Seed Systems Development Project and the National Fertilizer Project (World Bank, 1995, 1995a)
6   The SCRP is 'the national body with the mandate to conduct research in Ethiopia with reference to land degradation' and is supported by the Group for Environment and Development at the University of Bern (www.giub.unibe.ch/cde/projects/scrp.html, visited 5 January 2000). Set

up in 1981, the SCRP had seven research sites; it closed down in 1997 and
was reviewed in 1998.

7   The Ethiopian Highlands Reclamation Study began in 1983. It was funded
by the World Bank and was carried out by a team of international and
Ethiopian specialists under the FAO. Although the full report was never
formally ratified – in common with many other strategy documents – a
summary document was published in 1986.

8   For example, the NCS report quotes Hurni (1988) in stating that 'average
soil loss from arable land is appropriately six times the rate of soil
formation. The net result is a reduction in soil depth by 4mm per year'
(Wood and Ståhl 1989: 14). For a more recent reiteration of the Hurni
figures, see Bekele and Holden (1999)

9   Clapham, as early as 1988, comments on the 'extraordinary persistence. . .
of myths that can clearly be shown to be fictitious' and cites the deforestation statistic as an example (1988: xi). More recently, a decline from
40 per cent to 1 per cent forest cover in 40 years has been cited by Al Gore
in his high-profile *Earth in the Balance* as an example of a particularly
serious environmental catastrophe (Gore, 1992, cited in McCann, 1998: 1).
An environmental consultant commented to us on the persistence of
particular problematic data supporting entrenched policy narratives:
'The problem was that the 40 per cent figure gets into circulation and
becomes god-given; it gets recycled and accepted. People say it's so and
so it must be. I did the same in my work. I used certain data and recon-
firmed biases. But you have to build constituencies, how else do you get
things on the agenda? You have a job to do in a short time. . . I had to finish
a report in seven weeks. You accept things at face value and then you
question later. You tell a story and you want it to be coherent; if things fit
into it you accept them more easily. You get the figures to go along with
the story to create attention. The EHRS, for example, got information into
circulation and became a document to study.'

10   The NCS is, in fact, jointly housed by the EPA and the Ministry of Economic Development and Cooperation (MEDAC).

11   TGE (1994); FDRE (1996); FDRE (1997); FDRE (2000).

12   One of the aims of PADETES is 'to ensure the rehabilitation and conservation of the natural resource base of agriculture', principally through
biological measures such as 'use of legumes, crop rotations, alley-
cropping and use of compost' (*Ethiopian Herald*, 11 April 1998: 6, 8).

13   It should be noted that participation was also emphasized as essential to
environmental rehabilitation within the NCS Phase One report (Wood
and Ståhl, 1989: 61).

14   While PADETES is the result of a 'critical assessment of past extension
systems, including the recent effort by Sasakawa Global 2000', it is also
presented as a fusion of T&V and SG2000 approaches (*Ethiopian Herald*,
11 April 1998: 8).

15   For example, a number of donors have been supporting training in
participatory land-use planning activities, including the United Nations

Development Programme (UNDP), the UK Department for International Development (DFID) and others, with links to both government and NGOs. Various consultants and NGO players have also been active in training in participatory techniques, including participatory rural appraisal (PRA).

16 Consultations carried out as part of the PRSP (Poverty Reduction Strategy Paper) process, for example, did include significant engagement by civil society groups, it seems. Discussions included critiques of the government extension policy, but land tenure was again off limits, according to some informants.

17 See Young (1996, 1997: 203–204).

18 According to Young (1997: 204): 'Civil society in Tigray exerts few controls on the TPLF government and administration, and *gim gima*, even with its dangers of manipulation and human rights abuse, is a powerful weapon of control and accountability in the hands of the people.'

19 *Baitos* are assemblies at zonal *(zoba)*, *woreda* and Peasant Association *(tabia)* levels.

CHAPTER 5

1 The average for low-income countries is US$410 (World Bank, 2001a, b).

2 There has been an ongoing tussle between the World Bank/IMF and the Malian government/CMDT regarding the future of the parastatal. The pressure to move towards privatization has been intense. By mid-2002, the IMF reported the failure to meet the structural conditions on the reform of the cotton sector, and indicates that 'the new timetable for the liberalization of the cotton sector should be strictly adhered to' (IMF, 2002). Whether the release of very substantial debt relief under the HIPC initiative (totalling US$870 million) or continuation of the US$572 million World Bank project funding is reliant on this is not completely clear, but inevitably bound up in the ongoing negotiations.

3 'Successful' can be debated, of course; the 1997 presidential and political elections, for example, were boycotted by opposition parties. Nevertheless, Serra argues these problems notwithstanding, 'the democratic space has widened considerably in this decade' (Serra, 1999: 13). In 2002 a new president was elected – Amadou Toumani Toure – after an election contest involving 24 candidates.

4 The CMDT operates over an area of 15,105 square kilometres, involving 170,690 farm families in 5400 villages. It employees 2300 people full time and a further 2800 seasonally (CMDT, 1999).

5 This quote is from Bingen, citing the International Cotton Advisory Committee (1998: 271).

6 Production levels have been highly variable in recent years. A record harvest of 571,000 tonnes was recorded in 2001–2002, but this followed a low of 243,000 tonnes in the previous year. This was due to boycotts by

farmers in the cotton zone. This 47 per cent decline in output on the previous year resulted in a major jolt to the economy, with GDP growth dipping to only 1.5 per cent. In 2001–2002 a number of Malian and European banks intervened to offer credit to CMDT and prices were increased with a corresponding increase in production. In 2002–2003, prospects again look poor following bad rainfall, and exporting difficulties due to conflict in neighbouring Ivory Coast. This comes on top of low international prices for export cotton, depressed significantly by subsidies paid to US farmers.

7   Following the West African Franc (CFA) devaluation of 1994, the CMDT was flush with increased profits. Over 1 billion CFA are reported to be paid to the national exchequer annually.

8   The earliest French experiments with cotton date back to the 1860s in Senegal (Becker, 1994).

9   Colonial Minister Sarraut's policy of *mise en valeur* dates from 1922.

10 Gakou et al (1996) note: 'The introduction of improved varieties, pest and disease control, and fertilizers has raised the national cotton yield from 135kg/ha lint to over 1 tonne/ha in Mali' (1996: 57).

11 Mali-Sud is an area of 96,000 square kilometres bordering Guinea, the Côte d'Ivoire and Burkina Faso. It contains 4000 villages, 200,000 farms and 2 million inhabitants. Annual rainfall in the region varies between 600 and 1300mm (van Campen, 1991).

12 Penning de Vries and Djitèye (1982); Breman and Uithol (1984); Breman and Sissoko (1998); Breman and de Wit, (1983).

13 The website is www.info.usaid.gov/environment/greencom/mali.htm, visited February 2002.

14 Pyenson writes of the *'mission civilatrice'*, in which the display of scientific expertise is essentially a demonstration of the supremacy of French culture (Pyenson, 1993). However, colonial science had more immediately practical aspects: cartography and categorization of resources useful for export. See, for example, *Les Végétaux Utiles de l'Afrique Tropicale'* (Chevalier, 1905).

15 Others we spoke to argued that the creation of the Ministry of Environment meant it was technically possible to cut the size of the MDRE – in response to World Bank pressure – while moving jobs elsewhere.

16 A total of 16 projects were prioritized around four areas. Projects included Rational Management of Lands and Environmental Monitoring in the CMDT Area, with French, Swiss and Dutch funding. Other donors who pledged funds included the European Union (EU), the World Bank, USAID, the GTZ the African Development Bank (ADB), including technical support from the FAO and the United Nations Sudano-Sahelian Office (UNSO) (Ministère de l'Environnement, 1999).

17 One informant commented: 'PNT is not fertilizer, just mud, farmers said in the beginning, just "terre". They don't believe it is fertilizer. If they are convinced that application is the problem because of the wind, the solution is to mix with compost. By extension we can solve this.'

18 In actual fact, according to SFI steering committee representatives, the proposed fertilizer factory was likely to be a public–private partnership with a 20 per cent government investment, the rest coming from Hydrochem, and a fifth each from the ON, CMDT and Senchim.

19 For a World Bank critique of the CMDT as a managed monopoly, and an argument for greater competitiveness see, World Bank (2000).

20 In September 2000 Mali qualified for US$870 million HIPC debt relief (www.worldbank.org/hipc/country-cases/mali/mali.html, visited October 2001).

21 There are now estimated to be over 4000 NGOs and related organizations in Mali (UNDP, 1999).

22 Examples include village resource management projects supported by SOS-Sahel, which balance supporting agricultural production alongside negotiating environmental management and schemes for livelihood diversification; citizen action approaches by the NGO CARE, using literacy training and 'conscientization' approaches in order to empower communities to seek effective access to resources and make demands of government departments and other government officials; and initiatives by the League of the Cooperatives of the United States of America (CLUSA: an NGO training organization), concentrating on facilitating entrepreneurial activities by community groups with an emphasis on claiming rights that exist on paper but have not hitherto existed in practice.

CHAPTER 6

1 This chapter is based on research up to 2000. Since then, the political and economic conditions in Zimbabwe have changed dramtically. While we have attempted to offer some commentary on these new contexts, a full understanding of the implications for the policy process requires further investigation.

2 See Chapter 2 for a discussion of the term 'technocracy'.

3 See commentaries by, for example, Phimister (1986); Cliffe (1988); Alexander (1993); McGregor (1995); and Ranger (1999); among others, with the Zimbabwe debate reflecting a wider Africa-wide picture (see Anderson and Grove, eds, 1987).

4 A range of colonial legislation was premised on this assumption. For example, the Natural Resource Act (1941) and the Native Land Husbandry Act (1951) both sought to reverse the perceived negative environmental impacts of African farming practice through regulation and land-use planning.

5 'Communal areas' are the former reserves or Tribal Trust Lands to which indigenous populations were removed following land appropriation by the white settler class in Zimbabwe at the beginning of the 20th century. These areas are generally less fertile and with lower rainfall. These areas

contrast with the highly productive and formerly white-owned commercial farming areas.

6   For example, the publicity rhetoric of the Trees for Life campaign of the
NGO Environment 2000 is an example: 'Approximately 75,000 to 100,000
hectares or about 1.5 per cent of the total woodland area of Zimbabwe
disappears annually.' Equally, the popular outputs from the government
agencies have a similar tone (see Chenje et al, 1998), as do both academic
commentaries (for example, Moyo et al, 1991; Davies and Rattsø, 1996)
and donor agency documents (see DFID, 1999).

7   SARDC (1999), Communicating the Environment Programme, Factsheet
No 1

8   The Environmental Management Bill (now an Act of Parliament) has been
an attempt by the Ministry of Environment, Mines and Tourism to bring
together the range of environmental legislation in one framework (IUCN,
2000; Government of Zimbabwe, 2002).

9   Does this 'technocracy' always operate with specific interests in mind as
the Hill quote suggests? The answer is, at times, 'yes' and, at times, 'not
necessarily'. Particular policy directions may reflect routine practices and
norms. See Chapter 2 for an extended discussion of this point.

10 From the 1930s, the chief instructor for native agriculture, Emory Alvord,
was a key exponent of a view that traditional agricultural practices and
patterns of natural resource management needed root and branch reform
or modernization (see Alvord, 1948).

11 Popularization of scientific information through bureaucratic practice is
also key. Elwell's soil conservation manual, for example, used in training
Agritex staff, was cited by one informant as crucial to disseminating soil
loss information.

12 This characterization of the actor networks associated with soil fertility
work in Zimbabwe may be changing. In particular, through the activities
of the SoilFertNet supported by Rockefeller, a greater interest in more
applied developmental issues is being sparked, including a concern with
policy questions. It may be that, in the future, new, more solid and
extensive networks around this theme may start to form.

13 However, one feature of the current political crisis is more confrontational
NGO and state relations.

14 Today it is political connections and party affiliation that matters. New
social, economic and political networks are emerging, recasting the way
politics and policy is carried out in the country. For a rural case example,
see Chaumba et al (2002b).

15 A PRA network exists in Zimbabwe, hosted by the NGO SAFIRE
(Southern Alliance for Indigenous Resources). This has a resource
centre, newsletter and regular meetings. The network includes government officials, academic researchers, NGO workers and independent
consultants.

16 Work by the University of Zimbabwe (in collaboration with Lough-
borough University in the UK), trials by the Department of Research and

Specialist Services at Makoholi research station, the Zvishavane Water Projects demonstration work in Runde communal area, along with a range of meetings convened by international organizations such as the IUCN and the International Institute for Environment and Development (IIED), have together raised questions about the appropriateness of current regulations.

17   The Contill project was aimed at looking at conservation tillage options for dryland farming areas. It was established with GTZ funding at Makoholi Research Station near Masvingo, and involved a range of field-based activities in nearby communal areas, including Chivi, Zaka and Gutu. Its early phases were largely station based and technically oriented, although in its latter phases it became much more engaged in on-farm participatory research work (Chuma and Hagmann, 1997).

18   A large amount of work has recently been undertaken looking at local soil management practices under the auspices of the Indigenous Soil and Water Conservation Programme, coordinated by the Institute of Environmental Studies, UZ, and Intermediate Technology Development Group (ITDG), Zimbabwe (Reij and Waters-Bayer, eds, 2001). Other work by the Farming Systems Research Unit of the DRSS, Ministry of Agriculture and various university and NGO research groups has complemented this (Scoones, ed, 2001).

19   Under the Natural Resources Act, significant power is vested in the Department of Natural Resources, and particularly the Natural Resources Board, to both restrict and enable activities. In practice, this flexibility is rarely applied, given the complex procedures required to gain exemptions from statutory regulations. The board is appointed by the president and oversees the work of the department. It is made up of a range of people who are deemed to be knowledgeable and interested in resource management and environmental issues. Currently, no communal farmer is represented on the board, and it is composed mainly of academics, commercial farmers and NGO representatives.

20   The Intermediate Technology Development Group (ITDG) project in Ward 22 of Chivi district became a key demonstration site for alternative extension approaches during the 1990s (Murwira et al, 2000). Similar experiments were ongoing under the auspices of the Integrated Rural Development Programme (IRDEP) in Gutu. The Contill programme operated in Gutu and Chivi, and provided an important link between personnel and experiences. When the IRDEP programme wound down field activities, its strategic location in Masvingo and close connections with Agritex were key in gaining access to the department.

21   Consultants employed in preparing the Agricultural Services and Management Programme supported the idea of a major organizational review as a starting point for the programme. However, given the withdrawal of donor support in recent times, the programme has not progressed further. Instead, the major restructuring has gone ahead without the resources to support the new integrated research–extension agency AREX. The

consequence has been that the organizational change efforts within the former Agritex, and notably the development of a new participatory approach to extension, have not progressed. In 2000–2001, many extension workers were diverted to pegging the new resettlement areas and the emerging extension practice in the communal areas was abandoned. In the last few years, many staff have left or been transferred, and the networks established in the late 1990s, at the centre of the policy change process, have dissipated. The incapacity of the government organizations has been compounded by a lack of activity by NGOs, also resulting from lack of donor funds. The result has been a major loss of momentum.

22   The Land Tenure Commission reported in 1994 under the chairmanship of Professor Mandivamba Rukuni. During the period since then, few of the recommendations have been taken up. The political implications of the findings became increasingly apparent and the government ignored them. In an interview in Haramata, Rukuni commented: 'It is now exactly four years after we submitted the report. When I meet top politicians, including the president, they are still highly complimentary of the report we produced, but behind that it's a different story. The bureaucracy is generally sceptical. . . they say, it's nice on paper but difficult to implement' (Haramata, 1999: 7).

CHAPTER 7

1   In Zimbabwe, of course, this is now much less the case than during the past.

2   Such an approach comes under a variety of labels: the argumentative turn (Fischer and Forester, 1993; Dunn, 1993; Lapintie, 1998); collaborative planning (Healey, 1992, 1997, 1998); discursive democracy (Dryzek, 1990, 1993); deliberative democracy (Bohman and Rehg, 1997); institutional reflexivity (Mol, 1996); and frame reflection (Schön and Rein, 1994).

3   So-called deliberative inclusionary processes (DIPs), such as consensus conferences, citizens' juries, stakeholder platforms, citizens panels, scenario workshops and so on, are emerging in different parts of the world, therefore, as mechanisms aimed at opening the policy process to greater citizen participation and contributing to the redemocratization of the 'hard infrastructure' of government (Bloomfield et al, 1998; Holmes and Scoones, 2000; Munton, 2003).

References

Adam, B, Beck, U and Van Loon, J (eds) (2000) *The Risk Society and Beyond: Critical Issues for Social Theory*, London: Sage

Agcaoili, M and Rosegrant, M (1994) 'World Supply and Demand Projections for Cereals, 2020', *2020 Brief 2*, August, Washington, DC, IFPRI

Agarwal, A (1995) 'Dismantling the divide between indigenous and scientific knowledge', *Development and Change*, vol 26: 413–439

Agarwal, A and Sivaramakrishnan, K (2000) *Agrarian Environments: Resources, Representations and Rule in India*, Durham: Duke University Press

Alemayehu Konde, Data Dea, Ejigu Jonfa, Eyasu Elias, Fanuel Folla and Ian Scoones (2001) 'Creating Gardens: The Dynamics of Soil Fertility Management in Wolayta, Southern Ethiopia', in Scoones, I (ed), *Dynamics and Diversity. Soil Fertility and Farming Livelihoods in Africa* London: Earthscan

Alexander, J (1993) *The State, Agrarian Policy and Rural Politics in Zimbabwe: Case Studies of Insiza and Chimanimani Districts, 1940–1990*, DPhil thesis, Oxford: University of Oxford

Alexander, J (2000) 'Technical Development and the Human Factor: sciences of development in Rhodesia's Native Affairs Department' in Dubow, S (ed) *Science and Society in Southern Africa*, Manchester: Manchester University Press

Alexander, J and McGregor, J (2000) 'Wildlife and politics: CAMPFIRE in Zimbabwe', *Development and Change*, vol 31(3): 605–627

Alexander, J and McGregor, J (2001) 'Elections, land and the politics of opposition in Matabeleland', *Journal of Agrarian Change*, vol 1(4): 510–533

Allison, G (1971) *Essence of Decision*, Boston: Little, Brown

Alvord, E (1930) 'Agricultural demonstration work in native reserves', *Department of Native Affairs, Occasional Paper*, no 3, National Archives, Harare

Alvord, E (1948) 'The progress of native agriculture in Southern Rhodesia', *The New Rhodesia*, vol 15: 18–19

Andargachew Tiruneh (1993) *The Ethiopian Revolution, 1974–1987: A Transformation From an Aristocratic to a Totalitarian Autocracy*, Cambridge: Cambridge University Press

Anderson, D and Grove, R (1987) *Conservation in Africa: People, Policies and Practice*, Cambridge: Cambridge University Press

Appadurai, A (1996) 'Global Ethnoscapes: Notes and Queries for a Transnational Anthropology' in Appadurai A (ed) *Modernity at Large: Cultural Dimensions of Globalisation*, Minneapolis: University of Minnesota Press

Apthorpe, R (1996) 'Reading Development Policy and Policy Analysis: on framing, naming, numbering and coding', in Apthorpe R and Gasper D (eds) *Arguing Development Policy: Frames and Discourses*, London: Frank Cass

Apthorpe, R and Gasper, D (eds) (1996) *Arguing Development Policy: Frames and Discourses*, London: Frank Cass

Atkinson, M and Coleman, W (1992) 'Policy networks, policy communities and the problems of governance', *Governance*, vol 5: 154–180

Aubréville, A (1956) 'Un grand savant, un fervent ami de nos forêts tropicales, un grand colonial français n'est plus: Auguste Chevalier', *Revue Bois et Forêts des Tropiques*, no 48, Juillet–Aout: 3–6

Badiane, O and Delgado, C (eds) (1995) 'A 2020 Vision for Food, Agriculture and the Environment in Sub-Saharan Africa', *Food, Agriculture and the Environment Discussion Paper 4*, Washington, DC: IFPRI

Bahru Zewde (1991) *A History of Modern Ethiopia. 1855–1974*, London: James Currey

Barber, B (1984) *Strong Democracy: Participatory Politics for a New Age*, Berkeley: University of California Press

Barnes, B (1974) *Scientific Knowledge and Sociological Theory*, London: Routledge and Kegan Paul

Barnes, B (1977) *Interests and the Growth of Knowledge*, London: Routledge and Kegan Paul

Barnes, B, Bloor, D and Henry, J (1996) *Scientific Knowledge: A Sociological Analysis*, London: Athlone Press

Barnes, B and Shapin S (eds) (1979) *Natural Order: Historical Studies in Scientific Culture*, London: Sage

Bayart, J-F (1993) *The State in Africa: The Politics of the Belly*, London: Longman

Beck, U (1992) *Risk Society: Towards a New Modernity*, London: Sage

Beck, U (1995) *Ecological Politics in An Age of Risk*, Cambridge: Polity

Beck, U (1997) *The Reinvention of Politics: Rethinking Modernity in the Global Social Order*, Cambridge: Polity

Becker, L (1994) 'An early experiment in the reorganization of agricultural production in the French Sudan (Mali), 1920–40', *Africa*, vol 64(3): 373–390

Behnke, R, Scoones, I and Kerven, C (1993) *Range Ecology at Disequilibrium: New Models of Natural Variability and Pastoral Adaptation in African Savannas*, London: ODI

Beinart, W (1989) 'Introduction: the politics of colonial conservation', *Journal of Southern African Studies*, vol 15: 143–162

Bekele Shiferaw and Holden, S (1999) 'Soil erosion and smallholders' conservation decisions in the highlands of Ethiopia', *World Development*, vol 27(4): 739–752

Belshaw, D (1990) 'Food strategy and development planning in Ethiopia', *IDS Bulletin*, vol 21: 3

Benjaminsen, T (1997) 'Natural resource management, paradigm shifts and the decentralisation reform in Mali', *Human Ecology*, vol 25(1): 121–143

Berger, P and Luckmann, T (1972) *The Social Construction of Reality*, New York: Doubleday

Berhane Hailu (1995) *An Overview of Agricultural Development of Tigray: Existing Efforts and Future Prospects*, Mekelle: Tigray Bureau of Agriculture and Natural Resources Development, November

Bingen, J (1996) 'Leaders, leadership and democratization in West Africa: observations from the cotton farmers movement in Mali', *Agriculture and Human Values*, vol 13(2): 24–32

Bingen, J (1998) 'Cotton, democracy and development in Mali', *Journal of Modern African Studies*, vol 36(2): 265–285

Blake, R (1995) Letter on behalf of the Committee on Agricultural Sustainability for Developing Countries to James Wolfensohn, President of the World Bank, 2 October

Bloomfield, D, Collins, K, Fry, C and Munton, R (1998) 'Deliberative and Inclusionary Processes: Their Contributions to Environmental Governance', Paper presented at the first ESRC DIPs in Environmental Decision-Making Seminar, 17 December 1998

Bloor, D (1976) *Knowledge and Social Imagery*, Chicago: University of Chicago Press

Bohman, J and Rehg, W (1997) *Deliberative Democracy: Essays on Reason and Politics*, Cambridge, Massachusetts: MIT Press

Bourdieu, P (1977) *Outline of a Theory of Practice*, Cambridge: Cambridge University Press

Bojö, J and Cassells, D (1995) *Land Degradation and Rehabilitation in Ethiopia: A Re-Assessment*, AFTES Working Paper No 17, Washington, DC: World Bank

Bonneuil, C (1991) *Les Savants pour l'Empire. La Structuration de Recherches Scientifiques Coloniales au Temps de la Mise en Valeur des Colonies Françaises, 1917–45*, Paris: Orstom

Bonneuil, C and Kleiche, M (1993) *Du Jardin d'Essais Colonial à la Station Experiméntal 1880–1930: Eléments pour une Histoire du CIRAD*, Paris: CIRAD

Borlaug, N and Dowswell, C (1995) 'Mobilising science and technology to get agriculture moving in Africa', *Development Policy Review*, vol 13(2): 115–129

Bratton, M (1987a) 'Drought, food and the social organization of small farmers in Zimbabwe' in Glantz, M (ed) *Drought and Hunger in Africa: Denying Famine a Future*, Cambridge: Cambridge University Press, 213–244

Bratton, M (1987b) 'The comrades and the countryside: the politics of agricultural policy in Zimbabwe', *World Politics*, vol 49: 174–202

Braybrooke, D and Lindblom, C (1963) *A Strategy of Decision: Policy Evaluation as a Social Process*, New York: Glencoe Free Press

Brechin, S (1997) *Planting Trees in the Developing World: a Sociology of International Organizations*, Baltimore: Johns Hopkins University Press

Breman, H. and de Wit, C (1983) 'Rangeland productivity and exploitation in the Sahel', *Science*, vol 221: 1341–1347

Breman, H and Sissoko, K (eds) (1998) *L'Intensification Agricole au Sahel*, Paris: Karthala

Breman, H and Uithol, P (eds) (1984) *The Primary Production in the Sahel Project – a Bird's Eye View: Publicising the Results of a Study on the Sahelian Rangelands to Improve the Planning for Development Programmes for Animal Husbandry and the Management of Natural Resources*, Wageningen: Centre for Agrobiological Research

Brinkerhoff, D (1995) 'African state–society linkages in transition: the case of forestry policy in Mali', *Canadian Journal of Development Studies*, vol XVI(2): 201–228

Brock, K and Coulibaly, N (1999) 'Sustainable Rural Livelihoods in Mali', *IDS Research Report*, no 35, Brighton: Institute of Development Studies

Budelman, A (ed) (1996) *Agricultural R and D at the Crossroads: Merging Systems Research and Social Actor Approaches*, Amsterdam: KIT

Budelman, A and Defoer, T (2000) 'Not by nutrients alone: an alternative interpretation of the Soil Fertility Initiative', mimeo, Amsterdam: KIT

Bumb, B and Baanante, C (1996a) 'World Trends in Fertilizer Use and Projections to 2020', *IFPRI 2020 Vision Brief*, no 38, October

Bumb, B and Baanante, C (1996b) 'Policies to Promote Environmentally Sustainable Fertilizer Use and Supply to 2020', *IFPRI 2020 Vision Brief*, no 40, October

Burchell, G, Gordon, C and Miller, P (eds) (1991) *The Foucault Effect: Studies in Governmentality*, Hemel Hempstead: Harvester Wheatsheaf

Buresh, R, Smithson, P and Hellums, D (1997) 'Building soil phosphorus capital in Africa' in Buresh, R, Sanchez, P and Calhoun, F (eds) *Replenishing Soil Fertility in Africa*, SSSA Special Publication, no 51, Madison: Soil Science Society of America

Burgess, J (1990) 'The production and consumption of environmental meanings in the mass media: a research agenda for the 1990s', *Transactions of the Institute of British Geographers*, NS, vol 15: 139–161

Burgess, J and Harrison, C (1998) 'Environmental communication and the cultural politics of environmental citizenship', *Environment and Planning, A*, vol 30: 1445–1460

Callon, M (1986a) 'The Sociology of an Actor-Network: The Case of the Electric Vehicle' in Callon, M, Law, J and Rip, A (eds) *Mapping the Dynamics of Science and Technology: Sociology of Science in the Real World*, Houndmills: Macmillan

Callon, M (1986b) 'Some Elements of a Sociology of Translation: Domestication of the Scallops and the Fishermen of St Brieuc Bay' in Law, J (ed) *Power, Action and Belief: A New Sociology of Knowledge?* London: Routledge

Callon, M and Latour, B (1981) 'Unscrewing the Big Leviathan: How actors macro-structure reality and how sociologists help them to do so' in Knorr-Cetina, K and Cicourel, A (eds) *Advances in Social Theory and Methodology: Toward an Integration of Macro and Micro Sociologies*, Boston: Routledge and Kegan Paul, 277–303

Callon, M and Latour, B (1992) 'Don't Throw the Baby Out with the Bath School! A Reply to Collins and Yearley' in Pickering, A (ed) *Science as Practice and Culture*, Chicago: University of Chicago Press

Callon, M, Law, J and Rip, A (eds) (1986) *Mapping the Dynamics of Science and Technology: Sociology of Science in the Real World*, Houndmills: Macmillan

Catinot, R (1982) 'Hommage des forestiers tropicaux à André Aubréville', *Revues Bois et Forêts Tropiques*, no 195: 3–6

CGIAR (1995) *Renewal of the CGIAR: Sustainable Agriculture for Food Security in Developing Countries*, Washington: CGIAR

Chambers, R (1997) *Whose Reality Counts?* London: ITDG

Chaumba, J, Wolmer, W and Scoones, I (2002a) 'From jambanja to planning: the reassertion of technocracy in land reform in southeastern Zimbabwe?', *Sustainable Livelihoods in Southern Africa Research Paper Series*, no 2, Brighton: IDS

Chaumba, J, Wolmer, W and Scoones, I (2002b) 'New politics, new livelihoods: changes in the Zimbabwean lowveld since the farm occupations of 2000', *Sustainable Livelihoods in Southern Africa Research Paper Series*, no 3 Brighton: IDS

Chenje, M, Sola, L and Paleczny, D (eds) (1998) *The State of Zimbabwe's Environment*, Harare: MMET

Chevalier, A (1905) *Les Végétaux Utiles de l'Afrique Tropicale, T I*, Paris: Challamel

Chevenix-Trench, P, Moussa dit Martin, T and Woodhouse, P (1997) 'Land, water and local governance in Mali: rice production and resource use in the Sourou Valley, Bankass Cercle', *Working Paper* no 6, Institute for Development Policy and Management, University of Manchester

Chibudu, C, Chiota, G, Kandiros, E, Mavedzenge, B, Mombeshora, B, Mudhara, M, Murimbarimba, F, Nasasara, A and Scoones, I (2001) 'Soils, Livelihoods and Agricultural Change: The Management of Soil fertility in the Communal Lands of Zimbabwe', in Scoones, I (ed) *Dynamics and Diversity. Soil Fertility and Farming Livelihoods in Africa*, London: Earthscan

Chuma, E and Hagmann, J (1997) 'Conservation tillage for semi-arid Zimbabwe: results and experiences from on station and on-farm interactive innovation in Masvingo', *Zimbabwe Science News*, vol 31: 34–41

Clapham, C (1988) *Transformation and Continuity in Revolutionary Ethiopia*, Cambridge: Cambridge University Press

Clay, E and Schaffer, B (eds) (1984) *Room for Manoeuvre: An Exploration of Public Policy in Agriculture and Rural Development*, London: Heinemann

Clay, E and Schaffer, B (1984a) 'Conclusion: self-awareness in policy practice' in Clay, E and Schaffer, B (eds) *Room for Manoeuvre: An Exploration of Public Policy in Agriculture and Rural Development*, London: Heinemann

Cleaver, K and Schreiber, G (1995) *Reversing the Spiral: The Population, Agriculture and Environment Nexus in Sub-Saharan Africa*, Washington, DC: World Bank

Cliffe, L (1988) 'The conservation issue in Zimbabwe', *Review of African Political Economy*, vol 42: 48–56

CMDT (1996) *Utilization du Phosphate Naturel du Telemsi: Note Technique; Propositions pour la Vulgarisation du PNT*, November, Service Gestion des Terroirs, Division Défense et Restauration des Sols, Bamako: CMDT

CMDT (1998) *Info Coton: la Communion du Peuple Malien pour Célébrer le Coton*, La Revue Trimestrielle de la CMDT, Division Communication à la Direction Générale, Bamako: CMDT

CMDT (1999) *Maintien du potential productif dans les terroirs des zones cotonnières de la CMDT*, Direction Technique du Développement Rural, Service Gestion des Terroirs, Avril, Bamako: CMDT

CMDT (undated) *Le Coton: une Chance pour le Mali*, Bamako: CMDT

Cobb, R and Elder, C (1972) *Participation in American Politics: the Dynamics of Agenda-Building*, Baltimore, Maryland: Johns Hopkins University Press

Cohen, A, Fink, S, Gadon, H and Willits, R (1980) *Effective Behaviour in Organizations*, Homewood: Irwin

Cohen, J (1987) *Integrated Rural Development: The Ethiopian Experience and the Debate*, Uppsala: The Scandinavian Institute of African Studies

Collins, H and Yearley, S (1992) 'Epistemological Chicken' in Pickering, A (ed) *Science as Practice and Culture*, Chicago: University of Chicago Press

Collion, M-H (1995) 'On building a partnership between farmers and researchers', *ODI Agricultural Administration Network Paper*, no 54, January

Comaroff, J and Comoroff, J (1991) *Of Revelation and Revolution: Christianity, Colonialism, and Consciousness in South Africa*, Chicago: The University of Chicago Press

Comaroff, J and Comaroff, J (eds) (1999) *Civil Society and the Political Imagination in Africa: Critical Perspectives*, Chicago: Chicago University Press

Constable, M and Belshaw, D (1985) *A Summary of Major Findings and Recommendations from the Ethiopian Highlands Reclamation Study*, Addis Ababa: Ministry of Agriculture, Addis Ababa, Land Use Planning and Regulatory Department/FAO

Corbeels, Abebe Shiferaw and Mituku Haile (2000) 'Farmers' knowledge of soil fertility and local management strategies in Tigray, Ethiopia', *Managing Africa's Soils*, no 10, London: IIED

Crosby, B (1996) 'Policy implementation: the organizational challenge', *World Development*, vol 24(9), pp1403–1415

Dahl, R (1961) *Who Governs? Democracy and Power in an American City*, New Haven, Connecticut: Yale University Press

Dahl, R (1971) *Polyarchy*, New Haven: Yale University Press

Darier, E (1996) 'Environmental governmentality: the case of Canada's Green Plan', *Environmental Politics*, vol 5: 585–606

Davies, R and Rattsø, J (1996) 'Growth, distribution and environment: macroeconomic issues in Zimbabwe', *World Development*, vol 24(2): 395–405

De Alwis, K (1996) 'Recapitalisation of Soil Productivity in sub-Saharan Africa', *FAO Technical Investment Centre Occasional Paper Series*, no 5, February

De Valk, P and Wekwete, K (eds) (1990) *Decentralising for Participatory Planning? Comparing the Experiences of Zimbabwe and other Anglophone Countries in Eastern and Southern Africa*, Avebury: Aldershot

Defoer, T and Budelman, A (2000) *Managing Soil Fertility: a Resource Guide for Participatory Learning and Action Research*, Amsterdam: KIT publications

Defoer, T, Kanté, S, Hilhorst, T and de Groot, H (1996) 'Towards more sustainable soil fertility management', *AgRen Network Paper*, no 63, London: ODI

Defoer, T, Kanté, S and Sanogo, J-L (1999a) 'Cotton farming in southern Mali, part 2', *Case Studies of Soil Fertility Management in Africa: Resource Guide for Participatory Learning and Action Research*, KIT: Amsterdam

Defoer, T, Budelman, A, Toulmin, C and Carter, J (1999b) *Soil Fertility Management in Africa: Resource Guide for Participatory Learning and Action Research, Part 1*, Amsterdam: KIT

Degnbol, T (1996) 'The terroir approach to natural resource management: panacea or phantom?' *IDS Working Paper No 2*, Roskilde University

Degnbol, T (1999) *State Bureaucracies under Pressure: A Study of the Interaction between Four Extension Agencies and Cotton-Producing Farmers in the Sikasso Region, Mali*, PhD thesis, International Development Studies, Roskilde University

Dejene, A (1990) 'The Evolution of Rural Development Policies' in Pausewang S, Cheru, F, Brune, S and Chole E (eds) *Ethiopia: Rural Development Options*, London: Zed Press

Dembélé, I, Kater, L, Koné, D, Koné, Y, Ly, B and Macinanke, A (2001) 'Seizing new opportunities: soil-fertility management and diverse livelihoods in Mali' in Scoones, I (ed) *Dynamics and Diversity: Soil Fertility and Farming Livelihoods in Africa*, London: Earthscan

Dessalegn Rahmato (1994) 'The Unquiet Countryside: the Collapse of "Socialism" and the Rural Agitation, 1990 and 1991' in Zegeye, A and Pausewang, S (eds) *Ethiopia in Change: Peasantry, Nationalism and Democracy*, London: British Academic Press

DFID (1999) *Zimbabwe: Country Strategy Paper*, London: Department for International Development

Dimier, V (undated) *French Colonial Policy of Black Peasants in West Africa in the 1930s*, mimeo

Dobuzinskis, L (1992) 'Modernist and postmodernist metaphors of the policy process: control and stability vs chaos and reflexive understanding', *Policy Sciences*, vol 25: 355–380

Donham, D (1986) 'Old Abyssinia and the New Ethiopian Empire: Themes in Social History' in Donham, D and James, W (eds) *The Southern Marches of Imperial Ethiopia*, Cambridge: Cambridge University Press

Donham D and James W (eds) (1986) *The Southern Marches of Imperial Ethiopia*, Cambridge: Cambridge University Press

Donovan, G and Casey, F (1998) 'Soil Fertility Management in sub-Saharan Africa', *World Bank Technical Paper*, no 408, Washington, DC: World Bank

Dowding, K (1995) 'Model or metaphor? A critical review of the policy network approach', *Political Studies*, vol 43: 136–158

Dreyfus, H and Rabinow, P (1982) *Michel Foucault: Beyond Structuralism and Hermeneutics*, Brighton: Harvester

Drinkwater, M (1989) 'Technical development and peasant impoverishment: Land use policy in Zimbabwe's Midland Province', *Journal of Southern African Studies*, vol 15(2): 287–305

Drinkwater, M (1991) *The State and Agrarian Change in Zimbabwe's Communal Areas*, London: MacMillan Press

Dror, Y (1964) 'Muddling through – "science" or inertia?' *Public Administration Review*, vol 24: 153–157

Dryzek, J (1990) *Discursive Democracy: Politics, Policy and Political Science*, Cambridge: Cambridge University Press

Dryzek, J (1993) 'Policy Analysis and Planning: From Science to Argument' in Fischer, F and Forester, J (eds) *The Argumentative Turn in Policy Analysis and Planning*, London: University College London Press

Dryzek, J (1997) *The Politics of the Earth: Environmental Discourses*, Oxford: Oxford University Press

Dunn, W (1993) 'Policy Reforms as Arguments' in Fischer, F and Forester, J (eds) *The Argumentative Turn in Policy Analysis and Planning*, London: University College London Press

Dyson, T (1996) *Population and Food: Global Trends and Future Prospects*, London: Routledge

Easton, D (1965) *A Framework for Political Analysis*, New Jersey: Prentice Hall

Eden, S (1996) 'Public participation in environmental policy: considering scientific, counter-scientific and non-scientific contributions', *Public Understanding of Science*, vol 5: 183–204

Ehrlich, P (1968) *Population Bomb*, New York: Ballantine

Elwell, H A (1974) *Soil Erosion Survey: The Condition of the Arable Land in the Farming Areas of Rhodesia*, Hatcliffe: Soil and Water Conservation

Elwell, H A (1983) 'The degrading soil and water resources of the Communal Areas', *The Zimbabwe Science News*, vol 17(9/10): 145–147

Elwell, H (1987) 'Problems that have led to soil loss with specific reference to the communal areas', Paper presented to the Natural Resources Board Workshop on Conservation Tillage, Institute of Agricultural Engineering, 19 June 1987

Elwell, H A and Stocking, M A (1988) 'Loss of soil nutrients by sheet erosion is a major hidden farming cost', *The Zimbabwe Science News*, vol 22(7/8): 79–82

ENDA/ZERO (1992) *The Case for Sustainable Development in Zimbabwe: Conceptual Problems, Conflicts and Contradictions*, Harare: ENDA-Zimbabwe and ZERO

Epstein, S (1991) 'Democratic science: AIDS activism and the contested construction of knowledge', *Socialist Review*, vol 21: 35–64

Escobar, A (1995) *Encountering Development: The Making and Unmaking of the Third World*, Princeton, New Jersey: Princeton University Press

Ethiopian Herald (1998) 'Agricultural Extension Intervention in Ethiopia', Saturday, 11 April

Etzioni, A (1967) 'Mixed-scanning: a "third" approach to decision-making', *Public Administration Review*, vol 27: 385–392

Eyasu Elias (1998) 'Is soil fertility declining? Perspectives on environmental change in southern Ethiopia', *Managing Africa's Soils*, no 2 London: IIED

Ezrahi, Y (1990) *The Descent of Icarus: Science and the Transformation of Contemporary Democracy*, Cambridge, Massachusetts: Harvard University Press

Fairhead, J and Leach, M (1996) *Misreading the African Landscape: Society and Ecology in a Forest-Savanna Mosaic*, Cambridge: Cambridge University Press

FAO (1986) *Ethiopian Highlands Reclamation Study*, Final Report, 2 volumes, Rome: FAO

FAO (1990) *Conservation and Rehabilitation of African Lands: An International Scheme*, Rome: FAO

FAO (1995) *FAO Fertilizer Yearbook 1994*, vol 44, Rome: FAO

FAO (1996) 'World Food Summit, Towards Universal Food Security: Draft of a Policy Statement and Plan of Action', Rome: FAO

FAO, ICRAF, IFDC, IFA, IFPRI, USAID and the World Bank, (1996) *Soil Fertility Initiative*, Document released at the World Food Summit, November, Muscle Shoals, Alabama: IFDC

FDRE (1996) *Food Security Strategy*, Addis Ababa: Federal Democratic Republic of Ethiopia

FDRE (1997) *Environmental Policy of Ethiopia*, Addis Ababa: Environmental Protection Authority in collaboration with the Ministry of Economic Development and Cooperation

FDRE (2000) *Regional Conservation Strategy, Southern Nations, Nationalities and Peoples' Region*, volumes I to IV, Awassa

Ferguson, J (1990) *The Anti-Politics Machine. 'Development', Depoliticization and Bureaucratic Power in Lesotho*, Cambridge: Cambridge University Press

Fischer, F (1990) *Technocracy and the Politics of Expertise*, Newbury Park, California: Sage Publications Inc

Fischer, F (1993a) 'Policy Discourse and the Politics of Washington Think Tanks' in Fischer, F and Forester, J (eds) *The Argumentative Turn in Policy Analysis and Planning*, London: University College London Press

Fischer, F (1993b) 'Citizen participation and the democratization of policy expertise', *Policy Sciences*, vol 26: 165–187

Fischer, F (1995) *Evaluating Public Policy*, Chicago: Nelson Hall

Fischer, F (2000) *Citizens, Experts and the Environment. The Politics of Local Knowledge*, Duke University Press: Durham and London

Fischer, F and Forester, J (eds) (1993) *The Argumentative Turn in Policy Analysis and Planning*, North Carolina and London: Duke University Press

Foucault, M (1980) *Power/Knowledge: Selected Interviews and Other Writings, 1972-77*, New York: Pantheon

Foucault, M (1991) 'Governmentality' in Burchell, G, Gordon, C and Miller, P (eds) *The Foucault Effect: Studies in Governmentality*, London: Harvester/Wheatsheaf

Funtowicz, S and Ravetz, J (1993) 'Science for the post-normal age', *Futures*, vol 25: 739–755

Gakou, A, Kébé, D and Traoré, A (1996) *Soil Management in Mali*, Sikasso: Ministère du Développement Rural et de l'Environnement, Institut d'Economie Rurale, Centre Regional de la Recherche Agronomique

Garbett, K (1963) 'The Land Husbandry Act of Southern Rhodesia' in Biebuyk, D (ed) *African Agrarian Systems*, Oxford: Oxford University Press, 185–202

Giddens, A (1984) *The Constitution of Society: An Outline of the Theory of Structuration*, Cambridge: Polity Press

Gieryn, T (1995) 'Boundaries of Science' in Jasanoff, S, Marple, G, Petersen, J and Pinch, T (eds) *Handbook of Science and Technology Studies*, Thousand Oaks: Sage

Giller, K, Gilbert, R, Mugwira, L, Muza, L, Patel, B and Waddington, S (1998) 'Practical approaches to soil organic matter management for smallholder maize production in southern Africa' in Waddington, S, Murwira, H, Kumwenda, J, Hikwa, D and Tagwira, F (eds) *Soil Fertility Research for Maize-Based Farming Systems in Malawi and Zimbabwe*, Proceedings of the SoiFertNet Results and Planning Workshop, 7–11 July 1997, Harare: SoilFertNet and CIMMYT-Zimbabwe, 139–153

Gledhill, J (1994) *Power and its Disguises: Anthropological Perspectives on Politics*, London: Pluto Press

Goetz, A-M and Gaventa, J (2001) 'Bringing citizen voice and client focus into service delivery', *IDS Working Paper*, vol 138, July, Brighton: IDS

Goldstein, J and Keohane, R (1993) *Ideas and Foreign Policy: Beliefs, Institutions and Political Change*, Ithaca: Cornell University Press

Government of Zimbabwe (2002) 'Environmental Management Bill', Harare: Government Printers

Grillo, R (1997) 'Discourses of Development: The View from Anthropology' in Stirrat, R and Grillo, R (eds) *Discourses of Development: Anthropological Perspectives*, Oxford: Berg Publishers

Grindle, M and Thomas, J (1991) *Public Choices and Policy Change*, Baltimore: Johns Hopkins University Press

Haas, P (1990) *Saving the Mediterranean*, New York: Columbia University Press

Haas, P (1992) 'Introduction: epistemic communities and international policy coordination', *International Organization*, vol 46: 1–36

Haas, P, Keohane, R and Levy, M (eds) (1993) *Institutions for the Earth: Sources of Effective International Environmental Protection*, Cambridge, Massachusetts: MIT Press

Habermas, J (1973) *Legitimation Crisis*, Boston: Beacon Press

Hagmann, J with Chuma, E, Murwira, K and Connolly, M (1999) 'Putting process into practice: operationalising participatory extension', *ODI, Agricultural Research and Extension Network Paper*, no 94, London: ODI

Hajer, M (1995) *The Politics of Environmental Discourse*, Oxford: Clarendon

Halperin, M (1971) *Bureaucratic Politics and Foreign Policy*, Washington DC: The Brookings Institution

Handy, C (1976) *Understanding Organizations*, Harmondsworth: Penguin

Hannigan, J (1995) *Environmental Sociology: A Social Constructionist Perspective*, London: Routledge

Haramata (1995) 'Decentralisation in Mali', *Bulletin of the Drylands: People, Policies and Programmes*, IIED Drylands Programme, no 27, London: IIED

Haramata (1999) 'Interview with Mandivamba Rukuni', *Bulletin of the Drylands: People, Policies and Programmes*, IIED Drylands Programme, no 35, London: IIED

Haramata (2000) 'Mali's cotton farmers go on strike', *Bulletin of the Drylands: People, Policies and Programmes*, IIED Drylands Programme, no 38, London: IIED

Haraway, D (1991) 'Situated Knowledges: The Science Question in Feminism and the Privilege of Partial Perspective' in Haraway, D (ed) *Simians, Cyborgs, and Women: The Reinvention of Nature*, London: Free Association Books

Harding, S (1991) *Whose Science? Whose Knowledge? Thinking from Women's Lives*, Buckingham: Open University Press

Healey, P (1992) 'Planning through debate: the communicative turn in planning theory', *Town Planning Review*, vol 63(2): 143–162

Healey, P (1997) *Collaborative Planning: Shaping Places in Fragmented Societies*, Basingstoke and London: Macmillan

Healey, P (1998) 'Collaborative planning in stakeholder society', *Town Planning Review*, vol 69(1): 1–21

Held, D (1996) *Models of Democracy*, Cambridge: Polity

Helmsing, A, Mutiza-Mangiza, N, Gasper, D, Brand, C and Wekwete, K (1991) *Limits to Decentralisation in Zimbabwe. Essays on the Decentralisation of Government and Planning in the 1980s*, The Hague: ISS

Hempel, L (1996) *Environmental Governance: The Global Challenge*, Washington DC: Island Press

Henao, J and Baanante, C (1999) 'Nutrient depletion in the agricultural soils of Africa', *IFPRI 2020 Vision Brief*, no 62, October

Herbst, J (1990) *State Politics in Zimbabwe*, Harare: University of Zimbabwe Press

Herbst, J (2000) *States and Power in Africa: Comparative Lessons in Authority and Control*, Princeton, New Jersey: Princeton University Press

Herweg, K (1993) 'Problems of Acceptance and Adaptation of Soil Conservation in Ethiopia' in Baum Witzenhausen E (ed) *Acceptance of Soil and Water Conservation: Strategies and Technologies*, Witzenhausen: Deutsche Institut für Tropische und Subtropische Landwirtschaft

Hikwa, D and Mukurumbira, L (1995) 'Highlights of previous, current and proposed soil fertility research by the Department of Research and Specialist Services (DRSS) in Zimbabwe' in Waddington, S R (ed) *Report on the First Meeting of the Network Working Group*, Soil Fertility Research Network for Maize-Based Farming Systems in Selected Countries of Southern Africa, The Rockefeller Foundation Southern Africa Agricultural Sciences Programme, Harare: Lilongwe, Malawi and CIMMYT Maize Programme, 21–33

Hilhorst, T and Coulibaly, A (1999) 'Elaborating a local convention for managing village woodlands in southern Mali', *IIED Issue Paper*, no 78, Drylands Programme, London: IIED

Hilhorst, T and Muchena, F (eds) (2000) *Nutrients on the Move: Soil Fertility Dynamics in African Farming Systems*, London: IIED

Hill, K (1994) 'Politicians, farmers and ecologists: commercial wildlife ranching and the politics of land in Zimbabwe', *Journal of African and Asian Studies*, vol 29(3-4): 226–247

Hill, M (ed) (1993) *The Policy Process: A Reader*, Hemel Hempstead: Harvester Wheatsheaf

Hill, M (1997) *The Policy Process in the Modern State*, London: Prentice Hall

Hjern, B and Porter, D (1981) 'Implementation structures: a new unit of administrative analysis', *Organization Studies*, vol 2: 211–227

Hoben, A (1996) 'The Cultural Construction of Environmental Policy: Paradigms and Politics in Ethiopia' in Leach, M and Mearns, R (eds) *The Lie of the Land: Challenging Received Wisdom on the African Environment*, Oxford: James Currey

Hogwood, B and Gunn, L (1984) *Policy Analysis for the Real World*, Oxford: Oxford University Press

Holling, C (1993) 'Investing in research for sustainability', *Ecological Applications*, vol 34: 552–555

Holmes, T and Scoones, I (2000) 'Participatory Environmental Policy Processes: experiences from North and South', *IDS Working Paper 113*, Brighton: IDS

Howard, J, Demeke, M, Kelly, V, Maredia, M and J Stepanek (1998) 'Can the momentum be sustained? An economic analysis of the Ministry of Agriculture/Sasakawa Global 2000's experiment with improved cereals technology in Ethiopia', *Michigan State University Staff Paper*, September: 18–25, East Lansing, Michigan

Hudson, N (1961) 'An introduction to the mechanics of soil erosion under conditions of sub-tropical rainfall', *Proceedings of the Transactions of the Rhodesia Scientific Association*, vol 49: 15–25

Hultin, J (1989) 'The Predicament of Peasants in Conservation-Based Development', *Pastoral Development Network Paper*, no 27c, London: ODI

Hurni, H (1986) *Soil Conservation Manual for Ethiopia*, Addis Ababa: Ministry of Agriculture

Hurni, H (1988) *Ecological Issues in the Creation of Famines in Ethiopia*, Berne: University of Berne

Ibrahim Mohammed and Tamene Terfa (2001) 'Maize technologies: experience of the Ministry of Agriculture', paper presented at the Second National Maize Workshop of Ethiopia, 12–16 November 2001, Ministry of Agriculture, Addis Ababa

IFA (1995) *Fertilizers and Agriculture*, Bulletin of the International Fertilizer Industry Association, November

IFA (1996) *Fertilizers and Agriculture*, Bulletin of the International Fertilizer Industry Association, March

IFA (1998) *The Fertilizer Industry, World Food Supplies and the Environment*, published in association with UNEP (Revision of 1986 *The Fertilizer Industry – The Key to World Food Supplies*), Paris: International Fertilizer Industry Association

IFDC (1996) 'Restoring and maintaining the productivity of West African soils: key to sustainable development', *Miscellaneous Fertilizer Studies*, no 14, Togo: IFDC Africa

IIED (1998) *Desk Study of Donor Assistance to the Sahel Region in the Natural Resources Sector with Particular Reference to Mali and Burkina Faso*, Report prepared for SIDA, IIED Drylands Programme, March

Imber, M (1996) 'The Environment and the United Nations' in Vogler, J and Imber, M (eds) *The Environment and International Relations*, London: Routledge, 138–154

IMF (2002) 'IMF completes fourth review of Mali's PGRF arrangement and approves request for waiver of performance criteria', *News Brief No 02/78*, Washington, DC: IMF

Irwin, A (1995) *Citizen Science: A Study of People, Expertise and Sustainable Development*, London: Routledge

Irwin, A and Wynne, B (1996) 'Introduction' in Irwin, A and Wynne, B (eds) *Misunderstanding Science? The Public Reconstruction of Science and Technology*, Cambridge: Cambridge University Press

IUCN (2000) *Proceedings of the Workshop on Environmental Policies that Support Natural Resources Management and Practices*, held at the Sheraton Hotel, Harare, 30 June 2000, Lue Mbizvo, C and Mariga, R (eds), Harare: IUCN-ROSA

Izac, A (1997) 'Ecological Economics of Investing in Natural Resource Capital in Africa' in Sanchez et al (eds) *Replenishing Soil Fertility in Africa*, SSSA Special Publication Number 51, Madison, Wisconsin: Soil Science Society of America, American Society of Agronomy

Jamison, A (1996) 'The Shaping of the Global Environmental Agenda: The Role of Non-Government Organizations' in Lash, S, Szerszynski, B and Wynne, B (eds) *Risk, Environment and Modernity, Towards a New Ecology*, London: Sage, 224–245

Jasanoff, S (1987) 'Contested boundaries in policy-relevant science', *Social Studies of Science*, vol 17: 195–230

Jasanoff, S (1990) *The Fifth Branch: Science Advisors as Policy-Makers*, Cambridge, Massachusetts: Harvard University Press

Jasanoff, S (1996) 'Beyond epistemology: relativism and engagement in the politics of science', *Social Studies of Science*, vol 26: 393–418

Jasanoff, S, Marple, G, Petersen, J and Pinch, T (eds) (1995) *The Handbook of Science and Technology Studies*, Thousand Oaks: Sage

Jasanoff, S and Wynne, B (1997) 'Science and Decision-making' in Rayner, S and Malone, E (eds) *Human Choice and Climate Change: An International Assessment, vol 1, The Societal Framework of Climate Change*, Columbus, Ohio: Battelle Press

Jeune Afrique Economie (1998) 'La filière cotonnière est la clé du développement du Mali', Interview with Drissa Keita, PDG de la CMDT, 1–14 June

Jenkins, W (1978) *Policy Analysis: A Political and Organizational Perspective*, London: Martin Robertson

John, P (1998) *Analysing Public Policy*, London: Pinter

Jordan, G (1981) 'Iron triangles, woolly corporatism, and elastic nets: images of the policy process', *Journal of Public Policy*, vol 1: 95–123

Jordan, G (1990a) 'Policy community realism versus "new" institutionalist ambiguity', *Political Studies*, vol 38: 470–484

Jordan, G (1990b) 'Sub-governments, policy communities, and networks: refilling the old boots', *Journal of Theoretical Politics*, vol 2: 318–319

Jordan, G and Richardson, J (1987) *British Politics and the Policy Process*, London: Unwin Hyman

Kaplan, T (1990) 'The narrative structure of policy analysis', *Journal of Policy Analysis and Management*, vol 5

Keeley, J and Scoones, I (1999) 'Understanding Environmental Policy Processes: a review', *IDS Working Paper*, no 89, Brighton: IDS

Keeley, J and Scoones, I (2000) 'Knowledge, power and politics: the environmental policy-making process in Ethiopia', *Journal of Modern African Studies* 38(1): 98–120

Keeley, J and Scoones, I (2000a) 'Environmental Policy-making in Zimbabwe: Discourses, Science and Politics', *IDS Working Paper*, no 116, Brighton: IDS

Keeley, J and Scoones, I (2000b) 'Global Science, Global Policy: local to global connections in the policy process surrounding soil management in Africa', *IDS Working Paper*, no 115, Brighton: IDS

Kenis, P and Schneider, V (1991) 'Policy Networks and Policy Analysis: Scrutinizing a New Analytical Toolbox' in Marin, B and Mayntz, R (eds) *Policy Networks: Empirical Evidence and Theoretical Considerations*, Frankfurt: Campus Verlag

Kifle, L, Setargew, D and Tewolde Berhan, G E (1998) 'Ethiopia: National Conservation Strategy' in Wood, A (ed) *Strategies for Sustainability*, London: Earthscan

Kingdon, J (1984) *Agendas, Alternatives and Public Choices*, Boston: Little, Brown

Knoke, D (1990) *Policy Networks: The Structural Perspective*, Cambridge: Cambridge University Press

Knorr-Cetina, K (1981) *The Manufacture of Knowledge: An Essay on the Constructivist and Contextual Nature of Science*, Oxford: Pergamon Press

Knorr-Cetina, K (1999) *Epistemic Cultures: How the Sciences Make Knowledge*, Cambridge, Massachusetts: Harvard University Press

Kumwenda, J D T, Waddington, S R, Snapp, S, Jones, B and Blackie, M (1995) 'Soil fertility management research for the smallholder maize-based cropping systems of Southern Africa: a review', *Network Research Working Paper*, Harare: CIMMYT

Lapintie, K (1998) 'Analysing and evaluating argumentation in planning', *Environment and Planning B: Planning and Design*, vol 25: 187–204

Lasswell, H (1956) *The Decision Process: Seven Categories of Functional Analysis*, College Park, Maryland: University of Maryland

Latour, B (1986) 'The Powers of Association' in Law, J (ed) *Power, Action, Belief*, London: Routledge and Kegan Paul

Latour, B (1987) *Science in Action: How to Follow Scientists and Engineers through Society*, Milton Keynes: Open University Press

Latour, B (1988) *The Pasteurization of France*, Cambridge: Harvard University Press

Latour, B (1993) *We Have Never Been Modern*, Hemel Hempstead: Harvester

Latour, B (1999) *Pandora's Hope: Essays on the Reality of Science Studies*, London: Harvard University Press

Latour, B and Woolgar, S (1979) *Laboratory Life: the Social Construction of Scientific Facts*, Beverley Hills, California: Sage

Law, J (ed) (1986) *Power, Action and Belief? A New Sociology of Knowledge*, London: Routledge

Leach, M and Mearns, R (eds) (1996) *The Lie of the Land: Challenging Received Wisdom on the African Environment*, Oxford: James Currey

Leach, M, Mearns, R and Scoones, I (1997) 'Community-based sustainable development: consensus or conflict?', *IDS Bulletin*, vol 28: 4

Leach, M, Scoones, I and Thompson, L (2002) 'Citizenship, Science and Risk', *IDS Bulletin*, vol 33: 2

Levine, D (1965) *Wax and Gold: Tradition and Innovation in Ethiopian Culture*, Chicago: University of Chicago Press

Lindblom, C (1959) 'The science of "muddling through"', *Public Administration Review*, vol 2: 79–88

Lindblom, C (1980) *The Policy-Making Process*, New York: Prentice Hall

Lindblom, C (1990) *Inquiry and Change*, New Haven: Yale University Press

Lipsky, M (1979) *Street Level Bureaucracy*, New York: Russell Sage Foundation

Lipton, M (1999) 'Reviving the stalled momentum of global poverty reduction: what role for genetically modified plants?' Crawford Memorial Lecture, 28 October 1999, Washington, DC: CGIAR

Litfin, K (1994) *Ozone Discourses*, New York: Columbia University Press

Long, N (1992) 'From Paradigm Lost to Paradigm Regained?: The Case for an Actor-Oriented Sociology of Development' in Long, N and Long, A (eds) *Battlefields of Knowledge: The Interlocking of theory and Practice in Social Research and Development*, London: Routledge

Long, N and van der Ploeg, J (1989) 'Demythologising planned development: an actor perspective', *Sociologia Ruralis*, vol XXIX(3/4): 227–249

Lukes, S (1974) *Power: A Radical View*, London: Macmillan

MacKenzie, D (1990) *Inventing Accuracy: A Historical Sociology of Nuclear Missile Guidance*, Cambridge, Massachusetts: MIT Press

Majone, G (1989) *Evidence, Argument and Persuasion in the Policy Process*, New Haven, Connecticut: Yale University Press

Makumbe, J M (1996) *Participatory Development: The Case of Zimbabwe*, Harare: University of Zimbabwe

Makumbe, J M (1998) *Democracy and Development in Zimbabwe: Constraints of Decentralisation*, Harare: SAPES Books

Mamdani, M (1996) *Citizen and Subject: Contemporary Africa and the Legacy of Late Colonialism*, London: James Currey

March, J and Olsen, J (1984) 'The new institutionalism: organizational factors in political life', *American Political Science Review*, vol 78: 734–749

Marin, B and Mayntz, R (eds) (1991) *Policy Networks: Empirical Evidence and Theoretical Considerations*, Frankfurt: Campus Verlag

Marsh, D and Rhodes, R (eds) (1992) *Policy Networks in British Government*, Oxford: Oxford University Press

Masefield, A (1997) *Food Security in Ethiopia: An Update*, Brighton: Institute of Development Studies.

Maxwell, D (1999) *Christians and Chiefs in Zimbabwe: A Social History of the Hwesa People*, Edinburgh: Edinburgh University Press

Maxwell, S (1993) 'Can a cloudless sky have a silver lining? The scope for an employment-based safety net in Ethiopia', *Food for Development Discussion Paper*, no 1, Rome: World Food Programme

Maxwell, S and Belshaw, D (1990) *Food for Development: New Roles for Food Aid in Ethiopia*, Report of World Food Program Food for Development Mission. Rome: World Food Programme

Mazmanian, D and Sabatier, P (1983) *Implementation and Public Policy*, Chicago: Scott Foresman and Co

McCann, J (1995) *People of the Plow: an Agricultural History of Ethiopia 1800–1990*, Madison: University of Wisconsin Press

McCann, J (1998) 'A tale of two forests: narratives of deforestation in Ethiopia, 1840–1996', *Boston University, Africa Studies Centre, Working Paper*, no 209

McGregor, J (1995) 'Conservation, control and ecological change: the politics and ecology of colonial conservation in Shurugwi, Zimbabwe', *Environment and History*, vol 1(3): 257–279

McGregor, J (2002) 'The Politics of Disruption: war veterans and the local state in Zimbabwe', *African Affairs*, vol 101(402): 9–37

McLennan, G (1989) *Marxism, Pluralism and Beyond*, Cambridge: Polity Press

Meadows et al (1972) *The Limits to Growth: A Report for the Club of Rome's Project on the Predicament of Mankind*, London: Earth Island

Migdal, J (1988) *Strong Societies and Weak States: State-Society Relations and State Capabilities in the Third World*, Princeton, New Jersey: Princeton University Press

Miliband, R (1969) *The State in Capitalist Society*, London: Weidenfield and Nicolson

Ministère de la Développement Rurale et de l'Eaux, (1998) 'Plan d'action national pour la gestion de la fertilité des sols: preparation du volet fertilité des sols du PASAOP', *Termes de référence pour les groupes de travail*, vols 1–3, Bamako: MDRE

Ministère de l'Environnement (1998) *National Environmental Action Plan and CCD Program*, Bamako: Ministry of Environment

Ministère de l'Environnement (1999) *Environment Financing Sectorial Roundtable*, 27–29 May, Bamako: MoE

Mol, A (1996) 'Ecological modernisation and institutional reflexivity: environmental reform in the late modern age', *Environmental Politics*, vol 5: 302–323

Monga, C (1995) 'Civil society and democratisation in francophone Africa', *Journal of Modern African Studies*, vol 33(3): 359–379

Moorehead, R (1991) *Structural Chaos: Community and State Management of Common Property in Mali*, DPhil thesis, IDS, Sussex: University of Sussex

Morrissey, J (1996) *Citizen Participation in Environmental Policy: A Study of Landfill Siting in Two Appalachian Communities*, DPhil thesis, Knoxville: University of Tennessee

Moyo, S (2000) 'The political economy of land acquisition and redistribution in Zimbabwe, 1990–99', *Journal of Southern African Studies*, vol 26(1): 5–28

Moyo, S, Robinson, P, Katerere, Y, Stevenson, S and Gumbo, D (1991) *Zimbabwe's Environmental Dilemma*, Harare: Zero

Muir, A (1992) 'Evaluating the impact of NGOs in rural poverty alleviation: Zimbabwe country study', *Working Paper*, no 52, London: ODI

Mukahanana, M, Hoole, A, Monemo, M, Mhaka, E and Chimbuya, S (1998) 'Zimbabwe: National Conservation Strategy' in Wood A (ed) *Strategies for Sustainability*, London: Earthscan

Mungate, D and Mvududu, S (1991) 'Government and NGO collaboration in natural resources in Zimbabwe', *ODI AgREN Paper*, vol 24, London: ODI

Munro, W (1998) *The Moral Economy of the State: Conservation, Community Development and State Making in Zimbabwe*, Ohio: Centre for International Studies, Ohio University

Munton, R (2003) 'Deliberative democracy and environmental decision-making' in Berkhout, F, Leach, M and Scoones, I (eds) *Negotiating Environmental Change: New Perspectives from Social Science*, Aldershot: Edward Elgar

Murdoch, J (1997) 'Inhuman/nonhuman/human: actor-network theory and the prospects for a nondualistic and symmetrical perspective on nature and society', *Environment and Planning D: Society and Space*, vol 15: 731–756

Murdoch, J and Clark, J (1994) 'Sustainable knowledge' *Geoforum*, vol 25: 115–132

Murwira, K, Wedgewood, H and Watson, C (2000) *Beating Hunger, The Chivi Experience: a Community-Based Approach to Food Security in Zimbabwe*, London: ITDG Publications

Mutiza-Mangiza, N (1990) 'Decentralisation and district development planning in Zimbabwe', *Public Administration and Development*, vol 10: 1–13

National Conservation Strategy Secretariat (1994) *National Conservation Strategy*, vols 1–5, Ethiopia, Addis Ababa: The Secretariat

Ndiweni, M, MacGarry, B, Chaguma, A and Gumbo, D (1991) 'Involving farmers in rural technologies. Case studies of Zimbabwean NGOs', *ODI AgREN Paper*, no 25, London: ODI

Nelkin, D (1979) 'Scientific knowledge, public policy and democracy', *Knowledge: Creation, Diffusion, Utilization*, vol 1

Nelkin, D (1992) (ed) *Controversy*, Newbury Park, California: Sage

Newell, P (2000) 'Environmental NGOs and Globalisation: The Governance of TNCs' in Cohen, R and Rai, S (eds) *Global Social Movements*, London: Routledge

Nordlinger, E (1981) *On the Autonomy of the Democratic State*, Cambridge, Massachusetts: Harvard University Press

Nordlinger, E (1987) 'Taking the State Seriously' in Weiner, M and Huntington, S (eds) *Understanding Political Development*, Boston: Little, Brown and Co

Offe, C (1985) 'New social movements: challenging the boundaries of institutional politics', *Social Research*, vol 52: 817–868

Oldeman, R and Hakkeling, R (1990) 'World Map of the Status of Human-Induced Soil Degradation: an explanatory note', Nairobi: UNEP

Oram, P (1995) 'The Potential of Technology to meet World Food Needs in 2020', *2020 Vision Brief*, 13 April, Washington, DC: IFPRI

Ottaway, M (1990) 'Introduction: The Crisis of the Ethiopian State and Economy' in Ottaway, M (ed) *The Political Economy of Ethiopia*, New York: Praeger

Painter, T, Sumberg, J and Price, T (1994) 'Your *terroir* and my action space: implications of differentiation, mobility and diversification for the *approche terroir* in Sahelian West Africa', *Africa*, vol 64(4): 447–464

Parsons, W (1995) *Public Policy: An Introduction to the Theory and Practice of Policy Analysis*, Aldershot: Edward Elgar

Pateman, C (1970) *Participation and Democratic Theory*, London: Cambridge University Press

Paterson, M (1996) *Global Warming and Global Politics*, London and New York: Routledge

Penning de Vries, F and Djitèye, M (1982) *La Productivité des Pâturages Sahéliens: une Etude des Sols, des Vegetations et de l'Exploitation de Cette Ressource Naturelle*, Wageningen: Centre for Agricultural Publishing and Documentation

Phimister, I (1986) 'Discourse and the discipline of historical context: conservationism and ideas about development in Southern Rhodesia, 1930–1950', *Journal of Southern African Studies*, vol 12(2): 263–275

Pickering, A (1992) 'From Science as Knowledge to Science as Practice' in Pickering A (ed) *Science as Practice and Culture*, Chicago: Chicago University Press

Pickering, A (1995) *The Mangle of Practice: Time, Agency and Science*, Chicago: University of Chicago Press

Pieri, C (1989) *Fertility of Soils: a Future for Farming in the West African Savannah*, Berlin: Springer Verlag

Pieri, C, Dumanski, J, Hamblin, A and Young, A (1995) 'Land Quality Indicators', *Discussion Paper 315*, Washington: World Bank

Pinstrup-Andersen, P, Pandya-Lorch, R and Rosegrant, M (1999) 'World Food Prospects: Critical Issues for the early Twenty-First Century', *IFPRI 2020 Vision Food Policy Report*, Washington: IFPRI

Poulantzas, N (1973) *Political Power and Social Classes*, London: New Left Books

Pressman, J and Wildavsky, A (1973) *Implementation*, Berkeley: University of California Press

Price, D (1965) *The Scientific Estate*, Cambridge, Massachusetts: Harvard University Press

Prudencio, Y (1998) *The Soil Fertility Initiative: Progress and Issues in West Africa*, Progress report of the World Bank/SFI Coordinator for West Africa. October

Pyenson, L (1993) *Civilising Mission: Exact Sciences and French Overseas Expansion, 1830–1940*, Baltimore: Johns Hopkins University Press

Quiñones, M, Borlaug, N and Dowswell, C (1997) 'A Fertiliser-Based Green Revolution for Africa' in Buresh, R, Sanchez, P and Calhoun F (eds) *Replenishing Soil Fertility in Africa*, SSSA Special Publication Number 51, Madison, Wisconsin: Soil Science Society of America; American Society of Agronomy

Raftopoulos, B (2001) 'The State in Crisis: Authoritarian Nationalism, Selective Citizenship and Distortions of Democracy in Zimbabwe', Paper presented at the Rethinking Land, State and Citizenship through the Zimbabwe Crisis Conference held Copenhagen, Denmark, 4–5 September 2001

Ranger, T (1999) *Voices from the Rocks: Nature, Culture and History in the Matopos Hills of Zimbabwe*, Oxford: James Currey

Reij, C, Scoones, I and Toulmin, C (1996) *Sustaining the Soil: Indigenous Soil and Water Conservation in Africa*, London: Earthscan

Reij, C and Waters-Bayer, A (eds) (2001) *Farmer Innovation in Africa: A Source of Inspiration for Agricultural Development*, London: Earthscan

Rein, M and Schön, D (1993) 'Reframing Policy Discourse' in Fischer, F and Forester, J (eds) *The Argumentative Turn in Policy Analysis and Planning*, London: UCL Press

Rhodes, R (1997) *Understanding Governance: Policy Networks, Governance, Reflexivity and Accountability*, Buckingham: Open University Press

Rhodes, R and Marsh, D (1992) 'New directions in the study of policy networks', *European Journal of Political Research*, vol 21: 181–205

Ribot, J (1999) 'Decentralisation, participation and accountability in Sahelian forestry: legal instruments of political-administrative control', *Africa*, vol 69(1): 23–65

Richards, P (1985) *Indigenous Agricultural Revolution: Ecology and Food Production in West Africa*, Hemel Hempstead: Allen and Unwin

Roberts, R (1995) 'The Coercion of Free Markets: Cotton, Peasants and the Colonial State in the French Sudan, 1924–1932' in Isaacman, A and Roberts, R (eds) *Cotton, Colonialism and Social History in Sub-Saharan Africa*, London: James Currey

Roberts, R (1996) *Two Worlds of Cotton: Colonialism and the Regional Economy in the French Sudan. 1800–1946*, Stanford: Stanford University Press

Robins, S (1994) 'Contesting the social geometry of bureaucratic state power: a case study of land use planning in Matabeleland, Zimbabwe', *Social Dynamics*, vol 20(2): 91–118

Robins, S (1998) 'Breaking out of the straightjacket of tradition: the politics and rhetoric of "development" in Zimbabwe', *World Development*, vol 26(9): 1677–1694

Roe, E (1991) 'Development narratives, or making the best of blueprint development', *World Development*, vol 19: 287–300

Roe, E (1994) 'Deconstructing Budgets, Reconstructing Budgeting: Contemporary Literary Theory and Public Policy in Action' in Roe, E (ed) *Narrative Policy Analysis: Theory and Practice*, Durham: Duke University Press

Roe, E (1995) 'More than the politics of decentralization: local government reform, district development and public administration in Zimbabwe', *World Development*, vol 23: 833–843

SAA (Sasakawa Africa Association) (2001) 'Ethiopia country profile', www.saa-tokyo-org/english/country/ethiopia.html

Sabatier, P (1986) 'Top-down and bottom-up approaches to implementation research: a critical analysis and suggested synthesis', *Journal of Public Policy*, vol 6: 21–48

Sabatier, P (1988) 'An advocacy coalition framework of policy change and the role of policy-oriented learning therein', *Policy Sciences*, vol 29: 129–168

Sabatier, P (1998) 'The advocacy coalition framework: revisions and relevance for Europe', *Journal of European Public Policy*, vol 5: 98–130

Sabatier, P and Jenkins-Smith, H (eds) (1993) *Policy Change and Learning: An Advocacy Coalition Approach*, Boulder, Colorado: Westview Press

Sanchez, P, Shepherd, K, Soule, M, Place, P, Buresh, R, Izac, A-M, Mokwunye, A, Kwesiga, F, Ndiritu, C and Woomer, P (1997) 'Soil Fertility Replenishment in Africa: an investment in Natural Resource Capital' in Buresh, R, Sanchez, P and Calhoun, F (eds) *Replenishing Soil Fertility in Africa*, SSSA Special Publication Number 51, Madison, Wisconsin: Soil Science Society of America; American Society of Agronomy

SARDC (1994) 'Soil Erosion. Southern African Environmental Issues', *CEP Factsheet*, vol 1, Harare: SARDC

SARDC (1999) Communicating the Environment Programme, Factsheet No1

Sasakawa Africa Association (1996) *Facing the Future: the Sasakawa-Global 2000 Programme for Agricultural Development in Africa*, video produced for the SAA by Images First Ltd

Sasakawa Africa Association (1998) 'Feeding the Future', *Magazine of the Sasakawa Africa Association*, April, no 12

Scherr, S and Yadav, S (1997) 'Land Degradation in the Developing World: issues and policy options for 2020', *IFPRI 2020 Vision Brief*, no 44

Schön, D (1983) *The Reflective Practioner: How Professionals Think in Action*, New York: Basic Books

Schön, D and Rein, M (1994) *Frame Reflection: Towards the Resolution of Intractable Policy Controversies*, New York: Basic Books

Schram, S (1993) 'Postmodern Policy Analysis: Discourse and Identity in Welfare Policy', *Policy Sciences*, vol 26, pp249–270

Scoones, I (1996) 'Range management, science and policy' in Leach, M and Mearns, R (eds) *The Lie of the Land: Challenging Received Wisdom on the African Environment*, London: James Currey

Scoones, I (1999) 'New ecology and the social sciences: what prospects for a fruitful engagement?' *Annual Review of Anthropology*, vol 28: 479–507

Scoones, I (ed) (2001) *Dynamics and Diversity: Soil Fertility and Farming Livelihoods in Africa*, London: Earthscan

Scoones, I with Chibudu, C, Chikura, S, Jeranyama, P, Machaka, D, Machanja, W, Mavedzenge, B, Mombeshora, B, Mudhara, M, Mudziwo, C, Murimbarimba, F and Zirereza, B (1996) *Hazards and Opportunities: Farming Livelihoods in Dryland Africa. Lessons from Zimbabwe*, London: Zed Press

Scoones, I and Cousins, B (1994) 'The struggle for control over wetland resources in Zimbabwe', *Society and Natural Resources*, vol 7: 579–594

Scoones, I and Thompson, J (eds) (1994) *Beyond Farmer First: Rural People's Knowledge, Agricultural Research and Extension Practice*, London: IT Publications

Scoones, I and Toulmin, C (1999) *Policies for Soil Fertility Management in Africa*, London: DFID

Scoones, I and Wolmer, W (eds) (2002) *Pathways of Change in Africa: Crops, Livestock and Livelihoods in Mali, Ethiopia and Zimbabwe*, Oxford: James Currey

Scott, J (1998) *Seeing Like a State: How Certain Schemes to Improve the Human Condition Have Failed*, New Haven: Yale University Press

Serageldin, I (2000) 'The Challenge of Poverty in the 21st Century: the role of science' in Persley G and Lantin M (eds) *Agricultural Biotechnology and the Poor: An International Conference on Biotechnology*, Washington, DC: World Bank

Serra, R (1999) 'Creating a framework for reducing poverty: institutional and process issues in national poverty policy in selected African countries', *Mali Country Report*, Brighton: IDS

Shackley, S and Wynne, B (1995) 'Global climate change: the mutual construction of an emergent science-policy domain', *Science and Public Policy*, vol 22

Shackley, S and Wynne, B (1996) 'Representing uncertainty in global climate change science and policy: boundary-ordering devices and authority', *Science, Technology and Human Values*, vol 21(3): 275–302

Shapin, S (1979) 'The Politics of Observation: Cerebral Anatomy and Social Interests in the Edinburgh Phrenology disputes' in Wallis, R (ed) *On the Margins of Science: The Social Construction of Rejected Knowledge*, Sociological Review Monograph, No 27, Keele: University of Keele

Shapin, S and Schaffer, S (1985) *Leviathan and the Air Pump: Hobbes, Boyle and the Experimental Life*, Princeton: Princeton University Press

Shore, C and Wright, S (1997) 'Policy: A New Field of Anthropology' in Shore, C and Wright, S (eds) *Anthropology of Policy: Critical Perspectives on Governance and Power*, London: Routledge

Simon, H (1957) *Administrative Behaviour*, New York: Macmillan

Sivaramakrishnan, Kalayanakrishnan (1995) 'Colonialism and forestry in India: imagining the past in present politics', *Comparative Studies in Society and History*, vol 37: 1–40

Skalnes, T (1989) 'Group interests and the state: an explanation of Zimbabwe's agricultural policies', *Journal of Modern African Studies*, vol 27(1): 85–107

Skocpol, T (1985) 'Bringing the State Back In: Current Research' in Evans P, Reuschemeyer, D and Skocpol, T (eds) *Bringing the State Back In*, Cambridge: Cambridge University Press

Smaling, E, Nandwa, S and Janssen, B (1997) 'Soil Fertility in Africa is at Stake' in Buresh, R, Sanchez P and Calhoun F (eds) *Replenishing Soil Fertility in Africa*, SSSA Special Publication Number 51, Madison, Wisconsin: Soil Science Society of America; American Society of Agronomy

Smith, B (1976) *Policy-making in British Government*, London: Martin Robinson

Smith, G and May, D (1980) 'The artificial debate between rationalist and incrementalist models of decision making', *Policy and Politics*, vol 8: 147–161

Smith, J (1991) *The Idea Brokers: Think Tanks and the Rise of the New Policy Elites*, New York: The Free Press

Smith, M (1993) *Pressure, Power and Policy: State Autonomy and Policy Networks in Britain and the United States*, London: Harvester Wheatsheaf

Ståhl, M (1992) 'Environmental rehabilitation in the northern Ethiopian highlands: constraints to people's participation', in D Ghai and J Vivian (eds), *Grassroots Environmental Action: People's Participation in Sustainable Development*, London: Routledge

Stocking, M (1986) 'The cost of soil erosion in Zimbabwe in terms of the loss of the three major nutrients', *Consultants Working Paper*, no 3, Rome: FAO

Stoorvogel, J and Smaling, E (1990) *Assessment of Soil Nutrient Depletion in sub-Saharan Africa, 1983–2000, volumes I–IV*, Wageningen: the Winand Staring Centre

Suleiman, E (1974) *Politics, Power and Bureaucracy in France: the Administrative Elite*, Princeton, New Jersey: Princeton University Press

Swift, J (1996) 'Desertification: Narratives, Winners, Losers' in Leach, M and Mearns, R (eds) *The Lie of the Land: Challenging Received Wisdom on the African Environment*, London: James Currey

Tambora, B (1999) 'La CMDT "Ne Sera Pas Privatisée"', *Observateur*, 1 January, 1999

TGE (1994) *National Conservation Strategy, volumes I–V, Transitional Government of Ethiopia*, Addis Ababa: National Conservation Secretariat

The Ecologist (1972) 'Blueprint for Survival', special issue, London: Ecosystems

Thomas-Slayter, B (1994) 'Structural change, power politics and community organizations in Africa: challenging the patterns, puzzles and paradoxes', *World Development*, vol 22: 1479–1490

Throgmorton, J (1993) 'Survey Research as Rhetorical Trope: Electric Power Planning Arguments in Chicago' in Fischer, F and Forester, J (eds) *The Argumentative Turn in Policy Analysis and Planning*, London: UCL Press

Torgerson, D (1986) 'Between knowledge and politics: three faces of policy analysis', *Policy Sciences*, vol 9: 33–59

Toulmin, C (1995) 'The Convention to Combat Desertification: Guidelines for NGO Activity', *IIED Issue Paper*, no 56, April, London: IIED

Toulmin, C, Leonard, R, Hilhorst, T and Diarra, D (2000) *Mali Poverty Profile: Report prepared for SIDA*, IIED Drylands Programme, May

Toulmin, S (1958) *The Uses of Argument*, Cambridge: Cambridge University Press

Truman, D (1951) *The Governmental Process: Political Interests and Public Opinion*, New York: Knopf

UNDP (1999) *Appui à la Société Civile*, Bamako: UNDP

UNDP (2001) *Human Development Report*, New York: UNDP

UNEP (2000) *Global Environmental Outlook 2000*, London: Earthscan

Van Campen, W (1991) 'The long road to sustainable land management in southern Mali' in Savenjie, H and Huijsman, A (ed) *Making Haste Slowly: Strengthening Local Environmental Management in Agricultural Development*, Amsterdam: KIT

Van der Pol, F (1992) 'Soil mining: an unseen contributor to farm income in southern Mali', *Bulletin*, no 325, Royal Tropical Institute, Amsterdam: KIT

Van der Sluijs, J, van Eijndhoven, J, Shackley, S and Wynne, B (1998) 'Anchoring devices in science for policy: the case of consensus around climate sensitivity', *Social Studies of Science*, vol 28(2): 291–323

Van Reuler H and Prins, W (eds) (1993) *The Role of Plant Nutrients for Sustainable Food Crop Production in sub-Saharan Africa*, Leidschendam: Vereniging van Kunstmest Producenten

Van Veldhuizen, L, Waters-Bayer, A and de Zeeuw, H (1997) *Developing Technology with Farmers: A Trainer's Guide for Participatory Learning*, London: Zed Books

Ventgroff, R (1993) 'Governance and the transition to democracy: political parties and the party system in Mali', *Journal of Modern African Studies*, vol 31(4): 541–562

Vivian, J (1994) 'NGOs and sustainable development in Zimbabwe: no magic bullets', *Development and Change*, vol 25: 167–193

Vivian, J and Maseko, G (1994) 'NGOs, Participation and Rural Development. Testing the Assumptions with Evidence from Zimbabwe', *UNRISD Discussion Paper*, no 49, Geneva: UNRISD

Vogler, J (1996) 'The Environment in International Relations: Legacies and Contentions' in Vogler, J and Imber, M (eds) *The Environment and International Relations*, London: Routledge, 1–21

Vogler, J and Imber, M (eds) (1996) *The Environment and International Relations*, London: Routledge

Walt, G (1994) *Health Policy: An Introduction to Process and Power*, London: Zed Books

Wade, R (1997) 'Greening the Bank: The Struggle over the Environment, 1970–85' in Kapur, D, Lewis, J and Webb, R (eds) *The World Bank: Its First Fifty Years*, Washington, DC: Brookings Institution Press

Wapner, P (1996) *Environmental Activism and World Civic Politics*, Albany, New York: State University of New York Press

Warren, D, Slikkerveer, L and Brokensha, D (eds) (1995) *The Cultural Dimension of Development: Indigenous Knowledge Systems*, London: ITDG Publications

Weinberg, A (1972) 'Science and trans-science', *Minerva*, vol 10: 209–222

Weiss, C (ed) (1977) *Using Social Research in Public Policy Making*, Lexington, Massachusetts: D C Heath

Weiss, C (1992) *Organizations for Policy Analysis: Helping Governments Think*, Newbury Park, California: Sage

Whitlow, J (1988) *Land Degradation in Zimbabwe – a Geographical Study*, Report to the Natural Resources Board, Harare

Wiggins, S (1995) 'Change in African farming systems between the mid-1970s and the mid-1980s', *Journal of International Development*, vol 7(6): 807–848

Wildavsky, A (1974) *The Politics of the Budgetary Process*, Boston: Little, Brown and Co

Wildavsky, A (1979) *Speaking Truth to Power: The Art and Craft of Policy Analysis*, Boston: Little, Brown and Co

Winter, M (1998) 'Decentralised natural resource management in the Sahel: overview and analysis', *IIED Issue Paper*, no 81, December

Wood, A and Ståhl, M (1989) *Ethiopia: National Conservation Strategy: Phase One Report*, Prepared for International Union for the Conservation of Nature, Gland: IUCN

Woolgar, S (1988) *Science: The Very Idea*, London: Tavistock

Worby, E (2001) 'A redivided land? New agrarian conflicts and questions in Zimbabwe', *Journal of Agrarian Change*, vol 1(4): 475–509, October

Worku Tessema (2000) 'Stakeholder participation in policy processes in Ethiopia', *Managing Africa's Soils*, no 17, London: IIED

World Bank (1990) *Ethiopia's Economy in the 1980s and Framework for Accelerated Growth*, Report No 8062-ET, Washington, DC: World Bank

World Bank (1994) 'Ethiopia: Environmental Strategy Paper', draft, Washington, DC: World Bank

World Bank (1994a) 'Ethiopia: Environmental Strategy Paper. Background Paper on Institutional Arrangements', draft, Washington, DC: World Bank

World Bank (1995) *Ethiopia: National Fertiliser Project*, Staff Appraisal Report, Report No 13722- ET, Washington, DC, World Bank

World Bank (1995a) *Ethiopia: Seed Systems Development Project*, Staff Appraisal Report, Report No 137939-ET, Washington, DC: World Bank

World Bank (1996) *Restoration of Soil Fertility in Sub-Saharan Africa: Concept Paper and Action Plan*, Washington, DC: World Bank

World Bank (1996a) *La Coopération Mali-Banque Mondiale*, Bamako: World Bank

World Bank (1996b) 'Restoration of Soil Fertility in Africa: Concept Paper and Action Plan', Washington, DC: World Bank

World Bank (1998a) 'Ethiopia: Soil Fertility Initiative Concept Paper', Washington, DC: World Bank

World Bank (1998b) *Republique du Mali: Initiative Pour la Fertilité des Sols*, Mission Banque Mondiale du 5–9 Octobre, Aide memoire

World Bank (1998c) 'Ethiopia: Agricultural Growth', draft, AFTA1, Washington, DC: World Bank

World Bank (1999) 'The Soil Fertility Initiative: Taking Stock of Challenges, Framework for Action, International Facilitation Function: a proposal for donor funding', draft, Washington, DC: World Bank

World Bank (2000) *Cotton Policy Brief*, March, Washington, DC: World Bank

World Bank (2000a) *Cotton Policy Brief*, June, Washington, DC: World Bank

World Bank (2001a) *World Development Indicators*, Washington, DC: World Bank

World Bank (2001b) *World Development Report*, Washington, DC: World Bank

World Bank, ICRAF and IFDC (1994) *Feasibility of Rock Phosphate Use as a Capital Investment in Sub-Saharan Africa*, Washington, DC: World Bank

Wynne, B (1992) 'Uncertainty and environmental learning: reconceiving science and policy in the preventive paradigm', *Global Environmental Change*, vol 2(2): 111–127

Wynne, B (1996) 'May the Sheep Graze Safely?: A Reflexive View of the Expert-Lay Knowledge Divide' in Lash, S, Szerszynski, S and Wynne, B (eds) *Risk, Environment and Modernity: Towards a New Ecology*, London: Sage Publications (Theory, Culture and Society)

Yearley, S (1994) 'Social Movements and Environmental Change' in Redclift, M and Benton, T (eds) *Social Theory and the Global Environment*, London: Routledge

Yearley, S (1996) *Sociology, Environmentalism, Globalization*, London: Sage Publications Ltd

Young, C (1988) 'The African Colonial State and its Political Legacy' in Rothschild, D and Chazan, N (eds) *The Precarious Balance: State and Society in Africa*, Boulder, Colorado, and London: Westview Press

Young, C (1994) *The African Colonial State in Comparative Historical Perspective*, New Haven and London: Yale University Press

Young, J (1996) 'Ethnicity and power in Ethiopia', *Review of African Political Economy*, vol 70: 531–542

Young, J (1997) 'Development and change in post-revolutionary Tigray', *Journal of Modern African Studies*, vol 35(1): 81–99

Young, J (1998) 'Regionalism and democracy in Ethiopia', *Third World Quarterly*, vol 19(2): 191–204

Young, J (1999) 'Along Ethiopia's western frontier: Gambella and Benishangul in transition', *Journal of Modern African Studies*, vol 37(2): 321–346

Index

Note: The figure *n* following page references refers to material in the notes. Names of works are given in *italics*